FROM MAGIC TO METAPHOR

FROM THE LIBRARY OF

Patricia Rennie

D1225611

FROM MAGIC TO METAPHOR

A Validation of Christian Sacraments

George S. Worgul

with a Foreword by

Piet Fransen, S.J.

PAULIST PRESS
New York / Ramsey

The publisher gratefully acknowledges:

Material on the definition of a sacrament first appeared in "What Is a Sacrament?" in *U.S. Catholic* published by Claretian Publications, 221 W. Madison Street, Chicago, Ill., 60606, and is used with permission.

Material on the celebration model first appeared in the Fall 1977 *Chicago Studies*: "Celebrations: Models for Sacraments." This material has been revised and is used with permission.

Copyright © 1980 by
The Missionary Society
of St. Paul the Apostle
in the State of New York

All rights reserved. No part of this book may be reproduced or transmitted in any form or by any means, electronic or mechanical, including photocopying, recording or by any information storage and retrieval system without permission in writing from the Publisher.

Library of Congress
Catalog Card Number: 79–56753

ISBN: 0–8091–2280–4

Published by Paulist Press
Editorial Office: 1865 Broadway, New York, N.Y. 10023
Business Office: 545 Island Road, Ramsey, N.J. 07446

Printed and bound in the
United States of America

CONTENTS

*This book is dedicated to
Jeanne who is always a medium
of God's love for me*

PREFACE

This text is an invitation to explore the various dimensions of the Christian sacraments. Rather than investigating any one sacrament, it strives to present an overview or what has been traditionally called in theological handbooks: *Sacraments in General*.

In this exploration, every attempt has been made to correlate behavioral reflections on ritual with theological affirmations on sacraments. Hopefully, this procedure will foster both a continuing dialogue with the human sciences and a theology of sacraments that is commensurate to the demands of our present cultural era. Theology cannot be done in isolation. Concurrently, the human sciences cannot be authentic to their goals if they avoid dialogue with the theological discipline simply because it reflects on religion. Both fields of investigation study humankind and can retain their uniqueness within the exegency of cooperation.

Hopefully, the reader will finish this book sharing the author's profound beliefs that ritual is essential to human life and Christian sacraments are normal and natural for the Christian culture. Cultures will die without ritual.

Most importantly, this journey into sacramental theology will identify the most pressing issue challenging the Church today. It will suggest that the Church is experiencing a crisis of faith and membership which has been spawned by a general crisis of culture. In identifying this source of ecclesial turbulence, a beginning can be made in confronting the challenge of our age and furthering the vibrancy of the Church in the modern world.

Many individuals have encouraged the author in the composition of this text, to all of them I express my profound appreciation. I am especially thankful to my students at Siena College, St. Anthony on the Hudson, and Duquesne University, who struggled with this text as it was being developed and altered. It never would have seen the light of day without the warm friendship and support of the Graber family, Alice Dollard, Harriot Bridgeman, Frances Mohan, Rev. E. Sipperly, Rev. T. Saccone, Rev. J.

O'Grady, Rev. B. Beloin, and especially my family. Any theological insight which might be encouraged from this text is ultimately indebted to my fine teachers and friends at the Catholic University of Leuven, Belgium, especially Professors Fransen, Walgrave, and Blockx, whose seminal insights have always stimulated reflection.

Duquesne University
February 23, 1979

FOREWORD

During the second half of this century, many theologians chose to change their ways of reflection and study. The rather sudden disaffection with Latin as the common language of theological discourse, despite John XXIII's gallant defense of it in St. Peter's Basilica, forced theologians to turn to the scientific and common languages of their contemporaries. The way was paved for eventual interdisciplinary encounters between theologians and scholars of other disciplines.

The age-old "splendid isolation" between theology and other sciences was not easily broken. Most scholars were uneager to meet with theologians. They presumed their attitudes too "dogmatic" and supercilious. Theologians, even within modern neo-Scholasticism, were entrenched within a world of "supernatural" and therefore unreachable realities. They were not prepared to accept a fruitful and open dialogue. Furthermore, many scholars, whether theologians or not, were easily tempted to succumb to the almost inevitable imperialism which develops from the limiting pressures of specialization. One of the most infantile manifestations of this human weakness is the use of complex jargon that no one but the "initiated" themselves can understand. Our modern scientific world quite often resembles the little town of San Gimignano in Tuscany, south of Siena. Today, it still shows from the troublesome times of the fourteenth century, thirteen tall "Towers of Nobility," formerly seventy-two, depicting many small centers of power, riches and dignity. For these and other reasons, interdisciplinary activities, although growing and increasing, still present a problem.

Today, under the impulse of a growing anthropological concern, theologians are more and more drawn toward a greater openness to sciences, especially the human sciences of philosophy, psychology, sociology, and anthropology. What value is there to talk about faith, if this faith remains clothed in concepts and doctrines more congenial to a past age and therefore foreign to our actual concerns? The resolute new emphasis upon the function of human experience in the elaboration of any scientific or honest reflection on human life only deepens and strengthens the anthropological trends in theology. We should not forget that the rationalistic theology of grace of the eighteenth and nineteenth centuries contended that there was no experience of God's gracious presence in us for the majority of Christians, except for the extraordinary cases of infused mystical graces. The use of experience in theology was therefore radically excluded.

Finally, in a world where we discover the interdependency of all reality, any crude separation between the so-called natural forces and supernatural graces is unacceptable. It becomes an urgent duty for the theologian, whether he is engaged in more speculative and contemplative reflections or committed to more practical action and thought, to listen as attentively to the voices of modern science and experience as he did to the voices of the Fathers and great Scholastics. This kind of wholeness we meet in process theology and in some forms of liberation theology.

In light of the above considerations, we will undoubtedly understand the efforts of the present author, who deliberately introduces into his exposition of sacramental theology reflections and experiences borrowed from other modern sciences. The results, as the reader will discover by himself, far from disproving this kind of theological research and questioning confirm its utility and efficiency. Of course, some readers, less aware of the laws of human argumentation and thought, may regret that the authors psychological, sociological, and anthropological expositions were not fully intergrated into his theological expose. This kind of mixture, however, would have been totally impalatable and even quite confusing. To appeal to different sciences within the one effort of reflection can only establish a convergence of proofs, all pointing toward one common vision or understanding of reality. The proper object and method of every science is necessarily different from that of the others, and cannot therefore be mixed together, anymore than water and oil. This is a question of intellectual honesty. But, they confirm one another's basic conclusions, or better, the general perspective through which reality is being approached. Since they confirm one another, they also may warn one another and, particularly, make theology aware of some views to which it should turn its attention. There is indeed place for a serious dialogue, a reciprocal and enriching questioning of one's mutual ideas and more fundamental visions.

The present author is interested in one central understanding of human reality in relation to his sacramental theology. Namely, human growth and perfection is as corporate as it is undoubtedly personal. We might also express the idea this way: No one reaches his self-fulfillment or self-realization except in the meeting with others. If this is true, or from a different point of view, if God created us both as corporate and personal beings, it is clearly to be expected that he will redeem us in the same way. The mystery of grace is therefore a true mystery of both communal and personal authenticity and freedom. Consequently, the sacraments are not merely private means or individual ways to salvation, but in one way or another, according to their own nature and ecclesial function, they sanctify us *by bringing us together*. This is, of course, evident in the sacrament of the Eucharist.

The Old Testament includes this communal vision of salvation as one of the aspects of redemption. The tower of Babel is one of the most powerful myths for reminding us of the divisive forces of evil and sin. Conversely, being brought together as God's own people, as his heritage, as the people of God's choice or mercy is indeed a true form of redemption. This is the way John interpreted the so-called prophecy of Caiaphas: it is better that one man die for the people, and that the whole people should not perish. He concludes: "He did not say this of his own accord, but being high priest that year he prophesied that Jesus should die for the people (of the Jews), and not for the people only, but to *gather into one* the children of God who are scattered abroad" (Jn. 11:51–52). And it is, at least for us, a great satisfaction that most of the new Eucharistic Prayers created after Vatican II contain this idea of the people gathered by God himself and his Spirit.

We have too often and too easily considered grace as a kind of private form of sanctification, a private spiritual enrichment. Along the same lines, our sacramental devotion was primarily concerned with individual improvement and strength. This truncation of the multi-faceted richness of the sacramental mysteries was the result of medieval Scholastic thought, most probably initiated by Augustine himself. He may justly be called "Doctor gratiae." One may wonder, however, whether his concentration on God's gracious activities to liberate the sinner by some "spiritual help," did not reduce the whole reality of God's graciousness to a mere inner and spiritual aid which detaches us from "mass of damnation" individually. J. P. Jossua, O. P. calls this view the "festering boil" of our Western theology. Whatever one's evaluation, there is no doubt that we are prompted today from different sides, from the side of science and from the side of human experience of a world becoming ever smaller and more dependent on collaboration to realize that there is no salvation except in cooperation, solidarity, and brotherhood. If God created us as a human family, he will undoubtedly save us as a family. It would be rather remarkable, if not meaningless, if God's salvation brought to us by the sacraments of the Church would remain totally alien to this true aspect of our human condition.

One of the fundamental community-creating activities in human existence is symbolic activity. Symbolic activity is human activity par excellence. If it is true that we are a "personified body," a living unity and not a mere composition of body and spirit; if it is true by consequence that the most spiritual and intimate experiences do not emerge over the threshold of our subconscious without tangible, audible, or visible forms in which they are as it were, "incarnated," there is no human activity that would not be symbolic in one way or another.

The greatest tragedy of Western culture, at least in our estimation, lies in the fact that first the Enlightenment, and then the following rationalism still very much alive in some scientists, intellectuals, and especially pseudo-intellectuals, led us to neglect or even to despise the symbolic aspect of our human experience and activities. We believe that the true poverty of our Western culture, and many forms of our typical Western "neurosis," should be attributed to our depreciation of the symbolic functions of the body though, at the same time, we are obsessed by it as an object of pride and pleasure. "It is only a symbol" is probably the most silly and disasterous statement one hears so frequently. If we look around us, however, even when we underrate some forms of symbolic activity as primitive, infantile, or unworthy of a scientific and technical age, we cannot escape from using them. Our modern world is full of symbolisms we have newly created. We should yield whole-heartedly to their mysterious powers without any undue inhibition or self-consciousness.

Symbolism, however, being a type of language, has a history. It can become outdated and unadaptable to our needs and ways of life. This happened frequently with liturgical and sacramental symbolism. Comparative religion tells us, on the other hand, that no human aspect of life is as conservative as ritual tradition. This "conservatism" is, in our view, fundamentally rooted in the deep existential anxiety of man who amidst a threatened life refuses to imperil his deep need for security. But even the attempt to update our sacred symbolisms, as we discovered during the period after Vatican II, is a very delicate endeavor. The various liturgies we have are not a success as a whole. They were often worked out by committies of biblical and liturgical scholars who were not so well attuned to the wave-lengths of the Christian people. Our former liturgy grew during a time when the Church was not highly centralized. A greater participation of local churches, their theologians, their priests, and their artists was possible. As long as a centralized curial commission in Rome has to make the final decision for the whole world, there is indeed no hope for any improvement in the symbolic quality of our sacramental rites. Rome can check perfectly the orthodoxy of our rituals. But beauty was never created by a central authority, only by those who had the prophetic gift of discovering the creating beauty because they were true to themselves and their times.

Whatever the difficulties were and still are in elaborating a liturgy worthy of the beauty and truth of God, it is in and through the symbolic activities that human beings enter into and realize a true communion of life, that they are gathered together in sharing with one another the fundamental attitudes of a Christian in faith, hope, and love. For it is only when we enter freely into the mysteries of the sacraments that we are enriched by their gifts, fruits of the presence of God through his son, the risen Lord, and by virtue of the fulfilling activities of the Spirit.

Piet Fransen, S.J.
Leuven-Heverlee
September 21, 1978

PART ONE
INTRODUCING THE QUESTION

Beginnings are always important. They open a person to new horizons and possibilities. They also limit us insofar as they influence the perception and understanding of every new step we take. In this initial section of our theological endeavor, sacraments will be contextualized within the present crisis of culture. This viewpoint will allow the reasons for the sacamental crisis of our times to be properly identified.

In a second chapter, various methods for exploring sacramental theology will be offered and a particular method selected.

Finally, a third chapter will define the meaning of key terms that will appear throughout the pages of this text.

1 WHY THE CRISIS?

Many authors have described the *sacramental crisis* spanning the last two decades. Few, however, have undertaken a serious exposition and clarification of its cause. Far too often, instant solutions were constructed when the symptoms of the sacramental illness appeared. More often than not, this hasty reaction induced an application of the wrong medication to the misconceived illness. "Sure cures" have only complicated the problem.

Our search for a contemporary vision of sacraments will begin by undertaking the neglected task of identifying the reasons for the contemporary sacramental demise. A successful penetration into the origins of any discord often contains clues to the restoration of harmony and pinpoints issues which will require investigation in assuming the burden of reconstruction. If the origins of our sacramental crisis can be better understood, perhaps a solution to its turbulence can be proposed and a more adequate theology designed.

External and internal factors have given birth to the sacramental crisis. Externally, human history has entered a new cultural age with new and different presuppositions about the meaning, purpose, and style of life. This cultural shift has eroded the structures of the cultural-philosophical system upon which the former theology of the sacraments was based. Consequently, it is difficult to sustain questions and objections raised against the previous sacramental synthesis and the discipline is perceived as being in confusion if not chaos. Internally, theoreticians and practitioners within the Church have recognized and accommodated themselves to the cultural shift. They have attempted to rebuild a sacramental theology based on the new cultural presuppositions. This positive endeavor, however, required a certain abandonment and dismantling of the former synthesis. It also required a temporal process, a tentative grasping, which resists any *fait accompli* or total replacement. The actions of theoreticians and practitioners within the Church have only intensified the feeling of confusion and chaos.

3

A closer examination of these external and internal factors can teach us the areas where our efforts at reconstructing a sacramental theology can be valuably spent.

External Causes: The Cultural Crisis

Future historians may well have no choice than to label the twentieth century the "age of crisis." Modern culture exploits this magnetic term to consolidate a variety of experiences most of which are mildly described as distasteful and more vigorously as paralyzing. Every conceivable human discipline claims its own crisis. Economics possesses its "financial crisis." Transportation describes its "congestion crisis." Naturalists fight the "environmental crisis." Homeowners worry about the winter "fuel crisis." Psychiatric patients search through their "identity crisis." Marriage partners endure their "role" and "sex" crisis.

Religions possess no magical immunization from the contemporary contagia for crisis. The one time bastions of security have witnessed dwindling membership roles, aging congregations, and neutralization—if not total disregard—of moral directives. The churches also have their crisis: the "crisis of faith," the "crisis of membership."

How is this overriding concern for crisis to be explained? Three interpretations seem tenable. First, society is suffering from a mass neurosis which could be called *sociosis*.[1] The technological computer age has overwhelmed humankind's capacity for adaptation. Humankind is threatened by its own creative powers. The complexity and rapidity of contemporary life is impeding the formation of a necessary stability and integration of social life. All humankind can do is hope to cope.

Second, the present age of humankind is not radically different from former periods. The struggles of life, shrouded in the past, were as intense and challenging as our own. In short, humankind is always circumscribed by crisis and condemned to alienation. The form and features of the crisis will fluctuate from age to age, but its reality remains constant.

Third, the twentieth century is a rare age in the journey of human history. Its inhabitants are living simultaneously through the dying process of a past culture and the gestation period of a new self-understanding of humankind that will be expressed in a new culture. This interpretation maintains the "crisis" experience of individuals in the modern world. It supports their attestations that a profound change is occuring. But it interprets the present transformation more radically than ever imagined by the individual participants. No longer are parts of society or individual facets of culture in flux. The whole core and foundations of culture are seen as being recast. This event has infrequently been witnessed in human history and less frequently understood.[2] This third interpretation appears to correspond more accurately to the experience and data of our "cultural crisis" than the first two possibilities. What, however, is this culture "in crisis"? How is culture to be defined or described?

A culture is a construct of multiple layers reflected in diversified elements such as tools, language, art, institutions, economic practices, patterns of social behavior, religious beliefs, etc.[3] Culture is always more easily described than defined. Various concepts can serve as its substitute: world view,[4] horizon,[5] or operative model of reality. Yet, all the various descriptions and definitions of culture include two fundamental elements. First, culture is a perception of reality by social groups expressed in and through its social institutions and patterns of behavior.[6] Second, culture is essentially dependent on certain unconscious "principles" or "beliefs" which ground and sustain what is expressed in a conscious fashion in social institutions and patterns of behavior. This second element is more significant than the first, especially in attempting to comprehend the present cultural crisis and specific sacramental crisis.

An interdisciplinary consensus has emerged in the twentieth century on the significance of the unconscious elements in culture.[7] Two sages, John H. Newman and Jose Oretga Y Gasset, reflect this consensus. Newman called these unconscious elements "first principles." He explained, "... by first principles I mean the propositions with which we start in reasoning on any given subject matter."[8] These principles possess absolute control over all thought even though they are generally hidden and unconscious. Newman identified this hiddenness as the basis for their power and their power as the key to their hiddenness.

> You cannot see yourself; and in somewhat the same way the chance is that you are not aware of those principles or ideas which have the chief rule over your mind. They are hidden for the very reason that they are sovereign and so engrossing.[9]

Ortega Y Gasset called these unconscious presuppositions *creencias, beliefs*. He also argued for their hiddenness and absolute power. He noted that "beliefs constitute the basis of our lives, the ground on which they take place, because they put before us what is to us reality itself."[10] He continued:

> Everything we think about acquires for us *ipso facto* a problematic reality and occupies in our lives a secondary place if it is compared with our genuine beliefs. We do not think about the latter either now or later; our relation with them consists in something more efficient; counting on them, always, unceasingly. . . .[11]

Newman's "first principles" or Ortega Y Gasset's "beliefs" are simply the building blocks of culture. They are the key attitudes or interpretations of reailty which identify and sustain a particular culture and bond its members into a homogeneous group. They are the hidden judgments about life and reality which are the basis for the conscious expression of culture in its various forms. For example, from the birth of Christianity until the Renaissance man was presupposed to be a "being toward God." It was presupposed that human fulfillment would only be attained in relation to God. Consequently, when European culture during this period is examined, its concrete institutions and patterns of behavior are thoroughly expressive of this principle. From the Renaissance up until our present age man was presupposed to be a "being for himself." The institutions and patterns of behavior in European culture during this period aim at human fulfillment from within. Culture no longer relies on God or the supernatural. It turns to human reason and science.

There is a direct relationship between the unconscious presuppositions of culture and its conscious expression and integration. This relation is tender. A change in cultural presuppositions or in the social institutions will gcnerate the first stages of a process which could lead to the formation of a new culture on both the unconscious and conscious levels.

Any revision in the institutions of social life impinges on its "first principles" or "beliefs." When these revisions proliferate, a questioning of the validity of the unconscious presuppositions upon which the discarded social institutions were based will arise. Similarly, if there is a change in the unconscious presuppositions, "first principles," or "beliefs," the social institutions of a culture will gradually appear more and more hollow, archaic, and out of place. Cultural change can commence from the "top" or the "bottom."

Cultural change from the "top" is usually of long duration. The participants within a culture experience a gradual transformation of its individual institutions. Only in the final stages of the process will the full realization and depth of the transformation become apparent. Cultural change from the "bottom" is more dramatic and painful. In this situation one's whole culture appears to collapse. Every social institution appears beyond resuscitation. The turbulence of cultural "death" from the "bottom" is heightened by its unconscious characteristics. When the many social institutions of culture, e.g., family, religion, sexual roles etc., are threathened by new "ideas" and "models" some institutions will resist change and offer the hope of some stability and continuity. It will appear that the former age is still alive. In reality, however, these institutions are phantoms of the past doomed to yield to a new spirit which will finally and totally dismantle any remaining archaic and ossified institutional remnants.

There is no anesthetic for the pain of surrendering old "first principles" and embracing new ones. Because "first principles" are unconscious they are usually recognizable only when one tastes the anxiety of the middle time, the time between the last breath of the old age and the birth cry of the new age. "Only the Gestalt of a new world allows one to glimpse the first principles of the past which are perceived as tired and incapable of sustaining men and women in their new world."[12] Today, humankind is living in this middle time. We are historically situated between the postscript of a past age and the foreword of a new age. The experience of turmoil and crisis in all areas of cultural life, including religious life, is arising from the shift in "first principles" as humankind completes the journey from classical to contemporary culture.

The contrast between the "first principles" of classical culture and the emerging unconscious presuppositions of contemporary culture can be glimpsed by comparing the general goal, process, and judgment about reality in these two systems. Classical culture sought after the *absolute* and the *universal*. It searched for the "essence" of every reality, presupposing that these abstractions were real. The process of this quest was marked by *deductive reasoning*. Once universal principles were agreed upon and established, they could be further specified by application to particular situations and realities. Classical culture moved from the universal to the particular, from the general to the specific. It also made a judgment that reality was *permanent* or fixed. The "essence" of a reality never changed. Stability and completion were signs of perfection.

Contemporary culture is concerned with the *particular* rather than the universal. It is sensitive to the uniqueness of every reality and event as it appears. Only after focusing on the particular will contemporary culture turn to questions about the general interrelation of realities and even then it avoids absolutist claims. The process of knowledge in contemporary culture is *inductive.* One always begins with the facts and gradually constructs general principles which are continually evaluated in terms of the concrete realities under analysis. If a general hypothesis is attained, it is not perceived as absolute but tentative, since further investigation may require its revision or total abandonment. Contemporary culture envisions reality as *dynamic* and *evolving.* It stands ready to accept a newness, a freshness to existence. Change and growth are perceived as signs of perfection; completion is a sign of imperfection.

If our thesis that the social institutions and patterns of behavior are expressions of a culture's "first principles" or unconscious presuppositions is correct, it should be evident why classical culture's institutions have been abandoned by contemporary culture. They are simply inconsistent with the unconscious presuppositions of contemporary culture.

The debates over morality during the last two decades are classic examples of the above phenomenon.[13] For the móst part, adult Roman Catholics were educated according to an ethical system derived from classical culture. It emphasized a natural law which was universally valid, irreformable, and applicable to all situations. It should be of no surprise that they acted with confusion and unbelief when moral positions were exposed which claimed a relativity to moral norms, the absolute importance of the particular situation, and the evolutionary nature of the moral person. These new "ideas" were a foreign language to those educated within the classical culture with its presuppositions of absolutes, permanence, and deduction. In contradistinction, today's youth who are imbued with contemporary culture's presupposition of relativity, change, and inductive empiricism often identify classical moral teaching as equally foreign and incomprehensible. In both instances of this example, the conflict is deeper than a conscious disagreement about a particular type or fashion of morality. There is an unconscious battle of cultural "first principles." One can detect a superficial recognition of this phenomenon if close attention is paid to the comments made at meetings and discussions on the topic of our example. How often does one hear: "We're just in two different worlds," or "What you say is logical, but it contradicts everything I ever learned."

The change in cultural presuppositions, with a concurrent transformation of social institutions and patterns of behavior, is the external cause for the contemporary sacramental crisis. This becomes clear once the relationship of the Church to culture is realized and the central role of sacraments in the life of the Church is established. This theme is woven throughout the chapters of this text, but it is important that some initial comments be made immediately so that the cultural crisis and the sacramental crisis can be directly related.

The Church, whether it admits it or not, participates in culture. It always has and it always will. At one and the same time, the ecclesial community is a product of revelation and culture, of the divine and the human. The Church as a human community participates in the unconscious presuppositions of a particular culture and employs the language, patterns of behavior, and social structures which express these unconscious presuppositions. Moreover, "revelation" and the belief system of the Christian community are expressed in and through the medium of a culture's language, patterns of behavior, and social structures. Many examples of this fact can be marshalled from Christian history. Perhaps the clearest example is found in the New Testament itself. Biblical scholars have pointed out the cultural conditioning of revelation in the writings of St. Paul, especially in his reflections on the role of women in the Church. He places them, although not in every instance, in an inferior social position to men. Is this classification revelation or cultural conditioning? Contemporary critical biblical scholarship is leaning toward the latter.

A further example is the pyramid structure of the Church in the proposed draft of the *Dogmatic Constitution on the Church of Christ* at the first Vatican Council. It states:

> But the Church of Christ is not a community of equals in which all the faithful have the same rights. It is a society of unequals, not only because among the faithful some are clerics and some are laymen, but particularly because there is in the Church the power from God whereby to some it is given to sanctify, teach, and govern, and to others it is not (DS 190).

Is this pyramidical vision of the Church, the product of a terminal culture, swept by the revolutions' and nationalists' movements in Western Europe, searching for survival? One suspects it is, in view of the historical conditions surrounding the First Vatican Council and the remarkable recasting of ecclesial images by the Second Vatican Council which was not forced into a polemic with the French Revolution and the Enlightenment.

In his opening address to the bishops at the Second Vatican Council, John XXIII issued the clearest official admission in a formal ecclesial document of culture's effect on the Church and its teaching. After noting that the Vatican Council was not called to answer any particular heresy or to formulate new doctrines, he noted:

> In order, however, that this doctrine may influence the numerous fields of human activity, with reference to individuals, to families, and to social life, it is necessary first of all that the Church should never depart from the sacred patrimony of truth received from the Fathers. But at the same time she must ever look to the present, to the new condition and new forms of life introduced into the modern world which have opened new avenues to the Catholic apostolate.

Later, in the same speech, Pope John specifically distinguished the substance of the faith from its concrete form of expression. He pointed out that a council was necessary:

> ... from the revered, serene, and tranquil adherence to all the teachings of the Church in its entirety and preciseness, as it still shines forth in the acts of the Council of Trent and the First Vatican Council, the Christian, Catholic, and apostolic spirit of the whole world expects a step foward toward a doctrinal penetration and a formation of consciences in faithful and perfect conformity to the authentic doctrine which, however, should be studied and expounded through the literary forms of modern thought. The substance of the ancient doctrine of the Deposit of Faith is one thing, and the way in which it is presented is another.

It seems that Pope John hit on our key point in the relation of the Church to culture. As cultural elements change and die, religious doctrines and beliefs expressed through them require new expression if their "substance" is to survive.

Every element of ecclesial life can require revision. Authority structures, educational designs, communication networks, etc. . . . will demonstrate the need for adaptation to new cultural environments. But, the ritual life of the Church is peculiarly susceptable to cultural change and need for revision. There are two reasons for this situation. First, ecclesial ritual behavior is closely aligned with the unconscious presuppositions of a culture and the unconscious psyche of its individual participants. The language, patterns of behavior, and social structures of ritual are borrowed from culture and retain their dependency on culture. This has been theologically formulated in the principle that liturgy should reflect the life of the people i.e., the culture or world view of the people. Second, ritual behavior is at the same time a shared element in which all the participants have a stake, some experience, and some power. Ritual is the heart of the ecclesial community. This has been theologically formulated by insisting that where the Eucharist is celebrated, there is the Church.

When the unconscious presuppositions of a culture change, the Church will first recognize the threat in its ritual life. Therefore, it is not surprising that ecclesial communities turn to their worship patterns and religious rituals first, when they attempt to express their belief in the context of a new culture. This has recently been the case in both Roman Catholicism and the Anglical traditions. Why is ritual a nodal point in religious communities and culture? This question will be answered later in our text. At the present time, our aim is merely to identify the change in culture as the external cause of the present sacramental crisis.

Internal Causes: Church Theory and Practice

The title "internal causes" suggests that the Church has played a role in precipitating the sacramental crisis. It is our contention that the Church fulfilled this role in two ways. First, by working for the secularity of the world, the Church fueled the change from classical to contemporary culture and contributed to, if not initiated, the external cause for the sacramental crisis. Second, this general orientation of the Church has forced both theoretical reflection and pastoral practice to reevaluate and restructure ecclesial sacramental life and behavior.

It is probably strange and startling to think of the Church as a contributor to its own crisis. Perhaps it is more foreign to identify this contribution as an ecclesial support and embracement of secularity. Usually, one thinks of the Church as criticizing and opposing secularization.[14] Yet, in our own times, the German theologian J. B. Metz has effectively argued for a positive ecclesial interpretation of secularity in view of its ecclesial origins. Metz has claimed that:

> The secularity of the world, as it has emerged in a globally heightened form, has fundamentally, though not in all its individual historical forms, arisen not against Christianity but through it. It is originally a Christian event and hence testifies in our world situation to the power of the "hour of Christ" at work within history.[15]

Metz's whole position rests on a Christological interpretation. He understands the Christ event as the definitive acceptance of the world by God. In the Incarnation, God accepts the world as distinct from himself. The appearance of the "word made flesh" sets the world free to be itself.

Metz's interpretation makes statements about God and the world.[16] It claims that God is historical. God is Emmanuel, "transcendence itself becomes an event."[17] In the appearance of Jesus the meaning of history has been revealed. The Incarnation also reveals the world as anthropocentric. It is not a world of things or objects, but a world of people which has attained in Christ "an end that has already been promised to it."[18] In accepting the world as different and distinct in Christ, God has not swallowed up or sucked into the Godhead the reality of the world. He has allowed it to exist and guaranteed the permanence of its distinctiveness and difference from himself. Consequently, the Incarnation is the origin and continuing basis for secularity.

Metz's Christological vision has direct ecclesiological implications. The Church which continues the meaning and ministry of Jesus is the concrete "historical, tangible, and effective sign, the sacrament of the eschatologically final acceptance of the world by God."[19] In this perspective, one of the essential tasks of the Church is to continually guarantee and bring to perfection the liberation and secularity of the world. Metz has detected the partial historical attainment of this responsibility in three areas: the separation of Church and state; the autonomy of the human sciences from theology; and, the de-deification of nature.

First, there has been a gradual removal of "sacred overtones" from purely secular institutions e.g., civil governments, through the initiative of the Church. Worldly institutions have been stripped of their religious veneer and accepted at face value i.e., creations of man. Metz offers an example from the Middle Ages:

> ... the separating out of the *imperium* from the *sacerdotium* which began in the Middle Ages, the movement in which the world and its institutions, especially the state, made itself independent and distinct from the Church, must be seen as something fundamentally positive, from a Christian point of view. The state now appears no longer, as in the ancient world, as a sacred institution, but as a secular creation of God. It is divested of its direct and unquestioned numinousness and sacrality by Christianity, which proclaims itself to be the true coordinating point of all religious concerns of man, and the advocate of the secular world given its own authenticity and a genuine partnership with the Church.[20]

Second, the human sciences have attained a real independence and autonomy from the confines of theological reflection through the initiative of the Church. They have been freed to operate under their own methods and norms. Metz locates the inception of this independence in Thomas' use of Aristotle as an authority in his own right.[21] The fruition of the autonomy of the human sciences vis-à-vis theology is found in the Vatican II decree on the *Church in the Modern World* #59:

> This sacred synod, therefore, recalling the teaching of the first Vatican Council, declares that there are "two orders of knowledge" which are distinct, namely faith and reason. It declares that the Church does not forbid that "when the human arts and sciences are practiced they use their own principles and their proper method, each in its own domain." Hence "acknowledgement of this just liberty," this sacred synod affirms the legitimate autonomy of culture and especially of the sciences.

Third, through Christianity, nature has been divested of magical forces. Nature has been liberated from any interpretation which would understand it as being ruled by demiurges. Rather, nature has been freed to become the home of man's experience and understanding, a home subject to its own structures and flaws. Moreover, through Christianity, the value of the creative interaction of the human person and the world in work has attained its proper status. Man is no longer perceived as the slave of the forces and "god's" who control the world and its seasons, but the cooperator with nature in making the world a human residence.

In each of these three examples, the Church has initiated and fostered the growth of secularization and to this extent hastened the shift from classical to contemporary culture. It has quickened the transformation of cultural presuppositions which we have shown to be the basis for a crisis in culture. When this ecclesial activity is applied to a reflection on sacramentology, it is understandable how the Church has brought about its own sacramental crisis, how ecclesial activity is an internal factor in comprehending the contemporary sacramental crisis.

The internal contribution of the Church to the sacramental crisis has been further specified and intensified by recent theological reflection and pastoral practice. Sensing the inadequacy of the former sacramental synthesis in view of new cultural presuppositions "in the making," theoreticians and practitioners pointed out its deficiencies on the level of logic, meaning, value, and effectiveness. This allusion to the criticism of the past stops short of the full contribution of the Church to the sacramental crisis. The vacuum created by the valid criticism gave initiative for the creation of equally questionable sacramental theories and practices. With neither security in the "old" nor trust in the "new," the sacramental crisis only deepened. A closer look at both the negative evaluation of the former sacramental synthesis and the faltering attempts to replace it is quite revealing.

The catechetical traditions of both the Catholic and Protestant communions provide ready access to the main lines of the previous sacramental synthesis. Although there are variations in the particular denominational traditions both before and after the catechectical renewal of the 1960's,[22] the *Baltimore Catechism* and the *Larger Catechism* or *Westminster Larger Catechism* generally reflect the basic tendencies of the previous sacramental synthesis.

A Catechism of Christian Doctrine[23] more commonly known as the "Baltimore Catechism" was the Catholic catechetical workhorse in the United States for almost a century. It succinctly capsulized the essentials of Roman Catholic sacramental doctrine in a question-answer method. It taught:

Q. 136 What is a sacrament?
A. A sacrament is an outward sign instituted by Christ to give grace.

Q. 138 Whence have the sacraments the power of giving grace?
A. The sacraments have the power of giving grace from the merits of Jesus Christ.

The catcehism also placed the number of sacraments at seven.

The *Westminster Larger Catechism*[24] (1648) was a restatement of the "Westminster Confession" i.e., the Presbyterian profession of faith. In addition to the Presbyterians, it is followed by the Congregationalists and some Baptists. It taught:

Q. 162 What is a sacrament?
A. A sacrament is a holy ordinance instituted by Christ in his Church, to signify, seal, and exhibit to those who are within the covenant of grace, the benefits of his mediation; to strengthen and increase their faith, and all other graces; to oblige them to obedience; to testify and cherish their love and communion with one another; and to distinguish them from those who are without.

Q. 164 How many sacraments has Christ instituted in his Church under the New Testament?
A. Under the New Testament Christ has instituted in his Church only two sacraments: Baptism and the Lord's Supper.

In both catechisms there are common presuppositions and omissions. The foundation for the sacraments in both texts was the direct activity of

Christ. He was the institutor of the sacraments. The New Testament served as the common source for the substantiation of this affirmation. In this context, the New Testament was read in a typical pre-critical fashion indigenous to the classical theological synthesis. In this system, the New Testament was taken to be a historical-factual document. It was an instrument of documented "proof." Moreover, it was a polemical tool manipulated by both the Protestant and Catholic traditions to defend the exact number of the sacraments be it seven or two.

Both catechisms allude to Christ as the source of the sacraments, yet he appears to have a minimalized role. The sacraments are presented as realities distinct from his person rather than extensions of his person. Stated briefly, these catechetical sacramentologies are minimally influenced by Christology. The absence of any reflection on the relation of the sacraments to the Church is more glaring, as is the omission of the Holy Spirit and the relation of the sacraments to ordinary life and human behavior. It is not surprising that contemporary theological scholarship has negatively evaluated the classical sacramental synthesis which underpinned these catechetical traditions.

It is impossible to isolate one theological discipline as the "mastermind" in executing the downfall of the classical sacramental synthesis. The fatal blow to the former system has been the result of cross-disciplinary research and reflection. Biblical scholarship, historical criticism, Christological reflection, ecclesiological developments, liturgical explorations and ecumenical discussions have all contributed to its contemporary theological indictment.

Biblical scholarship has criticized a "fundamentalist" reading of the Bible as a strict factual documentary. Scriptural exegesis readily admits the impossibility of establishing from biblical texts the explicit factual institution of each sacrament by the historical Jesus. Most authors will admit the possibility of establishing two. Historical criticism has created a sensitivity to the difficult tasks of understanding the exact historical number of the sacraments, and, more important, the understanding of the general term "sacrament" and the particular meaning of each sacrament within its historical age and context. Christological investigations have finally accepted the full humanity of Christ and viewed him as the *sacrament of God*. Christ is portrayed as the primary sacrament. Any sacramental theology that does not see Christ as the center of sacramentology is judged inadequate. Developments in ecclesiology have underscored the intrinsic and necessary relation of the Church to Christ. The Church is the reality Christ instituted above and beyond any institution of sacraments. The sacraments are meaningful insofar as they are extensions of the Church. Liturgical explorations have underscored the worship character of the sacraments and their anthropological foundation. Liturgics has reminded us that sacraments are first and foremost prayers of the ecclesial community. Finally, ecumenical discussions have highlighted the inability of polemical sacramental theologies to bear fruit in our present age. Any sacramental synthesis which is merely polemical in character and chooses to ignore the "truth value" contained in the writings of members outside their particular ecclesial body will fall short of the exigencies of the present theological task.

With some minor adjustments, the classical sacramental synthesis may have survived the criticism emerging from one of the above theological disciplines. The combined force of their "attack," however, was mortal. A compilation of theological reflection in a collaborative synthesis further triggered the sacramental crisis on a theoretical level from within the Church.

Observers of concrete Christian living and sacramental practice could only agree with the theological judgment that the classical sacramental synthesis was inadequate and doomed. They detected a growing gap between sacramental performance and the verification of its "truth claims" by a commensurate Christian lifestyle. Serious discrepancies appeared. Why was it that only 50–60% of baptized members participated in the *minimum* worship pattern of the community i.e., the Sunday Eucharist? How was the failure of two out of five sacramental marriages to be explained? Why had the long Saturday confession lines vanished?

An analysis of the pastoral sacramental scene only verified the judgment of the theoreticians. If the sacramental economy was to survive, a change was in order. A repetition of the old order simply was not enough. A "new" way had to be found. The pastoral rush to bandage the sacramental wounds of the Church records the final element of the Church's internal contribution to its own sacramental crisis.

Spurred by the theological orientation of the Second Vatican Council, new sacramental programs and practices were designed. Although the strategy of reform and renewal may have been correct, the tactics employed only heightened the unrest experienced by the "faithful" and plunged sacramentology deeper into turmoil. The general principles of reform: the active and conscious participation of all the faithful in the liturgical celebration; a clear and facile understanding of the sacramental signs; the removal of any features which confuse and cloud the nature and purpose of the sacraments; and the restoration of Scripture to its proper place in sacramental celebrations, were laudable. The method of introducing these reforms, however, could be evaluated on a scale from "poor" to "disastrous".

A quick look at the publication dates of the various revisions tells the sad story. The Eucharist was first on the docket for change, being transformed in three revisions from 1966 until 1972. Next to appear was the Rite for the Baptism of Children in May 1969. The Rite of Confirmation appeared in August 1971. Two revisions appeared in 1972, the Rite of Christian Initiation of Adults on January 6th and the Rite for the Anointing of the Sick on December 7th. The revisions were completed on December 2nd, 1973 with the Rite of Reconciliation. Hopefully, no one will search for the theological logic behind the order in which the revisions were published. There simply does not appear to be any.

With the publication of each document, diocesan and parochial leaders established the machinery for new sacramental programs. "Parent nights" became requirements if children were to receive their first Communion, social action phases were incorporated into confirmation programs, the age of confirmation candidates was upped, etc. The effort to respond to the sacramental needs of the Christian community cannot be faulted, but the resulting programs were (and are) questionable. In the first place, the transformation and construction of programs were piecemeal and it seems without any desire for a sacramental overview or synthesis. This situation stemmed from the lack of coordination and correlation in the publication of the official *Rites*. Secondly, in place of an overall, integrated vision of the various sacraments, new "quasi-theologies" of individual sacraments made their appearance on the pastoral stage. Blame for this phenomenon can also be placed on the illogical order of the published official *Rites*. A good example of *A* for effort and *D* for results is the present state of the sacraments of Christian initiation i.e., baptism, confirmation, and the Eucharist.[25]

The three recent documents which mention the sacraments of initiation place them in their proper order i.e., baptism, confirmation, Eucharist. In practice, however, the sacraments are celebrated in the order of baptism, Eucharist, confirmation. In an attempt to justify this practice, some religious educators and theologians have constructed a new name and theology for confirmation. It is being called the sacrament of Christian maturity. This seems harmless enough. But when their claims are taken seriously and placed in relation to the two other sacraments of initiation, one realizes that a new, and not necessarily correct, understanding of Christian initiation as a whole is being proposed. The attempt to salvage the sacrament of confirmation by giving it a new title and altering its age requirement is a symptom of the pastoral hastiness which only complicates the sacramental crisis.

Unfortunately, the proponents of confirmation as Christian maturity have reflected on its meaning in isolation. Yet, it is impossible to propose a theology of confirmation void of reference to baptism and the Eucharist without dire consequences. Any change in the understanding of confirmation will demand a redesign of the whole initiation process, and a consequent altering of the meaning of baptism and the Eucharist. Four questions will demonstrate this point in the specific issue of confirmation as the sacrament of Christian maturity.

First, if confirmation is the sacrament of Christian maturity, what is the meaning of baptism? Second, if a person does not make a mature decision to live as a Christian until the time of confirmation, why should he or she be admitted to the Eucharist, the sign of full membership and active commitment to the Church? Third, if confirmation is the sacrament of Christian maturity, what is the distinctiveness of this sacrament in relation to baptism and the Eucharist? Most preparation manuals for confirmation do little more than present a theology of baptism and the Eucharist. Finally, how is one to make sense out of the word "mature" as distinct from "immature" within a sacramental system? Why should sacraments be administered to "immature" persons i.e., reception of the Eucharist before confirmation the "sacrament of Christian maturity"?

To understand confirmation as the sacrament of Christian maturity dramatically alters the theological understanding of initiation into the Church. It also creates an indefensible theological system. Baptism becomes an enrollment in a catechumenal process. The Eucharist, which has always been understood as the sign of full membership would become a preparation rite and replaced by confirmation as the premier sacrament. Yet these are the theological implications present in the current pastoral practice and reflection on the sacrament of confirmation. Given this disarray, a feeling of psychosis in the ecclesial community could well be a normal reaction.

Pastoral practice must be included as a factor in the internal contribution of the Church to the present sacramental crisis. Theology had undercut the former sacramental vision and, consequently, the former way of "doing" the sacraments. Unfortunately, many attempted replacements have left the sacramental system in a worse state of affairs. It is one thing to have an antiquated system which at least made sense in the past. It is another matter to have a new system without solid theological "roots." The theological and pastoral transition from the classical sacramental theory to a system for today takes time and perhaps incurrs mistakes. Until this time transpires, the sense of crisis will continue to prevail.

From Causes to Solutions

Unless one can clarify the causes for a particular crisis, solving the issue is pure chance. This is not the case in working toward a resolution of the sacramental crisis in the Church. Both external and internal factors for its existence are discernible. Understanding the effect of cultural change and the role of the Church in advancing cultural transformation avoids the error of attacking the wrong problems. For example, if one looks at the outside world as the secularized Goliath to be conquered by the ecclesial David, the true tension in sacramental theology will never be answered. Understanding the theological criticism of the former system and the desire for practical revisions focuses attention on the main elements which require inclusion in a new, well grounded, and contemporary theology and practice of sacraments within the Church.

The very causes for the sacramental crisis outlined in this chapter hint at the path which must be pursued out of the forest of confusion and crisis which has sprung up in the Church's sacramental life. First, it will be necessary to state accurately the presuppositions underpinning the investigation of our subject. This description must commence with an analysis of method, since method colors all one's research and thinking.

Second, the presuppositions of the emerging new culture must be looked at, since the unconscious presuppositions expressed in the language, patterns of behavior and social structures of contemporary culture will be the vehicle through which a contemporary theology of sacraments takes shape. Since the focus of this text is sacraments, the second part of the work will examine human ritual behavior from the vantagepoint of the behavioral sciences i.e., psychology, anthropology, sociology, and philosophy. We will show that ritual is indigenous to human cultural life, that there is an anthropological foundation to the ritual called sacraments by the ecclesial community.

Third, it will be necessary to construct a theological synthesis in terms of the contemporary cultural presuppositions. This data will constitute the third part of the work i.e., the theological dimension of sacraments. It could be viewed as a theological interpretation of the anthropological data. Hopefully, this synthesis will overcome any bandages or patch-work answers to the sacramental crisis by providing a coherent overview of the whole sacramental system.

The final part of our sacramental exploration goes beyond a solution to our specific sacramental crisis. It will examine the relation of our personal sacramental vision with other historical periods through a comparison of sacramental models. A new model for sacraments will be proposed which more adequately corresponds to the theological synthesis of the preceding section.

The causes of the present sacramental crisis are an important question of history. Solutions to the crisis are a task for the present, a present that is willing to learn from the past.

NOTES

1. The term sociosis is taken from the Dutch psychologist, van den Berg.

2. The *Aufklarung* appears to be the great movement that rang the death knell of the former culture and the birth cry of the new culture.

3. As a basic introduction to the idea of culture, cf. Harry L. Shapiro (ed.), *Man Culture and Society.* (New York: Oxford University Press, 1971); A. L. Krober, C. Kluckhohn, *Culture: A Critical Review of Concepts and Definitions.* (New York: 1963); A. L. Krober, *The Nature of Culture.* (Chicago: The University of Chicago Press, 1968).

4. Cf. William Luijpen, *Existential Phenomenology.* Duquesne Studies Philosophical Series 12, (Pittsburgh: Duquesne University Press, 1960).

5. Cf. Bernard Lonergan, "Metaphysics as Horizon," in *Collection.* F. E. Crowe (ed.), (New York: Herder and Herder, 1967), pp. 202-221.

6. Integration does not necessarily imply the resolution of conflicts and oppositions within a culture. However, cultural integration allows the participants to survive in the midst of conflicts.

7. Cf. T. Shannin, "Models and Thought," *Rules of the Game.* (London: Tavistock Publ., 1972), pp. 1-22; Thomas Kuhn, *The Structures of Scientific Revolutions.* 2nd ed., (Chicago: The University of Chicago Press, 1972); Herbert Butterfield, *The Origins of Modern Science.* (New York: Macmillan & Co., 1966); Ernst Nagel, *The Structure of Scientific Explanation.* (New York: Harcourt, Bruce and World, 1961); Max Black, *Models and Metaphors.* (Ithaca: Cornell University Press, 1964); Frederich Ferre, "Mapping the Logic of Models in Science and Theology," *New Essays in Religious Language.* D. M. High, (ed.), (New York: Oxford University Press, 1966), pp. 54-93; Robert P. Scharlemann, "Theological Models and their Construction," *The Journal of Theology.* 53 (1973), pp. 65-82.

8. John H. Newman, *Grammar of Assent.* (London: Longmans, Green and Co., 1903), p. 60.

9. John H. Newman, *Lectures on the Present Position of Catholics in England.* (Dublin: 1857), p. 26.

10. Jose Ortega Y Gasset, *Obras Completas.* Vol. V, (Madrid: Revista de Occidente, 1946-47), p. 383.

11. *Ibid.*, pp. 381-382.

12. Cf. my article, "The Ecclesiology of the 'Rite of Christian Initiation of Adults'", *Louvain Studies 6,* (1976).

13. For further examples cf. B. Lonergan, "Dimensions of Meaning," *Collection: Papers by Bernard Lonergan, S.J.,* (New York: Herder and Herder, 1967), pp. 252-267; "Dehellenization of Dogma," *Theological Studies.* 28 (1967), pp. 336-351; "Theology in its New Context," *Theology of Renewal.* L. K. Schook, (ed.), (New York: Herder and Herder, 1968).

14. J.B. Metz, *Theology of the World.* (New York: Herder and Herder, 1969) p. 15: "They all proceed on the (to them) obvious assumption that the secularity of the world is something that is actually contrary to the Christian understanding of the world and must therefore be totally overcome by Christian means. What is common to all of them is their fundamental rejection of the secularization of the world, which began in modern times and (*sic.*) is expressed in acute form in our present world situation."

15. *Ibid.*, pp. 19-20.

16. Cf. *Ibid.*, pp. 21-32.

17. *Ibid.*, p. 22.

18. *Ibid.*, p. 25.

19. *Ibid.*, p. 22.

20. *Ibid.*, p. 36.

21. *Ibid.*, p. 37.

22. Cf. my article "Surveying the Catechisms on Sacraments," *The Living Light.* (1978).

23. *A Catechim of Christian Doctrine No. 3.* (New York: Benziger Bros. Inc.) pp. 69-73.

24. The text can be found in T.F. Torrance, *The School of Faith.* (London: Camelot Press, 1959), pp. 183-185.

25. Cf. my article "Is Confirmation the Real Problem?," *Religion Teachers Journal.* 10 (1977), pp. 24-26.

2 IN SEARCH OF A METHOD

Even before theological reflection *per se* begins, the theologian must fight the battle of method. The contemporary theological enterprise requires that one clearly articulate the path one will pursue in research and reflection and clarify any presuppositions which accompany this endeavor. Should the theologian fail in this task, his or her work might become a mere exercise in futility. Far too often, the method employed by theologians in the past, especially from the seventeenth to the beginning of the nineteenth century, condemned their research and systems to faulty if not erroneous conclusion.

This chapter hopes to confront the issue of method. It will attempt to penetrate the meaning of the term "method." It will outline three potential methodological types. And, it will clarify the particular method employed in the present construction of a sacramental theology.

1. Method: Meaning and Types

Most spontaneous answers to the question: "What is method?" usually make reference to a set of procedures or rules. This response is not incorrect but is incomplete. It is valid to indicate that every scientific investigation contains certain rules or laws which govern the field under investigation. Yet, the term method possesses a deeper and more important meaning. Bernard Lonergan articulated this deeper dimension well:

> A method is a normative pattern of recurrent and related operations yielding cumulative and progressive results. There is a method, then, where there are distinct operations, where each operation is related to the others, where the set of relations forms a pattern, where the pattern is described as the right way of doing the job, where operations in accord with the pattern may be indefinitely repeated, and where the fruits of such repetition are, not repetitious, but cumulative and progressive.[1]

22

When speaking of a method then, two elements should be remembered. First, a method is not a process which exists independent of the methodologist or the researcher, but actually arises from and is continually grounded in his or her mental operations. An articulated method is the formal expression in words and/or symbols of the minds' operations in investigating a portion of reality. Second, a method is a framework for creative collaboration. It enables the discoveries within different functional specializations to interact and expand their perspective and understanding.

At first glance, this description of method can appear rather alien, but a brief example will reveal its validity. Imagine for a moment that there are no books on scientific research. You find yourself in a laboratory with Madame Curie. One morning you discover that some photographic film was mistakenly left out of its container overnight. The film demonstrates all the effects of having been exposed. Both of you are puzzled since there was no light whatsoever in the room. Immediately, you are faced with the question: Why? By trial and error, by different mental operations, you come to the discovery of radiation and you call the effect x (for unknown) rays. There was a process which lead to your discovery of X rays, and a more important process which was acted out by your mind.[2] These mental operations can be summarized under four headings: (1) experience; (2) understanding; (3) judgment; (4) decision. These four operations can take place simultaneously or in temporal spans. They can appear in a variety of orders. However, each of the operations is involved in human thought.

Experience refers to the sense data. Understanding refers to our attempt to understand what the data means, how it is to be interpreted or integrated. Judgment refers to the evaluation of whether our understanding of the data is valid, real, or a true understanding. Decision refers to our application of true data to our life activitites.

The above fourfold process of human knowledge is often hidden from our consciousness. The task of finding explanations for reality is provided for us by the various scientific disciplines. For example, textbooks preserve the discoveries and present the decisions which have proved valid. These texts, however, often exclude many elements of the process which were operative in the original struggle for conclusions. This is why many people know that 2 times 2 equals 4 or that $E = MC^2$, but few know why it does or the operations which have lead to the judgment that it is correct.

Throughout this text, method will be understood as a recurring process or pattern which yields continual insight and advancement of knowledge and results. The methodological pattern or process is understood to flow from the field or area under investigation but reflects the basic pattern of human thought which is a fourfold process of experience, understanding, judgment and decision. The goal of any method is to draw closer to the truth of any reality under investigation and to allow the correlation of knowledge within different functional specializations.

Three distinct methodological types can be isolated within the history of theological investigation: the psychological, the essential, and the existential.[3] A brief description of the general orientation of each type will provide a Gestalt for comprehending the method operative in the present investigation of sacramental theology.

Psychological Method

Everyone uses and is familiar with the psychological method. It utilizes a basic characteristic of human reflection. Generally, the human person has an immediate experience of his or her psychological life. The origins, motivations, and structures of our human personality or inner self are often unconscious, buried, or hidden. Yet, we still "see" or "experience" our inner self in our concrete activities, thoughts, and choices.

The correlation between our inner experience and our outer activity opens a path for dialogue between our individual self and the totality of our experience. Therefore, a human person turns to the inner self to understand and express many of the mysteries and realities of life, comparing them to and explaining them by reference to what he or she feels and thinks about himself or herself.

The psychological method presupposes that inner human life acts as a mirror reflecting the exterior mysteries of human existence and experience. The process of psychological explanation gives rise to one of the richest arenas of human existence: symbolization. Experience and explanation are embodied in expression. The human person symbolizes the meaning of reality discovered in the dialogue between the inner self and concrete action.

The description of grace in early Scholasticism serves as a good example of the psychological method:

> In early Scholastic theology, grace is described as a light, as an inner joy and peace of mind, as a stability of life. Sin, on the contrary, is the night of the soul, it is a sickness, a sluggishness, a weakness of the will, a blindness of the mind and a hardening of the heart, images which can be found in the Bible. . . . [4]

For early Scholasticism, the realities of grace and sin were understood by comparison with the inner psychological life-experiences of the human person.

The psychological method has both advantages and disadvantages. Positively, the method has pedagogical value. People readily comprehend psychological description and are continually living within the realm of symbolic language. Moreover, the psychological method is perceived as more vital and alive than strictly abstract thought. The psychological method also maintains the radical unity of reality, self-comprehension, and symbolic activity. The conglomeration of these facets thrusts the psychological method toward real concrete existence.

Negatively, the psychological method carries implicit dangers. Without a critical attitude toward one's inner feelings and self comprehension reality can be dangerously distorted and warped. An uncorrected egocentrism can annihilate the mystery, potential, and transcendence of reality by interpreting everything in terms of an inflated and glorified *I* which destroys the dialogue between self and reality and replaces it with a deceiving monologue.

When the psychological method is applied to theology, there will always be the danger of an "unarticulated Pelagianism." The anthropomorphic focus of the psychological method will tend to lead the researcher to place God and man on an equal plane. This tendency is intensified by the unique character of our age with its emphasis on "pop psychology," "T" groups etc. . . . where a fixation on self-understanding often degenerates into an individualism verging on monism. In this climate, the psychological method can be transformed into a manipulative tool for interpreting reality according to personal dreams and needs rather than as a vehicle for discovering truth through insight. All the above negative possibilities should warn against an exclusive or uncritical application of this method.

Essential Method

Essential method takes the opposite direction of psychological method. Where psychological method turned inward toward the self to understand reality, the essential method turns outward. Essential method attempts to discover through analysis what reality *must be like* in order for certain events or appearances to be possible. Stated more philosophically, essential method seeks to discover the a priori conditions for the possibility of any given fact or reality.

A presupposition that there are discoverable stable structures to reality lies behind the essential method. Reality will be understood when the researcher cracks this hidden, yet real, code. The pre-existent order or code of reality is envisioned by the essential method as universal and permanent. It is accessible through the use of reason, inference, and logic.

In a secondary thrust, essential method seeks to outline the mutual connections and organic unity of the a priori conditions which it reveals. In short, it aims at constructing a metaphysics. This endeavor lends credence to and reenforces the presupposition that an objective structure and order to reality actually exists.

Essential method has both asset deficits. It cannot be totally discounted as a potential methodology in theological reflection. In an age which walks a tight rope with total relativism, it can supply a needed recognition of some stability to reality. Yet, essential method can be employed only with great caution. This method in a decadent form stagnated and strangled theological reflection for too long. It lead to impersonal technical statements which bear no resemblance to experiential life. It can solidify the impression of a fixed and permanent universe void of change and dynamic elements. It can overlook the real dialectics and tensions which are the fabric of existence as human.

Existential Method

Existential method attempts to preserve the positive values of essential analysis while avoiding its pitfalls. Existential method considers human existence as a whole, as a web of interrelated realities and experiences. It turns away from the abstract and the universal to the individual and the concrete. It concentrates its efforts on performance and what is labeled "authentic existence."

Existential method can be defined as:

> The systematic exposition of the necessary and universal *a priori* conditions for the possibility of a given real existence in the wholeness of its human situation.[5]

The emphasis in this definition is on the phrase "a given real existence in the wholeness of its human situation." The focus on real existence as opposed to the abstract, on the wholeness of existence as opposed to the segmentation of reality, on the human situation as distinct from an objective world indifferent to the effect of human life differentiates existential method from essential method. At the same time, existential method is interested in investigating the structural elements within human existence which form a parcel of its content. Existential method, however, insists on their flexible and dynamic character. They are investigated with a note of tentativeness. They are checked and revised in view of actual experience.

Existential method has certain advantages and disadvantages. Its focus on real life and concrete experience places it in the locus of living truth rather than a world of abstractions. This is not to insinuate that abstraction is wrong or superfluous in itself; it serves an essential function in human thought. Abstraction, however, must terminate not in concepts or ideas, but reality as lived.

The emphasis on real life and concrete experience thrusts existential method in the direction of values and morals. It identifies personal responsibility and decision as components of reality which demand inclusion if an accurate reflection of reality is to be attained. Existential method is also amenable to a contemporary understanding of the world within which religious discourse unfolds and claims to bear meaning. In this respect, there is a certain openness to the content and expression of religious and theological queries.

The dangers confronting existential method are similar to those impinging on the psychological method. A hidden "Pelagianism" equating God and man can permeate existential method. There can also be a lack of precise meaning and thinking in existential method arising from its tendency to avoid ontological or metaphysical reflection which are necessary elements in the theological enterprise.

Variety and shades of difference can be detected when particular adherents within a methodological type are compared. Yet, a fundamental consistency will predominate. Since the present investigation into sacramentality will opt for an existential method, a brief outline of the main thrusts of three seminal thinkers within this method is opportune. Particular elements in our methodological approach to sacramentality have been gleaned in varying degrees from E. Husserl, M. Blondel, and D. Tracy. Hopefully, an exposition of their methodological uniqueness will further clarify our own.

Husserl

Husserl is well known as the father of phenomenology. It is within this context that his work is significant for our study of sacramental theology. The goal of phenomenology is faciley stated:

> Phenomenolgy is a work of reflection. Like any other philosophical work which aims to be radical and transcendental, it finds itself confronted with a variety of tasks. The first is that of *phenomenological reduction,* whose purpose. . . . is first to uncover hidden assumptions in positions which are being criticized, and second, to discover the significant "primitive fact" whith its character of irreducibility, inevitability and primacy.[6]

Husserl has left his mark on phenomenology through his development and explanation of eidetic reduction.

Husserl's philosophical goal was a knowledge and understanding of reality liberated from the experiential or theoretical prejudices of the knower. He observed the bias our experiences, unconscious influences and preconceptions exerted on the comprehension and meaning of appearing reality. Therefore, he devised a method composed of phenomenological description and *eidetic reduction* to correct these potential distortions.

In this method, one proceeds by describing the experienced or appearing phenomenon. Slowly, the researcher works his way back through his previous experience of the phenomenon until he arrives at the first experience of the phenomenon or the "primitive fact." While this *eidetic reduction* is carried out, the researcher brackets any prejudicial coloring which may have transformed or influenced the meaning of the phenomenon. Ultimately, the researcher will attain the "essence" of the reality free from distortion. From this vantage point, one can investigate the import and effect of the bracketed prejudices and reintegrate them into the knowing experience.

Husserl's contribution to our theology of sacraments is his insistence on phenomenological description and acknowledgment of the influence of the knower on the object known. Throughout this work, sacraments will be understood as appearing phenomenon that first and foremost require description. In a secondary fashion, Husserl alerts us to be conscious of hidden prejudices in our knowledge and cautions us against any quick identification of reality with what we spontaneously see and think.[7]

Blondel

In creating a sacramental theology, we are undertaking an analysis of realities which are at the same time human and divine, "natural and supernatural", present in the human condition yet free gifts. It will be argued throughout this text that sacraments are the most normal realities and human activities in human existence. How, then, are they divine? It will also be argued that the sacraments are comprehendable within the purely human behavioral sciences. However, how can human science sustain a living belief in a divine reality? The particular path pursued in our sacramental journey raises serious methodological questions both from the human sciences and from theology. In a general way, these issues have already been explored by the French genius M. Blondel.

Blondel was a philosopher by training and practice.[8] One fundamental question dominated his intellectual effort. It has been expressed in his classic philosophical principle: nothing can enter into man which does not go out from him and which in a certain sense corresponds to an inner need for expression.[9] This principle places a challenge before the Christian philosopher since revelation is claimed to be factually supernatural and any refusal of the supernatural is interpreted as a positive decay. Blondel's problem was to demonstrate how he could be faithful to his philosophical principle and at the same time demonstrate the acceptability of the Christian claims concerning revealed realities.

Blondel attempted to situate properly the issue confronting him. First, he proposed a method identified by the word *immanence*. He proposed to study human destiny from within. The method of immanence did not imply that man possesses everything needed for his life within himself, nor did it reject what is traditionally referred to as the "transcendent." For Blondel, the word "immanent" was equivocal i.e., making the equation in our consciousness between what we seem to think and will and what we actually do think and will.[10] If the supernatural was to be justified, it required a reflection which commenced and moved within immanence i.e., by going back to things in themselves in order to understand what every man thinks and wills and through analysis arrive at the ground or basis which makes all conscious thought and will possible. Herein lies Blondel's unique contribution to philosophical method in general and the method which will be operative in this particular work on sacraments.

Blondel proposes that there are ideas one necessarily and really thinks since they are implicit in one's conscious thoughts and activities. It is almost as though there were two tiers of thinking and willing. One has as its referent my concrete conscious thoughts and choices. The other has, as its referent, my unconscious, or better, my preconscious power of thinking and willing. Blondel writes of the *volonte voulanté* (the willing will) and the *volontés voulues* (the willed will). It is the willing will which makes possible and sustains the concrete choices of the willed will. The willing will is the general power or faculty which enables individual concrete choice. An example will clarify Blondel's scheme.

It often happens that an individual suddenly comes to realize that ideas or conviction he thought he believed are not the true thoughts or convictions he unconsciously held. Converts often speak of always having believed the tradition or tenets of their "new" religious tradition as latent convictions which were unconscious or hidden. At the time of conversion, these veiled beliefs become clear and conscious. In this situation the willing will of the convert was always oriented to his "new" religious tradition even though his willed will was not. After conversion, his willed will is in conformity with his willing will or fundamental power of choice.

Blondel applies his distinction between the willing will and willed will to the issue of the supernatural within philosophical reflection. Man is an agent for Blondel. He is directed toward the fullness of existence of which he is not the author. Humankind seeks the possibility of all thought and all choice. This human orientation is not the product of man's desire but a necessity of his peculiar type of being and existence.

In spite of the intense drive for the fullness of thought and will, man is fallible. He can deviate from the goal for which he is destined. His willed will can opt for less than the infinite which lays hold of his being. Only the power of human tradition spanning the eons of human civilization keeps humankind as a global reality in pursuit of its destiny. The willing will will never settle for less than the infinite which surpasses any particular reality the willed will might embrace.

Blondel claims that his analysis of the human condition from within demonstrates the presence of the *idea* of the supernatural. This idea is the goal of human destiny i.e., the object of all possible thought and will which supersedes all actual thoughts and choices. This idea is present in the autonomous immanent i.e., in the human person independent of an appeal to revelation or a sphere outside the world in which humanity resides.[11] Blondel is at the threshold of the supernatural detecting its idea in human existence from within that existence.

For our present task of constructing a sacramental theology, the method of immanence is significant for its faithfulness to remaining within the actual natural world without leaping to a supernatural realm. It begins from an anthropological inquiry and arrives at the idea of the supernatural without arguing from revelation. The method of immanence demonstrates that the philosopher by application of his own methods can demonstrate that the answers of Christian faith "fit" the unquenchable quest of human destiny. In a similar fashion, our method will commence with the human situation, the "immanent," and attempt to demonstrate that the theological claims about sacraments "fit" the data which emerges from an anthropological analysis of human "ritual behavior."

Tracy

One of the most recent theories on theological method and, one which has exerted a profound influence on the present investigation of sacramental theology, has been David Tracy's *Blessed Rage for Order*.[12] Tracy summarizes his vision in five theses. First, "the two principle sources for theology are Christian texts and common human experience and language."[13] Second, "The theological task will involve a critical correlation of the results of the investigation of the two sources."[14] Third, "the principle method of investigation of the source 'common human experience and language' can be described as a phenomenology of the 'religious dimension' present in everyday and scientific experience and language."[15] Fourth, "the principle method of investigation of the source 'the Christian tradition' can be described as an historical and hermeneutical investigation of classical Christian texts."[16] Fifth, "to determine the truth-status of the results of one's investigation into the meaning of both common human experience and Christian texts the theologian should employ an explicitly transcendental or metaphysical mode of reflection."[17]

Each of the above theses fleshes out the central affirmation of Tracy's tome i.e., Christian theology seeks to reflect philosophically on the meaning present in the Christian fact.[18] The initial step is to identify the data from Christian texts and clarify the human existence to which it is proposed as a meaning system.[19] The cry for a correlation of the two sources of theology recalls Tillich's method of correlation. Tracy, however, insists on a distinctiveness from Tillich. Tracy believes that Tillich merely juxtaposed questions from the human sphere of existence with answers from the religious sphere. In his evaluation this is insufficient. A critical correlation is more than a coupling of Christian answers with human existential questions. The revisionist method requires that the Christian answers be critically compared with all other potential answers, whether they arise from non-Christian religions or even from within the human situation itself.[20]

Tracy's third and fourth theses are the heart of his methodological vision. The theologian must search the human experience in an attempt to detect a dimension of life which can be called the "religious dimension." Here the revisionist orientation is akin to Blondel and Husserl. Theology must begin by describing what appears in human experience. This prerequisite arises from the universalist claim of Christianity. If Christianity is the answer to the meaning of life, an answer available to all persons, then there should be a trace of the questions-answers present within the Christian horizon in common human experience and language.

The theologian must also critically confront his own tradition through history and hermeneutics. History will determine what the Christian texts are. Hermeneutics will allow a comprehension of the meaning, interpretation, and contemporary application of the established text. In the arena of hermeneutics the theologian must be concerned not only with the meaning of the textual words, but also with the general world view or horizon, the rituals, symbols, or cultural peculiarities which contextualize the text. The hermeneutical goal can be summarized in a question: "what is the mode-of-being-in-the-world *referred to* by the text?."[21]

The final task of the revisionist method is the most difficult to sustain. Tracy argues that the truth claims of the critical correlation between common human experience and language and the Christian tradition must be verified by a metaphysical mode of reflection. Only metaphysics can serve as an adequate criteria to test the claims of the correlation, since only a metaphysics can establish criteria which apply to all situations.[22]

Blessed Rage for Order reflects the present status of method within the theological enterprise. It presents the maturity of a scientific endeavor begun at the turn of century and which is currently reaping interest.

The issue of theological method has an explicit bearing on sacramental theology. Of all the theological disciplines, sacramentology lends itself to close analysis and scrutiny from the viewpoint of the human behavioral sciences. This situation arises not only from the theoretical nature of this theological arena, but more importantly from the performative character of sacraments i.e., their actual ritual-symbolic acting out. The actual application of the human sciences of anthropology, psychology, and sociology to sacraments, however, has been a recent phenomenon. It has appeared in our times primarily due to the methods which have been proposed for theological analysis. It is insufficient for our present purpose to look at method in general. Our attention must turn to the specific method germaine to our peculiar labor i.e., the development of a sacramental theology for our age.

2. A Method for Sacramental Theology

It should be clear from our discussion of method in general that two elements necessarily comprise the content of any contemporary investigation into a sacramental theology: those which are anthropological and those which are theological. By distinguishing these elements, we are not attempting to create a dichotomy between them. Rather, we hope to demonstrate the real foundation for sacraments within concrete human existence.

Our methodological option for sacramental theology can be classified as existential and in the direction of Blondel and Tracy. We will proceed in two stages. First, an attempt will be made to uncover those areas of human existence which could be labeled "religious" and "sacramental" i.e., involved with ritual behavior which purports to supply a meaning to the human experience of "the Other," "ultimate concern," "God" etc. This data will be gleaned and evaluated from the viewpoint of the behavioral sciences of anthropology, sociology and psychology. As C. Kiesling has pointed out:

> A sacramental theology which does not approach the sacraments within the horizon of religious rites of non-Christian religions and secular activities of every kind is no longer adequate for a true explanation and evaluation of the Christian sacraments.[23]

Second, our method will explore the theological dimension of sacraments by constructing a system which will allow an integrated vision. This dimension will correspond to an analysis of Christian texts and lead to a correlation of the theological elements with the anthropological results.

In both our anthropological and theological investigation, no single focus will suffice. ". . .no one method can lead to a satisfying grasp of the issue, due to the fact that the sacraments themselves are highly complex, involving a number of dynamics from the various dimensions of both human and divine life."[24] Yet two elements can be signaled out for special emphasis in our understanding of the Christian sacraments: the phenomenological and the Christological. The phenomenological focus stems from the insight of G. van der Leeuw who defended the thesis that sacraments are rooted in human nature. Every sacrament takes up within itself a particular human phenomenon be it initiation, a meal, forgiveness, care of the sick, human consent, or service. Consequently, the sacraments are initially to be understood in light of and in the context of the human phenomenon which gives rise to and remains present in the sacramental action. In a sense, the phenomenological focus highlights the sacramental nature of all reality.

> Man must articulate the religious experience of the sacramentality of all created agents and activities. They elaborate a hierarchy of perfection and value among all created agents and activities as sacramental. This articulation is expressed not only in theoretical knowledge, but more fundamentally in institutionalized action. Specific agents and activities are institutionalized as paradigms of the sacramentality of all other agents and activities. God's self-giving and transformation of man are seen with special clarity in these institutionalized agents and activities which serve as reminders of, and norms for the sacramentality of all other created agents and actions.[25]

The Christological focus maintains that an understanding of the activity of God in the sacraments is impossible without a comprehension of what God has factually done in Christ. God does not act directly in the sacraments or in any other arena of human existence. God mediates his activity through the humanity of Christ.

> Indeed, God is using the humanity of Jesus, and it is for this very reason that Christ is called the *Ursakrament*, the original sacrament. His *humanness* is *the* sign, *the* symbol, *the* sacrament of God's self-communication to us; all the other signs, symbols, and sacraments are secondary to the humanness of Jesus.[26]

A valid penetration into the mystery of the sacraments presupposes a comprehension, no matter how limited, of the mystery of Christ as the unfolding of salvation. The humanity of Jesus is the core of sacramental theology since it binds together the human phenomenon of symbolic activity with the offer and attainment of divine life. The Christological focus in no way negates the path of phenomenological description and anthropological analysis of human ritual and symbolic activity. Rather, Christology requires a study of the human personality and human community plunged into social life and behavior.

Christology is not complete without the added dimension of ecclesiology. A Christological sacramental theology implies an ecclesial sacramental theology. The risen Lord continues to be alive and operative in human history through the Church. The Church continues the ministry of Christ in the world. One could say that the Church is the sacrament of Christ the *Ursakrament*. Consequently, one's understanding and image of the Church will radically influence one's vision of sacraments. This ecclesiological note also directs us to a phenomenological focus. The Church is a community of persons and therefore a sociological entity with all the roles, patterns of behavior, and social structures which constitute any sociological entity. At the same time, the human reality of the Church, through the power of the Holy Spirit, is the medium for divine love and life. Consequently, a discernment of the mutual cooperation between the human and the divine in the Church will enlighten the relation of the human and the divine in sacramental activities.

The remaining chapters of this work will expose the phenomenological, Christological and ecclesiological dimension of sacraments. The phenomenological approach will appear most clearly in Part Two of this text: The Anthropological Dimension of Sacraments. The Christological-Ecclesiological approach will predominate in Part Three: The Theological Dimension of Sacraments. This particular methodological division does not arise only from the traditional division of content within sacramental theology, but also, and more importantly from the peculiar sacramental crisis of our cultural age as outlined in the last chapter.

By a phenomenological examination of the anthropological dimension of ritual and ritual behavior, the flavor and direction of the present cultural presupposition can become more conscious as they are expressed in growing cultural integration. A correct understanding of the cultural stance of contemporary humanity is indispensable for an accurate formulation and expression of the theological claims about sacraments in a language and paradigmatic model comprehensible by and communicative to persons of the twentieth century. The inclusion of Christology and ecclesiology within the theological dimension of sacraments situates them within the larger scope and vision of an integrated theological enterprise. This option affords not only a mutual and interrelational embellishment, but adhears to the heart of the critical corrective introduced into sacramentology during the last three decades.

NOTES

1. B. Lonergan, *Method* . . . ,p. 4.
2. For a descriptive analysis and examples of this process of B. Lonergan, *Insight* . . ., pp. 3-32.
3. Cf. P. Fransen, *Intelligent Theology,* Vol. i, (London: Dunton, Longman & Todd, 1967), pp. 9-39.
4. *Ibid.*, p. 21.
5. *Ibid.*, p. 31.
6. Albert Dondeyne, *Contemporary European Thought and Christian Faith.* (Pittsburgh: Duquesne University Press, 1963), pp. 33-34.
7. For further information on phenomenology and Husserl, cf. Pierre Thévenaz, *What is Phenomenology?* James Edie (ed.), (Chicago: Quadrangle Books, 1962).
8. For an introduction to Blondel's thought, cf. Jean Lacroix, *Maurice Blondel, An Introduction to the Man and his Philosophy.* (New York; 1968); also, Rogeri Aubert, *Le Problème de L'acte de Foi.* (Louvain: Editione Nouvelaerts, 1969), pp. 277-294.
9. M. Blondel, *Lettre Sur Les Exigences de la Pensée Contemporaine en matiere d'apologetique.* (Paris: Presses Universitaires de France, 1956) p. 34: " . . .que rien ne peut entrer en l'homme qui ne sorte de lui et ne corresponde en quelque facon à un besoin d'expansion, et que ni comme fâit historique, ni comme traditionnel, ni comme obligation surajoutée du dehors, il n'y a pour lui vérité qui compte et précepte admissible sans être, de quelque manière, sutonome et autochtone."
10. *Ibid.*, p. 39ff.
11. *Ibid.*, pp. 87-95.
12. David Tracy, *Blessed Rage for Order.* (New York: The Seabury Press, 1975); cf. also Thomas Ommen, "Verification in Theology: A Tension in Revisionist Method," *The Thomist* 43 (1979), pp. 357-384.
13. *Ibid.*, p. 43.
14. *Ibid.*, p. 45.
15. *Ibid.*, p. 47.
16. *Ibid.*, p. 49.
17. *Ibid.*, p. 52.
18. *Ibid.*, p. 43.
19. *Ibid.*, p. 45, "The major insight (of contemporary theology) remains the insistence present in theological reflection at least since the time of Schleiermacher; the task of a Christian theology involves a commitment to investigate critically both the Christian faith in its several expressions and contemporary experience in its several cultural expressions."
20. *Ibid.*, p. 46.
21. *Ibid.*, p. 52.
22. *Ibid.*, pp. 55-56.
23. C. Keisling, "Paradigms of Sacramentality," *Worship* 44 (1970), p. 537.

24. K. Osborne, "Methodology and Christian Sacraments," *Worship* 48 (1974), p. 537.

25. Keisling, p. 425.

26. Osborne, p. 538.

3   A CLARIFICATION OF TERMS

Key terms will constantly recur throughout our search for the meaning of ritual and sacraments. It is well known that many theological battles have been waged and condemnations issued simply over the misconception of words and misinformation on the meaning of terms. For this reason alone, it is prudent to describe how these key terms are to be understood in our investigation of Christian sacraments. Prudence is transformed to necessity when one recalls that the past and present history of sacramental theology vividly testifies to terminological confusions and resulting condemnations. A moment's reflection on the eucharistic controversies surrounding Berengar of Tours or the heated controversy over "transubstantiation" vs "transsignification" in the last two decades impels us, even "frightens" us, to undertake a description of recurring key terms. More positively, this description should facilitate a comprehension of the anthropological and theological content of Parts Two and Three of this study by exposing the reader to some of its focal points.

Sign Image Symbol

Three recurring terms in our investigation form a natural cluster: sign, image, and symbol. All three have been extensively employed in sacramental theology. In our own age they have been frequently confused and misused, generating needless estrangement among theologians and churches. By explaining them in terms of their similarities and differences, their distinctive meanings can be better elucidated.

The human world teems with *signs*. They are essential to survival. Every sphere of existence is permeated with signs. Every individual uses signs. Signs tell us whether to add (+) or subtract (−). They direct us to stop (red light) or advance (green light). They inform us whether we are linked (kiss) or rejected (fist). They warn us of danger (smoke) and tell us of peace (treaty). We use signs to communicate vocally (language) and to understand invisible realities (o₂, oxygen). There are an infinite possible number of signs. Yet, all signs share common features.

Any analysis of signs can trace its origin to the reflection of St. Augustine. He wrote:

> Signum est enim res, praeter speciem quam ingerit sensibus, aliud aliquid ex se faciens in cogitationem venire.

> A sign is a thing which, besides the species it imposes on the senses, leads to a knowledge of something other than itself.[1]

In this definition, Augustine isolated the essential function and effect of a sign. It is a directional pointer which makes an unknown reality known. Through the experience and knowledge of a particular sign, the receiver has knowledge of another reality which is not immediately present. A sign acts as a substitute for an unknown reality to which it is related. The example of smoke as a sign of fire clarifies these affirmations.

If you were hiking in a woods and saw smoke billowing above a hill, you would spontaneously think there was a fire on the opposite side. How do you know there is fire on the other side? One could appeal to the saying: "Where there's smoke, there's fire." But, you have not seen or smelt the fire. You have really only seen and smelt the smoke. Let's look at the situation more closely. The reality you know or the reality present in your cognitive faculty is the smoke. Yet the fire, an unknown reality, is also present in your cognitive faculty by its relationship to the smoke. Smoke functions as a sign vis-à-vis the fire, and in being known makes the unknown fire present in your cognitive faculty.

One further question must be posed in our smoke-fire example. How is it that the unknown fire becomes present in your cognitive faculty through a knowledge of the smoke? It happens precisely because you have grasped the smoke as a signifier of fire. Through past experience, you know the relationship between smoke and fire and now you apply it to your immediate concrete experience of the smoke.

The above observation leads to two final notations on *signs*. First, signs can both uncover and hide the reality they signify. Second, there are different classifications of signs, distinguished by the quality of their relation to the reality they signify. Our smoke-fire example can explain these two points.

In our example, you know there is a fire behind the hill because you have grasped the smoke as a sign for fire. Suppose another individual had never seen or heard of the relationship of smoke and fire. For him/her, the smoke would not immediately point to fire. Moreover, the smoke would actually hinder a knowledge of the fire by turning attention exclusively to itself, the smoke. Consequently, the smoke, as a sign, can either reveal or hide the fire. It depends on whether one grasps the signifying power of smoke in relation to fire. Vaggaggini expressed this point well:

> The instrumental sign is not perfectly translucid but offers a resistance, as it were, to the knowledge of the thing signified; one must pass through the sign to arrive at the signified. The sign is like a veil, though transparent; for the eyes that do not know how to penetrate the veil, the sign is a screen. To penetrate the veil means to grasp the sign precisely in its value as signifying the thing. Hence for one who does not grasp the value the sign acts as a screen; for one who does grasp it, on the other hand, the sign acts as a bridge and informant.[2]

In our example of smoke-fire, the relation between the sign and the reality signified arises from nature. This can be called a *real* sign. There are, however, signs which do not arise from nature which can be called *conventional* signs. Conventional signs are the product of human reason. They are the creations of human persons with no necessary relation between the sign and the reality signified. For example, a red light is a sign for stop. It is a conventional sign, since there is no inner necessity for red to mean stop. It could as easily have been agreed upon that red would mean go. It should be clear that conventional signs are fixed by human agreement.

An *image* is a particular type of sign. It functions as a directional pointer and has the effect of making a reality different from itself known. The goal of an image is more specified than many other types of signs. It aims at reproducing as accurately as possible the reality it signifies. A photograph of a spouse should not only make one think of him/her, but should bear his/her resemblance. An architect's scale model of an office building should be a miniature replica of what the building will actually look like. Even a hastily sketched caricature traced by an artist on the Champs Élyseés should be identifiable by the purchaser as a likeness of himself/herself.

Why is it that a marble sculptured bust of an individual is called an image, and smoke is never referred to as an image of fire? What is the distinctive feature which differentiates images from other signs? Signs that are images have a likeness of *species* with the realities they signify. An image emulates the distinctive features which specify a reality within its particular group or *genus*. A self-portrait by Van Gogh is recognizable as such because of its likeness to his particular characteristics as a human person. The portrait is therefore an image. On the other hand, smoke bears no likeness to the features which specify fire. Consequently, smoke is not referred to as an image. The important element to keep in mind about images is their goal of being as identical as possible to the reality they signify.

A *symbol* is another classification of signs. Its distinctiveness can be grasped in its difference from both conventional signs and images. Unlike a conventional sign, a symbol is not grounded in an arbitrary human agreement. Symbols are not made by humankind. They are discovered in reality. Unlike an image, a symbol does not aim at exact reduplication or identity. *A symbol points to a reality different than itself and makes it present without being identical to it.*

Symbols share the common characteristic of all signs i.e., a directional pointer which makes an unknown reality known. Not all signs, however, are symbols. Signs which are symbols are characterized by their *power and depth to disclose a reality by actually making it present*. Symbols could be labeled *"supercharged" realities*. By packing so much into itself, a symbol "opens up a level of reality, of being and corresponding meaning, which otherwise we could not reach, and in doing so that symbol participates in that which it opens to new awareness."[3]

Symbols are primarily agents of unity and convergence. Only in a secondary fashion are they substitutes, a meaning more accurately ascribed to other signs.[4] This is suggested in the etymology of the word. The term symbol is derived from the Greek work *sum-ballo, sum-ballein*. The verb literally means "thrown together." The noun form refers to a mark or tally employed for the purpose of identification. An object was broken and at a later date joined by the respective holders to form a unity and authenticate their identities. Martelet explains this well:

> The symbol, therefore, is an agent of unity. It is broken, but only in order to unite. It divides a single element, but only in order, sooner or later, to overcome confusions or misunderstandings, and lack of knowledge, too, that distance or forgetfulness has produced among the different persons.[5]

The verbal form *sum-ballein* also suggest the idea of unity. The prefix *sum* in Greek suggests a bringing together. *Sum-ballein*, therefore, implies assembling or making one what was fractured or divided.

The clearest and most readily available example of a symbol is the human body. If you were asked the question: Are you your body? How would you respond? After some reflection you would probably answer: Yes and no. You realize that your body is a necessary part of you. It situates you in the world. It is a vehicle for your communication with others. It plays an intrinsic role in the formation of your self-image and personality. If it ceases to function, you will die. Yet, you would also insist that your body is not identical with everything that makes you you. Your body does not exhaust your meaning. In short, your body is a symbol of the reality that you are. Your body points to you and makes you present, without being identical to you. Your body, as a symbol, is an agent for the unity of you as a person. In and through your body, the disparate elements of your unique reality converge to form a whole.

Signs, images, and symbols are naturally clustered, but they should not be confused by using them synonymously. They should be envisioned as varying in intensity as they relate to the realities they signify. Above all, symbols should not be reduced to the level of images or conventional signs. Throughout this text, a symbol will be understood as an agent of unity which *really* makes present the reality it symbolizes.

Sacrament

The term *sacrament* is so common to Western religious traditions that its original meaning and evolution have often been forgotten. The English word sacrament is derived from the Latin *sacramentum*. The Latin term had its own secular history and meaning. It was also taken over to translate the Greek word *mysterion* (mystery) and explain the Christian rituals known as "sacraments."

Originally, the Latin word *sacramentum* referred to a deposit placed before a court when two parties entered into litigation. The loser forfeited his share of the deposit which was often then used for religious purposes and called a *sacramentum*, a sacred thing. Perhaps the closest English expression to this phenomenon is a pledge. The term was also used in the sense of a pledge with the overtones of a promise. Soldiers and citizens would often take a solemn oath of loyalty to the emperor and the state which was called a *sacramentum*.

Sacramentum was specifically used by Christian authors to translate the New Testament term *mysterion*. This Greek term generally referred to either some hidden decree of God to save the world or "liturgical rites" kept secret from the uninitiated through which the followers of a particular cult hoped to enter into unity with the deity.

> *Mysterion* in the Greek-speaking culture was a dedication to a god by means of a ritual initiation during which the secret meaning of certain symbols was revealed. In the mystery cults of Greece (Eleusis) or the ones of Egypt (Isis) and the Middle East (Attis, Mithra) which flourished in the Hellenistic and Roman worlds, the dedication centered on a ritual imitation of the god's suffering and death. Initiation established a direct contact with the godhead and assured participation in his immortality.[6]

In Greek religious practice, *mysterion* lay between the ideas of myth and divine superstition. The Greeks possessed a keen sense of fate, *moira*. Fate determined and controlled all human history. This theme permeated all the Greek tragedies. Paralleling this fixation on fate was a desire to escape, a desire for salvation, *soteria*. Salvation was available to those who participated in the Greek mystery religions, those who had learned the secret during their initiation. One can sense that the secret was a pledge or promise and hence the use of the Latin *sacramentum* to translate the term *mysterion*.

When the early Christian authors employed the word *sacramentum* for *mysterion*, they were not suggesting that the Christian sacraments were identical to the initiation rites of the Greek mystery religions. Rather, they were highlighting the Christian "mysteries" as pledges. During the Middle Ages the Latin term *sacramentum* became more and more specifically linked with the seven rituals of the Church which we know today as the "Christian sacraments" and as "sacred signs." For example, Peter Lombard explains *sacramentum* in terms of the seven rituals of the Church called the sacraments of the new law:

> Jam ad sacramentum novae legis accedamus, quae sunt: Baptismus, Confirmatio, pania benedictionis id est Eucharistia, Poenitantia, Unction Extrema, Ordo, Conjugium.[7]

Thomas Aquinas, following the tradition of Augustine, understood the sacraments to be sacred signs:

> (Sacramentum) est enim signum rei sacrae inquantum est sanctificians homines. A sacrament is a sign of a sacred thing, insofar as it makes men holy.[8]

With the insights of Lombard and Aquinas, the classical understanding of the term *sacramentum* became fixed. Unfortunately, its original overtone of pledge or promise was often overlooked or forgotten in the emphasis placed on its sign-quality or character. Once the sacraments were understood as signs, the question had to be broached: What type of signs are they? Are sacraments conventional signs, images, or symbols? This text will argue in Chapter Seven that the sacraments are properly understood as symbols.

Liturgy Rubric Ritual

The final set of terms which require clarification are liturgy, rubric, and ritual. In many "quasi-theological" circles and discussions, these terms are often hurled about with a modicum of understanding. Frequently, they are wrongly interchanged and defined.

Liturgy is the translation of the Greek word *lietourgia*. The Greek word itself is a composite of *laos* (people) and *ergein* (work or service). "The fundamental meaning is activity performed not for private ends, but for the sake of the people."[9] This meaning permeated the ancient religious use of the term. In the Septuagint, the Greek translation of the Hebrew Bible, and the New Testament *leiturgia* is the technical term for worship. R. C. D. Jaspers notes:

> In the singular the word "liturgy" denotes an act of worship, more specifically the Eucharist. Derived from the Greek *Leiturgia*, it was used in Hellenistic Greek as an act of public service. In the New Testament it is employed as an act of service or ministry (e.g., Phil. 2:30). In time it was confined in Christian usage to the idea of service of God and finally, since worship was regarded as the supreme service to God, it was applied to the Eucharist. . . . [10]

In both its secular and religious usage, liturgy has a communal rather than individual thrust and focus.

Rubrics comes from the Latin *ruber* meaning red. The word refers to the ceremonial directions for conducting a service. They were labelled rubrics since they were inscribed in the liturgical books in red ink as opposed to the prayers which were primarily in black.

Rubrics have often been wrongly conceived as ritual. Correctly understood, ritual far surpasses directions for liturgical celebrations. In fact, ritual is a more potent and embracing term than liturgy. Ritual is present in both secular and religious behavior. Urban Holmes has defined ritual:

> . . . as the repetition of those symbols which evoke the feeling of that primordial event which initially called the community into being with such power that it effects our presence at that event. . .in other words, represents the primordial event.[11]

Rituals attempt to express meaning. As V. Turner has pointed out, ritual is fundamentally a bundle of symbols which

> prescribed formal behavior for occasions not given over to technological routine, having reference to beliefs in invisible beings or powers regarded as the first and final causes of all effects.[12]

The following three chapters will examine the multiple dimensions of ritual in detail. At this point, we only wish to state the three types of religious ritual and the four elements which are at work in them. Religious rituals fall into the categories of either *magic, taboo,* or *relations.* Magic rituals attempt to control the divine. Taboo rituals seek to isolate an individual or community from the "holy" or the "other" which is considered to be dangerous. Relation rituals endeavor to form a relational nondestructive bond between a community and the "divine." In each of these religious rituals, four elements are present: symbolism, consecration, repetition, and remembrance. Symbols from the natural order make the "divine" present in the ritual without being identical to the "divine." Consecration enables a natural situation to share in a power or principle which transcends the natural and is its basis. Repetition of the ritual links the participants to their past and allows them to return to the original religious event the ritual is celebrating. Remembrance bonds the community together by preserving the religious tradition expressed in and through the ritual.

It should be obvious that ritual is never to be confused with rubrics. These two realities are on two totally different levels. We will discover that ritual is a more significant and universal reality than is popularly imagined.

As we proceed in the next part of our sacramental investigation, the importance of the clarification of terms undertaken in this chapter will be more clearly understood. Moreover, the date from psychology, anthropology, sociology, and philosophy will assist in further penetrating the rich meaning of certain terms singled out in this chapter, notably symbol and ritual. Hopefully, these initial remarks will minimize terminological confusion.

NOTES

1. St. Augustine, *De Doctrina Christiana II,* 1; PL 34, 35.

2. C. Vagaggini, *Theological Dimensions of the Liturgy.* (Collegeville: The Liturgical Press, 1976), p. 33.

3. Terrence Toland, "Christian Sacrament: Sign and Experience," in *Readings in Sacramental Theology,* Stephen Sullivan (ed.), (Englewood Cliffs: Prentice-Hall Inc., 1964), p. 23; also C. Froekle, *The Idea of the Sacred Sign According to Abbot Anscor Vonier.* (Rome: Catholic Book Agency, 1971), p. 32; and Susan Langer, *Philosophy in a New Key.* (Cambridge: Harvard University Press, 1957).

4. Gustave Martelet, *The Risen Christ and the Eucharistic World.* (New York: Seabury Press, 1976), pp. 19-22.

5. *Ibid.,* p. 18. For an interdisciplinary discussion of symbol cf. The International Colloque of 1974 published in *Revue Des Sciences Religieuse* 49 (1975), pp. 3-161; also, on the relation of symbol and metaphor, cf. Paul Ricoeur, *Interpretation Theory: Discourse and the Surplus of Meaning.* (Fort Worth: The Texas Christian University Press, 1976).

6. Louis Dupré, *The Other Dimension.* (New York: Doubleday, 1972), pp. 179-180; also, Herbert Mursurillo, "Sacramental Symbolism and the Mysterion of the Early Church," *Worship,* 39 (1965), p. 266.

7. Peter Lombard, *Libri Sententiarum,* Bk IV, d.2, c.1.

8. St. Thomas Aquinas, *Summa,* III q. 60, a. 2.

9. Gerhard Podhradsky, *New Dictionary of the Liturgy.* (New York: Alba House, 1966), p. 123.

10. R. C. D. Jaspers, "Liturgies", in *A Dictionary of Liturgy and Worship.* J. G. Davies (ed.) (New York: Macmillan, 1972), p. 222.

11. Urban Holmes, "Ritual and Social Drama," *Worship* 51 (1977), p. 198; also Raimundo Panikkar, "Man as a Ritual Being," *Chicago Studies* 16 (1977), p. 5-28.

12. Victor Turner, "Ritual, Tribal, Catholic," *Worship,* 50 (1976), p. 504.

PART TWO
THE ANTHROPOLOGICAL
DIMENSIONS OF SACRAMENTS

The three chapters which comprise Part Two of this study will examine the human experience of ritual. They attempt a synthetic survey of the behavioral sciences' and philosophy's findings on the central phenomena which are operative in ritual and, consequently, sacramental performance. The content of this survey corresponds to what Tracy called "common human experience and language." The method corresponds to what he described as a "phenomenology of the 'Religious Demension' present in everyday and scientific experience and language." Although the insights of psychology, sociology, anthropology and philosophy are valuable in their own right, their *lines of convergence* on the meaning and significance of ritual for individuals and communities are of utmost importance for a proper understanding and evaluation of the Christian rituals called sacraments.

4 PSYCHOLOGY: RITUAL AND THE INDIVIDUAL

Today, the scientific basis of psychology and its significant role in understanding the human person is commonly accepted by both the "secular" and "sacred" communities. This was not always the case. Psychology had a rocky beginning in the scientific community. It was even more suspect by religious groups and either benignly neglected or explicitly rejected until very recently.

August Comte, the founder of French Positivism, generated the initial scientific opposition to psychology. At the time of its inception in the nineteenth century, he vigorously denied even the possibility of psychology as a science. Comte was thoroughly imbued in the scientific rationalism of the first half of the nineteenth century. He formulated a comprehensive theory of intellectual evolution called the "Law of Three Stages,"[1] i.e., a religious, a metaphysical, and a positive phase to human thought.

> By a religious (or theological) stage, Comte understood a period of mythic thought and apprehension; by a metaphysical state, a period in which objective rational but abstract categories and concepts are used to organize the world of experience; by a positive stage, a period in which the modern scientific mode of apprehension and concept formation are developed.[2]

Psychological theories appeared to Comte as regressive elements impeding the flow of intellectual and social history.

Even though many scholars were less disposed to accepting Comte's totally negative evaluation of psychology, they were influenced by his radical criticism. They were inclined "through the influence of positivism to reduce psychology to a simple appendage of physiology."[3]

Religious groups have shared Comte's disdain for psychology. This "new" science was often perceived as undermining religious belief in God.

49

It was frequently interpreted as challenging a religious understanding of the human person as a spiritual being. It was viewed as a foreign invader infringing on religion's field of expertise. The reductionist tendencies of the early psychological theories only intensified the negative religious bias. Consequently, any serious and mutually enriching dialogue between religion and psychology was negated by fear and polemicism.

Comte's positivism and religion's rebuke were not to "win the day" against psychology. Through the work of Freud, Adler, and Jung there was a resurgence of this discipline. Interestingly, one discovers many seminal ideas in these authors which are significant in our investigation of religious ritual. A brief look illustrates this point.

Freud discovered that neurosis originated in mental trauma which were no longer present in the patient's consciousness. He found that the neurosis could be dissipated once the trauma returned to consciousness. This process led Freud to postulate what he originally called the "subconscious" and later the "unconscious." He called the removal of the trauma from the conscious level to the unconscious repression. Repression was the genesis of all neurosis.

Freud proceeded further. He noted that repressions could form clusters which he named complexes. This title was only applicable, however, when the repression arose from the conscious mind's endeavor to respond to some moral prohibition. The discovery of complexes led Freud to understand the significance of dreams. Dreams disclosed the hidden and unconscious drives of the human mind.[4] Dreams were not rooted in reality as such, but in symbolic wishes which were also the seedbed for religion. This was why Freud referred to religion as an illusion.

> The content of religion has no roots in rational thoughts, but in wish-dreams: that all events may be guided toward the good of man, that justice may prevail and than at eternal life awaits us at the end of the present one. The term "illusion," by which Freud refers to these dreams, does not imply that religious ideas are false, but only that they have their origin in wishes rather then experience.[5]

Freud portrayed the human person as seeking a resolution on frustration through dreams and religion was the product of this effort. Why was humankind frustrated? In *The Future of an Illusion*, Freud identified man's environment as a source of human discord. In *Civilization and its Discontent*, he added a "social" source for frustration i.e., his famous "Oedipal complex."

According to Freud, every male naturally experiences a preconscious attachment to his mother which is accompanied by a parallel hostility to his father. The "Oedipal complex" was not a metaphysical judgment but a biological given. "Being born of women and being nourished and protected by this woman and the man to whom she belonged would inevitably introduce the male child into the Oedipal constellation."[6]

The weakness of Freud's system lay in his ultimate reduction of the human psyche to sexuality. He explained all the various elements of human psychological life in terms of the role of sexuality in one's inner life. Freud's theory suffered from "sexual" reductionism. Positively, Freud reopened the road to symbolism. He fostered the rediscovery of symbolism as the foundation for human existence.[7] From Freud onward, positivism was gradually reversed.

It was precisely the disagreement over the role of the "sex drive" in the unconscious that led Adler and Jung to form their rival schools of psychology. Adler added the "inferiority complex" to the "Oedipal complex." He asserted that the thwarted desire for a perfect harmonious physical integrity seeks its compensation in aggressive behavior. Jung pursued a different direction. He interpreted the psychological life of the human person globally and, in a sense, metaphysically.

Jung was a universalist. He claimed that no individual will attain full stature until he or she personally confronts the meaning of man in the universe, until he or she measures himself/herself against the whole of reality. Underpinning all reality was the "sacred." Jung believed that in the individual unconscious there was a "collective unconscious" composed of "archetypes." The unconscious consisted of an inherited transhistorical symbolism relating all people, no matter what their culture, to the same metaphysical reality. Religion originated in the impact of this "collective unconscious" on consciousness. Religion proposed to answer the psychological experience which confronted every human person and lived on in humankind's "collective unconscious."[8]

One of the first of the archetypes to interest Jung was the *anima*, or the supreme aspiration for that which will complete our own being, our own existence. The human attraction to the *anima* finds its conscious counterpart in the attraction to the mother in dependency.

> Jung who had originally accepted Freud's idea that "the personal God is psychologically nothing other than a magnified father" was later forced to qualify this identity even for the "paternal" god and increasingly felt to introduce feminine elements into religion.[9]

Jung also noted an *animus*, expressed through a dependency on the father who always surpasses. The "father" always expresses himself through an intermediary, his spirit. It would be impossible to overlook the structural comparision between Jung and the Christian "Trinity."

In a positive fashion, the work of Jung overcame an exclusive individualism in the psychological drama. He demonstrated a certain solidarity in humankind's struggle to make sense out of life and the world. He also correctly situated religion in the context of ultimate meaning or a metaphysics.

Religious groups have come to respect and employ the findings of psychology. In our own age it has been a tremendous asset for comprehending many communal and individual aspects of religion. Once the principle that "grace builds upon nature" was taken seriously and psychology solidified its position as a legitimate science, the use of psychological theories and findings in religion was inevitable. Today, one finds the names of W. James, A. Maslov, and K. Kohlberg appearing regularly in theological lectures, courses and written manuscripts treating a variety of religious themes.

Our purpose here is not to survey the literature on the psychology of religion. It is quite specific. This chapter hopes to demonstrate the role of ritual in the formation and development of the human personality. Since sacraments are fundamentally ritual behavior, this data will be indispensable to an anthropological understanding of sacraments.[10] Erik Erikson's studies on the "Ontogenetic Foundation of Ritual" and Bernard Bro's investigation into "Binary Oppositions" will focus on this investigation.

Erikson: Ontogeny of Ritualization

In her famous work, *Natural Symbols*, M. Douglas articulated the prevalent negative attitude toward ritual in contemporary culture. She wrote:

> One of the gravest problems of our day is the lack of commitment to common symbols. If this were all, there would be little to say. If it were merely a matter of our fragmentation into smaller groups, each committed to it proper symbolic forms, the case would be simple to understand. But more mysterious is a wide-spread, explicit rejection of rituals as such. Ritual is become a bad word signifying empty conformity. We are witnessing a revolt against formalism, even against form.[11]

The neglect of ritual is dangerous. A "revolt against ritual" is potentially a precursor to individual and social psychological cataclysm. Ritual is endemic to the formation of individual personality and social life. Recent investigations in psychology and anthropology have verified these affirmations, especailly the work of Erik Erikson.

Erikson is well known for his theory on the five stages of personality development and integration i.e., infancy, early childhood, play age, school age, and adolescence. In a seminal article, he outlined the powerful and essential role ritual plays in each stage of development and its continuation in adult behavior. Erikson believed that ritual had an "ontogenetic" foundation i.e., emerging from the biological development of the human person and his or her ontological characteristics.

For a behavior to be classified as ritual, Erikson required the presence of three elements. It must be interpersonal, repetitive, and adaptive.

> We should, therefore, begin by postulating that behavior to be called ritualization in man must consist of an agreed-upon interplay between at least two persons who repeat it at meaningful intervals and in recurring contexts; and that this interplay should have adaptive value for both participants.[12]

Erikson detected these conditions in such diverse activities as the simple relations of human infancy and the complex relations of public ceremonies and festivals. He presented a chart labeled the "Ontogeny of Ritualization" which schematized his correlation of ritual with its appropriate stage of personality development and its continuance in adult life.

ONTOGENY OF RITUALIZATION

Infancy	Mutuality of Recognition					
Early Childhood		Discrimination of good and bad				
Play Age			Dramatic elaboration			
School Age				Rules of performance		
Adolescence					Solidarity of conviction	
Elements in Adult Rituals	Numinous	Judicial	Dramatic	Formal	Ideological	General Satisfaction

In each age period, a value is introduced through ritual behavior that advances personality development and that is reinforced in succeeding stages of adult ritual behavior.

Infancy: Personality Emergence and Ritual

The biological and emotional needs of child and mother are the spawning ground of ritual in infancy. Physical necessities for survival require the mother's interaction with the child and are the occasion for the initial emergence of the infant's personality and identity. Erikson claimed that the "greeting" ritual between mother and child effected a "mutuality of recognition" which was the basis for all healthy psychological growth.

The "greeting" ceremony which marks the beginning of an infant's day is familiar to everyone. With a surprising consistency, the waking infant communicates to the mother that he/she is awake. This message triggers a conglomeration of emotions, feelings, and behavior in the mother. She marshals her senses, congnitive powers, and intuitive feelings in an attempt to ascertain the child's condition and initiates "services to be rendered."

Several days of observation reveal that this event is highly ritualized: " . . . the mother seems to feel obliged, and not a little pleased, to repeat a performance which arouses in the infant predictable responses, encouraging her, in turn, to proceed."[13]

An analysis of the various elements which comprise the "greeting" ritual reveals that this behavior is both individual i.e., focused on the needs of the particular infant, and stereotyped i.e., typical of mothers. Physical needs are the foundation for the whole activity, yet emotional needs of the child and mother are concurrently fulfilled.

In the "greeting" ritual the mother calls the infant by name. The name has usually been selected with care and perhaps given in a name-giving ceremony e.g., during baptism. The repetition of the name and the care the mother renders the child have a special meaning for the child and the mother. "Daily observation . . . suggests that this mutual assignment of very special meaning is the ontogenetic source of one pervasive element in human ritualization, which is based on mutuality of *recognition*."[14]

Mutual affirmation and certification are constitutive elements of a healthy human personality and psyche. The repetitive achievement of mutual recognition, positive evaluation, and meaning in and through the "greeting" ritual launches an infant on the path to individual and social maturation. On the other hand, the absence of affirmation and recognition in early infancy will radically injure an infant by "diminishing or extinguishing his or her search for impressions which will verify his or her senses."[15] Once mutual recognition is established, however, the aroused need for stimulation will perdure throughout life as a hunger for new and evermore formalized and extensive ritualization. Once an infant tasts face-to-face recognition, he or she will have a felt need for its fulfillment in a reinforcing repeatable cycle.

The face-to-face mutual affirmation or mutual recognition of infancy pervades all future ritualization. Erikson has identified it as a sense of a *hallowed presence* or *numinous*, and noted its clear operation in religious rituals:

> We vaguely recognize the numinous as an indispensable aspect of periodic religious observances, where the believer, by appropriate gestures, confesses his dependence and his childlike faith and seeks, by appropriate offerings, to secure a sense of being lifted up into the very bosom of the supernatural which in the visible form of an image may graciously respond, with the faint smile of an inclined face. The result is a sense of *separateness* transcended, and yet also of distinctiveness confirmed.[16]

On a psychological level, the mutuality of recognition required for psychological growth and stability in infancy finds continued expression and reinforcement in adult religious rituals by a sense of the *numinous*.

In both the "greeting" ritual of infancy and the adult rituals which convey the mutuality of recognition and the *numinous*, ritualization reconciles opposites. This can be observed in four areas. First, the mutuality of reciprocal needs is between two quite unequal organisms and minds i.e., adult vs baby; man/women vs the "divine." Second, the mutuality of recognition is highly personal yet communal. Each child and mother is unique, yet their behavior is stereotyped. Religious rituals affect each of the participants differently, yet the ritual is communal. Third, the mutuality is playful yet formal. The repetitive character of the mutuality makes it familiar, yet there is still a sense of surprise when the expectations are fulfilled. An infant still smiles at the repeated games of its mother. A worshiper is still overcome by the "love of God" he has experienced in previous religious services.

Finally, ritualization helps to overcome ambivalence. An infant elicits love from its parents, but also feelings of confinement. An infant loves its parents but will eventually experience them as possessive and arbitrary.

The "divine" is attractive and loving, yet a reality that can be threatening. Erikson points out:

> For as we love our children, we also find them unbearably demanding, even as they will soon find us arbitrary and possessive. What we love or admire is also threatening, awe becomes awfulness, and benevolence seems in danger of being consumed in wrath. Therefore, ritualized affirmation, once instituted, becomes *indispensable* as a periodic experience and must find new forms in the context of new developmental activities.[17]

There is a growing consensus in the social sciences that the overcoming of ambivalence and the resolution of opposites is not only the effect of ritualization but also its origin and reason for existence. The human person and human society are confronted by oppositions. Ritual is the human vehicle for coping and discovering meaning in this situation. As d'Aguili and Laughlin have written:

> Ritual aims at uniting opposites in an effort to gain control over an essentially unpredictable universe. The *Ultimate* union of opposites which is the aim of all human religious ritual is the union of contingent and vulnerable man with a powerful, possibly omnipotent, force. In other words, we propose that men and a superhuman power are the ultimate poles of much mystic structure, and that polarity is the basic problem that ritual must solve existentially.[18]

More will be said on this point later in this chapter and in the one that follows.

One might naturally inquire how it is possible for an infant to cope with all the elements that are involved in the first stage of human development. Isn't it too much to ask of an infant? Fortunately, infancy is only the beginning or initiation into a lifelong process. Its importance, however, cannot be underestimated. Psychopathological finds record tragedies that an absence of mutual recognition will produce. The loss or absence of mutuality of recognition in the earliest stages of life can lead to psychic withdrawal and repression. Erikson explains:

> . . . the earliest affirmation is already a reaffirmation in face of the fact that the very experience by which man derives a measure of security also exposes him to a *series of estrangements* which we must try to specify as we deal with each developmental stage. In the first stage, I submit, it is a

sense of *separation by abandonment* which must be prevented by the persistent, periodic reassurance of familiarity and mutuality. Such reassurance remains the function of the numinous and thus primarily of religious ritual or of the numinous element in any ritual. Its perversion or absence, on the other hand, leaves a sense of dread, estrangement, or impoverishment.[19]

The mutuality of recognition begun in infancy remains as a need throughout adult life. It's presence, brought about through ritual, engenders psychic health.[20] Ritualization assists the human person in dealing with human instinct. Instinct in humans is different from that of animals. Animal instinct is always expressed. Human instinct can either be expressed or controlled. Ritualization represents "a creative formalization which avoids both impulsive excess and overly compulsive self-restriction.... "[21] Erikson assigned three vital functions to ritualization which further specify its creativity in view of the uniqueness of human instinct. First, ritualization allows dangerous complexity to be simplified. Second, it secures a consistent identification of one human generation with another. Third, it provides a psychological foundation for "ego" development which is essential for the eventual total personality integration in adulthood. Ritualization, he explained,

... binds instinctual energy into a pattern of mutuality which bestows convincing simplicity on dangerously complex matters. In establishing mutuality in the immediacy of early needs, ritualization also does the groundwork for lasting mutual identification between adult and child from generation to generation ... ritualization also provides the psychological foundation for that inner equilibrium which, in psychoanalysis is attributed to a "strong ego"; and thus also a first step for the gradual development (to be sealed only in adolescence) of an independent identity which, guided by various rituals of "confirmation" representing a "second birth," will integrate all childhood indentifications, while subordinating those wishes and images which have become undesirable and evil.[22]

Ritualization also advances psychological growth by bonding an infant to what Erikson called the "pseudospecies." Unlike the animal kingdom, humankind has not evolved into different species. Rather, humankind has evolved into "pseudospecies" i.e., clans, tribes, nationalities, etc. At birth, a human infant can be placed in any of the human "pseudospecies" and become "specialized" in it. The identity or bond with the specific "pseudospecies" will be formed in many ways, but primarily through participation in the group's ritualizations. Ritual is the vehicle par excellence for an individual's identification with his or her particular unit of humankind.

Early Childhood: Judicious and Negative Identity

A child gains increased locomotion and language as infancy gives way to early childhood. Biological and psychological advances bring new challenges to the child and the parent. Ritualization is again relied upon to transmit needed elements for maturation and survival.

Erikson sees two important elements introduced to the child through ritual during this period of development: the *judicious* and the *negative identity*. The term *judicious* refers to and encompasses "methods by which *discrimination* between right and wrong is ontologically established."[23] Negative identity refers to what the child is not to become if he or she is to be accepted within the social group.

Increased mobility and autonomy in the child find a parallel establishment of defined limits of acceptable behavior by the parent. A child must learn to cope with his/her new situation and environment. As in the case of infancy, the child faces a possibility of estrangement:

> ... standing upright, the child realizes that he can lose face and suffer shame; giving himself away by blushing, he feels furiously isolated, not knowing whether to *doubt himself* or his *judges.*[24]

Yet, the potential estrangement has changed. The *judicious* recognizes more and more the emerging free will of the child. More and more responsibility is placed on his or her shoulders. In the rituals of infancy, avoidance of danger, harm, etc., was the mother's responsibility. In early childhood, the child is trained through ritualization to be responsible for himself or herself.

In a repeated, interpersonal, and value-centered fashion a child's parents and elders remind him or her what will happen if he or she does not "be careful" or "watch out.". Erikson claims that this is the ontogenetic foundation for the *negative identity*. Although this term sounds negative, it actually serves a positive function. The "pseudospecies" uses the *negative identity* as a means of group cohesion and coherence. "The *negative identity* furnishes explicit images of the "pseudospecies" which one must *not* resemble in order to have a chance of acceptance in one's own."[25] Negative identity is reinforced in the individual and the group through ritualization, as is clear in taboos and rites of initiation.

The establishment of the *judicious* and the *negative identity* in early childhood find their adult continuation in ritualizations of law. The offender or suitable culprit is placed before the public eye as an example to the whole "pseudospecies," the parental judge, the peers of the jury, and the whole populus. He is an example of what a member of the "pseudospecies" should not be, and what will happen to others who pursue such behavior.

Erikson's analysis and explanation of childhood and the *judicious* suggests a structural-functionalist interpretation of ritual i.e., explaining its causes in terms of its function in the social group (pseudospecies). One has the impression that ritual necessarily preserves order and the status quo. There is, however, a second possible interpretation of ritual. Ritual can challenge the status quo and initiate conflict and/or change.

> Ritual can have two sorts of consequences for the society in which it takes place: either it can provide a process whereby people become more attached to the basic way of life and values of society, or to the major sub-groups within it of which the participants in ritual are a part; or ritual can lead to people making new demands on the way of life in society, and a desire to see change both in action and in the values society pursues.[26]

Ritual can either sustain or transform a "pseudospecies" way of life.

Play Age—School Age: The Dramatic—The Formal

In their classic works, *Homo Ludens*[27] and *Man at Play*[28], Johan Huizinga and Hugo Rahner portrayed the cultural and theological significance of play. Erikson contributes a psychological importance to play by locating its origin within his stages of personality development. He demonstrates how the ritualization of play adds creativity and the *dramatic* to the child's world. The distinguishing feature of the *dramatic* in play age is the child's ability to form a coherent plot with dramatic turns and a climatic conclusion.[29]

Play age affords the child an opportunity to create his or her own world with its own ritualizations. The first stirrings of the imagination and a familiarity with adult ritualizations enables the child to create his or her own rituals with themes borrowed from the adult world, yet exhibiting a freedom and autonomy from their adult structures. Erikson notes:

> ... this age offers the child a microreality in which he can escape adult ritualization and prepare his own, reliving, correcting and recreating past experiences, and anticipating future roles and events with the spontaneity and repetitiveness which characterize all ritualization.[30]

This ritualization of play usually centers around the theme of guilt. It enables the child to express, aggravate, or resolve the experience of inner estrangement which can arise from a sense of guilt. Psychopathological findings again verify this interpretation. Unresolved excessive guilt in a child will lead to his or her inhibition of thought and action.

The elements of play ritualization in childhood find their adult counterpart in the theater. The stage is humankind's arena for play, the setting where the drama of life is reenacted. Anyone familiar with the "Greek Tragedies" or a host of more contemporary dramas e.g., *Equus*, will detect that adult drama still focuses on and attempts to resolve guilt.

The free expressions of play age quickly give way to school. A child's capacity for further cognitive and emotional growth increases. At school, however, play undergoes a transformation. School provides a structure whereby previously experienced elements in the child's life are disciplined into a sequence and arrangement of performance. In the formalized rituals of school,

> ... play is transformed into work, game into cooperation, and freedom of imagination into duty to perform with full attention to all the minute details which are necessary to complete a task and to do it "right."[31]

Erikson believes that it is in school age that the child is introduced to the *formal* dimension of ritualization. The *formal* is an "order" both perceived by the child and participated in by the child.[32]

Adolescence: Solidarity of Conviction

In adolescence, the child becomes the adult ritualizer. At this stage of development, an individual prepares fully to embrace the world of his or her "pseudospecies" i.e., to accept its irreversible commitments and consequently, to reject any "foreign" ideologies. Adolescence requires a greater cognitional and emotional acceptance of the various elements of ritualization which appeared in the preceding stages of development. This is not to suggest that the adolescent merely reverts back to infantile behavior. It is to say that the elements of the *numinous, judicious, dramatic,* and *formal* are experienced and accepted on a higher or more mature plane of existence. These elements are no longer passively accepted but personally embraced as one's own.

During the stage of adolescence, one discovers the introduction of what has been labelled "rites of passage." These rituals secure the transition of the individual from adolescence to adulthood. The goal of these ritualizations is the same as that of all ritualization in adolescence, *solidarity of conviction* of the individual with the "pseudospecies." Through these ritualizations the individual embraces and is embraced by the group as one of its own. Among "primitive" tribes initiation rituals function to attain these goals. In contemporary Western civilization, educational institutions have assumed the tribal functions. Yet, the same structures and elements of tribal initiation rites can be discerned in education i.e., separation from the old way of life, a period of transition and testing, and ritual celebrations marking the completion of the process with concrete signs and symbols of recognition.[33]

The transition from adolescence to adulthood does not complete the process of psychological growth and maturation. Moreover, it does not halt ritualization. The values and elements which permeated the whole process of development through ritualization require continual reinforcement. The attained integration accruing from ritual requires bolstering by continued performance. Ritualization will continue to be the medium and vehicle for the sustenance of the "pseudospecies'" values.

Erikson does not shy away from commenting on the present status of adult rituals. In many ways he evaluates them as empty and incapable of reinforcing the ontogenetic elements unveiled in the development and formation of the human personality within the context of its "pseudospecies." This unfortunate circumstance makes contemporary youth prone to abandon the dead rituals of a past age and search for new forms of communication which will supply what is lacking in the "traditional" rituals.

Erikson's comments directly correlate with our contentions on cultural change in the introduction. The *numinous,* the *judicious,* the *dramatic,* and the *formal* are all defined and comprehended within the cultural context of a particular "pseudospecies." They assume the shape and form designated by a particular age for their concretization. As a culture changes, the designations for these ontogenetic elements will be transformed to correspond to the "new" self-understanding of the "pseudospecies."

Significance of Ritual

Ritual, from a psychological perspective, is neither foreign nor extrinsic to the human person or the human community. Ritual is integral and necessary for the attainment of an integrated and healthy psycho-social existence. The absence or severe dimunition of ritual can lead to psycho-social personality disorders.

Reflection on Erikson's vision of ritual in the development of the human person suggests that ritual is instructional, interpretive, and indoctrinating. Ritual teaches "mutuality of recognition," discrimination of good and bad, dramatic elaboration, and the rules of performance by allowing these elements to be experienced by the developing person. Ritual interprets one's experience of reality by placing the experience within its structural relationships. It slants one's views to those of a particular "pseudospecies." Ritual indoctrinates individuals into the world view of a particular community and makes them members of it. It leads to a "solidarity of convictions," a lived-through unity with the "pseudospecies" which is itself permeated with reinforcing rituals.

Without participation in ritual or appropriation of the elements which it mediates, the human person faces psychological conflict, personality impairment, and estrangement from the inner self and outer society. Correspondingly, hollow or weak rituals will threaten the ability of the "pseudospecies" to incorporate new members and maintain a stable existence in the flow of history. Neither individuals nor communities can survive psychologically without ritual.

Bernard Bro: Binary Oppositions

Erikson's work on the ontogenetic basis for ritualization demonstrated the importance of ritual for personality development and stabilization. Anthropological studies have further developed and specified the insights which can be gleaned from his work. In this respect, the studies of Ferdinand de Saussere and Claude Levi-Strauss are seminal. The introduction of what has been labelled "structuralism" in linguistic and anthropological studies lends both justification and support to the key place of ritual in human existence.

Structuralism claims that there are certain organizations of data within any given culture that are enshrined in cultural myths. These organizations of data frequently remain on the unconscious level. Humankind creates these cognitive structures in order to identify, explain, relate and solve the forces which impinge on their existence, forces which are antinomies.

The resolution of the antinomies is cognitively realized in and through the structure of the cultural myths.

The unconscious organizations of data or thought patterns are the basic code through which the meaning of various realities and experiences within the culture can be interpreted. If the code can be "cracked, the anthropological system, and its meaning, of any particular "pseudospecies" becomes accessible. Levi-Strauss goes so far as to claim a cross-cultural character for this code. He believes that there are only so many fundamental thought structures which are within the potential of the human species, and they are employed by any person who thinks.

The cognitive resolution of antinomies in cultural myths has been theoretically accepted in the anthropological-sociological fields. Levi-Strauss's position, however, has been critiqued for not paying attention to ritual's role in the resolution.

> Although there is evidence supporting the contention that antinomies are cognitively resolved within the myth, we contend that the only resolutions which are psychologically powerful to both individuals and groups are those which have an aspect of existential reality. We will attempt to show . . . that such a powerful effective resolution arises primarily from ritual or mediation and rarely from a cognitive fusion of antinomies alone, although such a cognitive fusion may be a necessary precursor in human religious rituals.[34]

The forces which confront the human person effect not only cognition, but also volition and action. A merely cognitive resolution of antinomies overlooks the full dimensions of humankind's capacity to integrate opposing forces, capacities which include choice and action. As Aquili and Loughlin note:

> But in and of itself, this organization of reality into mythic structures does not give man genuine control over the overwhelming forces of nature which confront him. Satisfying the cognitive imperative, although necessary, is not sufficient. Since man obtains mastery of his immediate environment by motor action, he attempts to achieve mastery over disease, famine, and death by some form of motor action as well. It is thus that religious ritual will necessarily arise out of the structuring of myths.[35]

Our present interest is not structuralism as an anthropological school. Rather, our focus is on a particular dimension uncovered in the investigations undertaken by structuralism i.e., binary oppositions and the drive for integration in human existence. Humankind needs to resolve experienced opposing forces and ritual is the medium for this resolution.

Cultural and cross-cultural studies uncover opposing forces, feelings, concepts and realities which reflect juxtaposing poles of human experience. Although these elements of experience are opposing, they are also related in the sense that they define the opposite meaning of each other e.g., light—darkness, life—death, holy—profane, father—mother, tribe—alien, etc. Each "pseudospecies" must somehow find a means to hold these opposing but related experiences and realities together, a way to integrate these binary oppositions into a unified, even if tenuous, system. Ritualization serves as a key instrument in this task. Ritualization opens the possibility of overcoming the fractured existence of humankind, a fracture which is attested to by the conflict of the drive for unity with the experience of opposition and disharmony.

> Considered as a continuous series of actions oriented to an end, life is an incomplete process, its true essence lies in its relation to the whole which it constantly strives to express. Ritual from this point of view may be regarded as an expression of a primordial existential urge for integration with the whole that transcends and transfigures it.[36]

This point was made clearly in Erikson's exposition of ritualization in infancy. Bernard Bro in investigating the anthropological substructure for ritual identified three sectors where the human person seeks the resolution and eventual integration of opposition: himself, others, and the world. He also noted that the desired resolution and integration only takes place on the unconscious level of human existence.[37]

A drive and dynamism for wholeness and unity permeates the human potential. The human person, however, experiences disproportions and incongruity in the normal condition of his or her existence. A corresponding experience of negativity and limitations matches the drive for unity. Bro envisioned three possible responses to this situation: forgetful oblivion, conflict or flight, and "embracing negativity and moving beyond it."

Forgetful oblivion is an attempt to seek relief from oppositions in an imagined form of intoxication e.g., a pretended unreal self-image, workaholism, or physical possessions. Conflict or flight seeks relief either in submission to those forces which oppose the drive for unity or condemnation of those realities or persons which limit or prohibit the attainment of wholeness. The third response, which for Bro is the decisive foundation for a ritualization which will resolve experienced oppositions is to "embrace

negativity and move beyond it."[38] The meaning of this term will become
clear in a discussion of the three sectors which require integration i.e., self,
others, and the world.

From birth, each person stands face to face with his or her ideal self,
that reality which is within his or her potential to become. Each person has
a dependence on the ideal self. Self-understanding emerges in relation to it.
It is a stimulus for growth and personal expansion. As Bro notes:

> . . . we are "subjects," who cannot help but stand in a relation of depen-
> dence to something else. We discover this dependence and we master it
> by means of this image of the ideal self. It is the self we would like to be,
> although we are not it yet, and we already possess it as an image inside
> us. We turn back to this image constantly through our plans, our fears,
> and our regrets. It is here that the fate of each man is played out, as he
> runs into the inevitable obstacles posed by existence.[39]

Yet, the ideal self is really an illusion. It cannot be the ultimate of human
existence. The only real possibility of actualizing human potentials is to
relativize the ideal self and move beyond it. Every concrete attainment of
one's potentials necessarily implies that the totality of the ideal self is denied for a partial, yet real, realization of it. To wait for the opportunity to
realize the totality of the ideal self would be tantamount to waiting for
Godot.

Ritual offers the human person the possibility of breaking through
one's ideal self-image. Bro explains this in term of religious ritual. He
writes:

> As we encounter each of the great experiences offered to man, the sacra-
> ments offer us the possibility of cooperating in this experience in all its
> concreteness, but in the name of another's power. Without repudiating
> our most personal elements, indeed for the sake of our total integration
> and our total retrieval of existence, the sacraments offer us a chance to
> cooperate completely in our own fulfillment, while demanding that we
> distinctively relativize our self-image.[40]

This negation of the ideal self by a recognition of the other, the holy, corresponds to the *numinal* element of Erikson's ontogeny of ritualization, an
element developed in infancy and reeforced throughout life by the rituals
of the "pseudospecies." It is important to note that the negation of the ideal self is not the terminal point. One must move beyond negation to posi-

tive action and appropriation, a step, however, which is impossible without the initial negation of the ideal self.

The second opposition which confronts the human person is his or her peers or species. The human person concurrently feels a need for a relationship with others and a fear of others. There is a twofold source for this fundamental opposition. First, the individual human person can never adequately form or exhaust the image of the other. The other always remains free and elusive. In the language of Gabriel Marcel, the other always is a mystery and not a problem. Second, the individual human person also recognizes that the other person cannot totally respect him or her when intervening in his or her existence. The other's existence comes first in the relationship. I count for nothing in their existence, it is independent from me.

Bro sees ritual as a way of overcoming this dual opposition and attaining communion with other persons without domination. Ritual allows one to respect the difference of the other and independence of the other, yet effects a positive relationship with the other. It is interesting that in the establishment of a relationship with another through ritual, a negation of the ideal self is realized since one ceases to be the sum total of the universe. One also moves beyond negation to participation in the richness of the other.

The third opposition confronting the human person is the world. Human existence is thoroughly sensible and worldly. The world is humankind's home. Yet the world is an uncomfortable home. It can be foreign, restrictive, and limiting. The world can prohibit humankind's integral wholeness.

Bro envisions ritual as a means for its participants to enter into this strange world without destruction. Through ritual, the world can be employed symbolically. The world is not merely a place of dead, static reality, but a vibrant situation in which humankind makes meaning. It becomes the place or locus where humankind concretizes itself and interprets its existence.

Bro is not alone in affirming the presence of alienation which hypnotizes human existence. The great "thinkers" of Western civilization all include the ingredients of anger, fear, and separation within their intellectual formulas.[41] Feuerbach, Marx, Hegel, Freud, Jung, Sartre, Camus, Heidegger, Levinas, Marcuse, etc., seek to interpret this experience with positions ranging from spiritualism to materialism, ontologism to psychologism.

Multiple levels of "absurdity" or alienation stand as one element of bi-polar human life. No person can escape the power of this element which pervades human existence. Ritual, however, allows its integration into a higher framework, a perspective in which alienation can be transformed from a negation to a source of creativity. Ritual can lead from estrangement to communion. Through ritual, the human person can embrace a negativity and move beyond it to positive meaning.

Conclusion

Through the work of Erikson and Bro, one could dismiss the importance of ritual only with dire consequences. Ritual is not an indifferent or non-essential ingredient to human life. It is at the basis of what it means to be human.

From a psychological point of view, ritual is a necessary vehicle from the healthy maturation of the human personality. It transmits necessary values for personal and communal life. It binds together the fabric of a particular world view so that reality is experienced as meaningful rather than absurd.

Moreover, ritual opens the possibility for an individual or community to resolve the experience or fragmentation and bi-polar oppositions which define human existence. It neutralizes the negative power of the ideal self, others, and the world and transforms it into an occasion for growth and maturation. Ritual is not immature or escapist behavior, but an attempt by the power of human transcendence to discover positive value to life.

NOTES

1. Auguste Comte, *Cours de Philosophie Positive. Vol. 1, La Societé Positiviste.* (Paris: 1892), p. 243. On Comte, cf. Alen Inkles, *What is Sociology?* (Englewood Cliffs: Prentice-Hall Inc., 1969), pp. 2-6; Gregory Baum, *Religion and Alienation: A Theological Reading of Sociology.* (New York: Paulist Press, 1975), pp. 43-44.

2. Thomas O'Dea, *The Sociology of Religion.* (Englewood Cliffs: Prentice-Hall, 1966), p. 43.

3. Louis Boyer, *Rite and Man: Natural Sacredness and Christian Liturgy.* (Notre Dame: University of Notre Dame Press, 1963), p. 39.

4. Sigmund Freud, *The Interpretation of Dreams.* (New York: Avon Books, 1965), pp. 155-167.

5. Dupré, p. 87.

6. Baum, p. 121.

7. *Ibid.*, pp. 115-125.

68 FROM MAGIC TO METAPHOR

8. There is a development in Jung's understanding from the *Psychology of Unconsciousness* (1911) through *Two Essays on Analytic Psychology* (1926) to *Psychology and Religion* (1930) cf. Raymond Hostie, *Religion and the Psychology of Jung*. (New York: Sheed and Ward, 1957).

9. Dupré, p. 92.

10. Eric Erikson, "The Development of Ritualization," in *The Religious Situation*. (Boston: Beacon Press, 1968), pp. 711-733; and *Identity: Youth and Crisis*. (New York: W. W. Norton, 1968), pp. 91-141; also cf. Erving Goffman, *Interaction Ritual: Essays on Face to Face Behavior*. (Garden City: Doubleday, 1967); and David M. Rafky, "Phenomenology and Socialization: Comments on the Assumptions Underlying Socialization Theology," *Sociological Analysis* 32 (1972), pp. 7-19. For an overview of the different sociological understandings of ritual cf. S. P. Nagendra, *The Concept of Ritual in Modern Sociological Theory*. (New Delhi: The Academic Journals of India, 1971); and Robert Bococh, *Ritual in Industrial Society*. (London: George Allen and Unwin, Inc., 1974).

11. Mary Douglas, *Natural Symbols*. (London: Barrie and Rockliff, 1970), p. 1.

12. Erikson, "The Development. . .," p. 712.

13. *Ibid.*, p. 713.

14. *Ibid.*, p. 714.

15. *Ibid.*

16. *Ibid.*, pp., 714-715.

17. *Ibid.*, pp. 715-716.

18. Eugene d'Aquili and Charles Laughlin, Jr., "The Biopsychological Determinants of Religious Ritual Behavior," *Zygon* 10 (1975), p. 41; also Nagendra, p. 7; and Bococh, pp. 174-175.

19. Erikson, "The Development. . .," p. 716.

20. For the relation between parental images and images of the *numinous* cf. A. Vergote and C. Aubert, "Parental Images and the Representations of God," *Social Compass* 19 (1972-1973), pp. 431-444.

21. Erikson, "The Development. . .," p. 718.

22. *Ibid.*, pp. 718-719.

23. *Ibid.*, p. 721.

24. *Ibid.*

25. *Ibid.*, p. 722.

26. Bococh, p. 174.

27. Johan Huizinga, *Homo Ludens: A Study of the Play-Element in Culture*. (London: International Library of Sociology and Social Reconstruction, 1949).

28. Hugo Rahner, *Man at Play*. (New York: Herder and Herder, 1972).

29. Erikson, "The Development. . .," p. 723-4.

30. *Ibid.*, p. 725; also cf Jerome Singer, *The Child's World of Make-Believe: Experimental Studies of Imaginative Play*. (New York: Academic Press, 1973).

31. *Ibid.*, pp. 726-727.

32. A difference can be noted between boys and girls 6-12 in their religious attitudes and ritual performance, cf. Jean-Marie Jaspard, "Loi Ritualle et Structuration de L'attitude Religieuse Chex Enfant," Social Compass 19 (1972-'73), pp. 459-471.

33. Cf. Brian Wicker, "Ritual and Culture: Some Dimensions of the Problem Today," in Roots of Ritual. James Shaughnessey (ed.), (Grand Rapids: William B. Eerdmans Publ. Co., 1974), pp. 13-46.

34. d'Aquili and Loughlin, p.41.

35. Ibid., p. 49.

36. Nagendra, p. 7.

37. Bernard Bro, "Man and the Sacraments: The Anthropological Substructure of the Christian Sacraments," Concilium 31 (1968), pp. 33-50.

38. Ibid., p. 39.

39. Ibid., p. 40.

40. Ibid.

41. Cf. Baum, pp. 7-61. On the various dimensions of alienation cf. William C. Bier, S. J. (ed.), Alienation: Plight of Modern Man? (New York: Fordham University Press, 1972).

5 SOCIOLOGY-ANTHROPOLOGY: THE FUNCTION OF RITUAL IN THE HUMAN COMMUNITY

The need for ritualization is not confined to the individual human person. By operation and definition, ritual is a social phenomenon. It implies group interaction. Ritual is an interpersonal behavior that has social effects.

In the preceding chapter, ritual was presented as an imperative for personality development which functioned as the medium for resolving experienced binary-oppositions. This chapter will examine *how* ritual functions to attain this goal of an integrated world view or world hypothesis. Such an inquiry can only be successful when ritual is analyzed in reference to the social community. Consequently, this investigation must enter and explore the domain of sociology and anthropology.

The very basis for sociology and anthropology is the existence of social units, groups, or "pseudospecies." These two sciences articulate three main components which make up the basic composition and world vision of a particular community: language, patterns of behavior, and social structure. Ritual operates in each of these components. A study of each area will allow the function of ritual in the whole social life to emerge. Moreover, this endeavor will demonstrate how ritual fulfills its task.

Language: Disclosure of Meaning

The intensification of the information explosion through the continued growth of the mass media has sensitized contemporary humankind to language. A plethora of verbiage has invited humankind to take a closer look at what it does with words. Common sense tells us that language is a medium or vehicle for communication. Common sense, however, does not

70

explain the process, complex functions, and elements that comprise language. This task falls to linguistics and philosophy, especially the Anglo-American tradition. This particular stream of reflection has presented a basic vision or theory of language which can contextualize our analysis of religious language and ritual.

In his book, *How To Do Things With Words*,[1] J. L. Austin sketched an original framework for understanding language and its various functions. He devised what is now generally known as Speech Act Theory. Through this scheme, Austin sought to analyze what things are accomplished through the use of words and how they are accomplished. His goal was clear and simple:

> ... to analyze and categorize speech acts. Analysis reveals the parts and structure of one kind of act, while categorization reveals the parts and structure of several kinds of acts. An analysis of a speech act consists at least of a statement of the individually necessary and jointly sufficient conditions for the successful performance of a speech act.[2]

Austin delineated three "acts" in speech i.e., *locutionary acts*, *illocutionary acts*, and *perlocutionary acts*. A locutionary act is performed when a sentence is spoken with a meaning e.g., he said: "The cat is up the tree." Every sentence which has a reference of meaning is a locutionary act.[3] When a locutionary act is "put to use," Austin calls it an illocutionary act. An illocutionary act is something we *do* in performing a locutionary act. For example, an illocutionary act might inform, warn, order, or undertake. Illocutionary acts are important for they signal out the performative element of speech. Illocutionary acts are not merely statements. They are utterances which bear a force or power.[4] A perlocutionary act is "what we bring about or achieve *by* saying something, such as convincing, persuading, deterring and even, say surprising or misleading."[5] Illocutionary acts have an impact or effect. This is their perlocutionary characteristic. For example, if I say: "You will be punished if you continue to steal from the department store," I am making a statement that has a meaning. I am also issuing a warning in making the statement. Furthermore, I am attempting to deter the robber.

Every illocutionary act is composed of two elements: illocutionary content and illocutionary force. Content refers to the data that is communicated through the statement. Force refers to how the content is conveyed. For example, the four following propositions can be stated:[6] Sam smokes habitually; Does Sam smoke habitually?; Sam smokes habitually!;

Would that Sam smoked habitually. In each of these propositions, the same content is being coveyed. A different force, however, is employed to convey the content. In the first statement, the force is a statement, in the second a question, in the third a command, in the fourth a wish.

In his Speech Act Theory, Austin groups various utterances according to their illocutionary force. He develops five categories: verdictives, exercitives, commissives, behabitives, and expositives. A. P. Martinich has added two further categories, constantives, which purport to represent facts, and master speech acts which control other speech acts. Three of these categories are of immediate importance for our investigation of religious language and ritual: exercitives, commissives, and master speech acts. When one examines ritual and especially religious ritual language utterances cluster around these forces.[7]

Exercitives exercise rights, power, or influence. They focus on "appointing, voting, ordering, urging, advising, warning, etc."[8] Commissives are typified by promising or undertaking. They are directed toward commitment or statement of intention. Master speech acts determine and delineate other speech acts by determining the context within which they are to be interpreted. "Some master speech acts announce the beginning of some type of activity ('starters'); examples: 'Once upon a time,' 'Let us pray.' Other master speech acts announce the end of that activity ('stoppers'); examples; 'The end,' and 'Amen'."[9]

This cursory glance at Austin's Speech Act Theory should make clear that speech is more than the use of words or the communication of content. There is a power or force to language which accompanies every human utterance and which in many ways controls the meaning of the utterance. If this is true for language in general, it is especially apparent in religious language.

The importance of language lies not only in a logical and correct comprehension of its use. There is a fuller dimension to language and religious language in particular which highlights its function for the individual and the social group. Language *discloses* meaning. It articulates experience in such a fashion that its depth of meaning is expressed. The disclosive power or language is most apparent in the type of discourse called "religious." In brief, religious language identifies or brings one to the "limit situations" of human existence. "The function of religious language is to bring to speech such experiences even to provoke them, and in its own way to answer them. Religious language is the primary language of the limits. It meets dread and allows faith."[10]

Ian Ramsey [11] and Frederick Ferre[12] uniquely responsible for advancing the analysis and evaluation of religious language in a post-verification and post-falsification study of religious discourse.

Ramsey is mesmorized by one question in his reflections on religious language. He seeks to determine the locus or situation that religious language attempts to address. He:

> sets forth his central understanding of the "uses" of religious statements in his book *Religious Language: An Empirical Placing of Theological Phrases.* As the title indicates, Ramsey is principally concerned to answer two questions about religious language: to what kind of empirical situation does religious language appeal; for such situations, what kind of language is appropriate?[13]

Ramsey discovered that religious language addresses what he calls "odd" situations which require total commitment. By "odd" Ramsey means those personal situations for which indicative language and statements are insufficient. A literal description of the situation simply does not express its significance; yet, the reality of the situation cannot be denied. For example, one might scale the heights of a great mountain. While scanning the horizon, there is suddenly the sense of a power abstractly present yet hidden in the panoramic beauty of the canyons below. Overwhelmed, one speaks of God, the Creator. A geologist, artist, and physician might collaborate to construct an exact description of what was perceived and the effect it produced. But, this description will not exhaust or explain the experience of the mountain climber who will insist there was more involved.

If ordinary discourse fails in communicating the experience of an "odd" situation, what form of language would be appropriate? Ramsey believes that an "odd" language is demanded of an "odd" situation. The "odd" character of this language consists in the qualifications which are placed on its content i.e., the use of concepts of infinity to express universality and total commitment. The application of these qualifiers is an attempt to express or disclose through language whatever has been experienced but at the same time evades reduction to usual or ordinary explanations or reports.

Ramsey offers an example of the disclosive power of religious language by citing the story of Nathan the prophet and David. David had slept with Uriah's wife while Uriah was at battle fighting for the king. When David learned that Uriah's wife was pregnant, he called Uriah back from the front, hoping that he would have relations with his wife and think the child was. During his furlough, Uriah would not have relations with his wife since Israel's religious laws prohibited relations for soldiers during war. When David learned of Uriah's refusal of sexual relations, he devised a new plan of action. He placed Uriah in command of the troops which would be the first to confront the enemy in battle. This increased the chances that Uriah would be slain. David's plan worked. Nathan the prophet, however, learned of David's plan. He went to the king and asked him a question.

> The Lord sent Nathan the prophet to David, and when he came to him he said: Judge this case for me. In a certain town there were two men, one rich and the other poor. The rich man had flocks and herds in great numbers. But the poor man had nothing at all except one little ewe lamb that he had bought. He nourished her, and she grew up with him and his children. She shared the little food he had and drank from his cup and slept in his bosom. She was like a daughter to him. Now, the rich man received a visitor, but he would not take from his own flocks and herds to prepare a meal for the wayfarer who had come to him. Instead he took the poor man's ewe lamb and made a meal of it for his visitor. David grew very angry with that man and said to Nathan: As the Lord lives, that man who has done this deserves to die. He shall restore the ewe lamb fourfold because he has done this and has had no pity. Then Nathan said to David: You are the man.[14]

The encounter with Nathan is a disclosure situation for David. With Nathan's words: "You are the man," the "ice breaks" and truth is disclosed. David is pushed to the *limit* and understands more deeply the meaning and responsibilities implied in his actions. It is important to notice that the disclosure not only reveals a deeper level of meaning to David but demands a response or commitment on his part.

The disclosive character of religious language takes human reason to the brink, the limit of human experience. At the limit, the human person is confronted by experiences and questions which appear to have no complete answer within the range of human experience; yet, an answer is demanded. In a sense, the disclosive power of religious language in general and ritual language in particular leads to a relativization of ordinary human experience and its explanations. It directs humankind beyond the ordinary and the explainable as the ultimate answer to life by activating the power of force that is inherent in language, a power which can be directed into different sectors by the various types of illocutionary acts and illocutionary forces.

Ritual or sacramental language as a subdivision of religious language is rich, supercharged and polyvalent. "Worship is a way of providing a group of occasions whereby we may be enabled to see ourselves. The interpretation of life and the relation to the transcendent that are the distinctive marks of liturgy are grasped by images."[15] The images of religious ritual are transmitted through language, gesture, and space.

Ritual language is metaphorical. The metaphors of religious ritual language disclose something about God and something about the participants. The metaphors are freely mixed. Although they are numerous, they are not random with a concentration or focus on metaphors which depict and speak of transformation. In almost all cases, the metaphor is tied to an event.[16] The metaphors of religious ritual possess imperative as well as indicative force, not only informing but also enjoining and commanding.

A dynamic creativity prospers in religious ritual language as it describes the "odd" situations which require total commitment. The symbols of ritual language can be clustered for additon or coalesced for condensation.

> Sacramental language, from the way it behaves, shows several signs of being extraordinarily creative. It carries no power of self-verification. Its transitive and indefinite reference, as well as its polysemy, cannot for good or ill be directly refuted or falsified. But within the believers' sphere of discourse it carries many signs of being concerned, like miracles, with a power; and there corresponds with that assumption of the presence or operativeness of a divine power an imperative incumbent on the believer to respect the holiness of the situation he directly or indirectly invokes.[17]

B. R. Brinkman has proposed three primary and two secondary characteristics of religious ritual language. This discourse is primarily (1) descriptive, narrative, or mythical; (2) heuristic; and (3) prescriptive. Secondarily, the discourse is (4) promissory or fiduciary; and (5) performative.[18]

The term *descriptive* refers to the narrative or myth which accompanies ritual performance. Usually, the descriptive element or narrative operates as an explanation of exegesis of the ritual action. It sets the context for a correct interpretation of the performance.

The term *heuristic* refers to the power of language to arouse interest and evoke discovery of a reality which is not immediately observed in the ritual action. Through the heuristic power of religious ritual language, "the believer is led to consider a different symbol than the one first presented."[19] For example, at the celebration of the Christian Eucharist one could specify the following transmission of symbols: priest—host—Body of Christ—grace—love. The observation of one reality within the context of religious discourse activates the human power of transcendence to move beyond one reality to another. "The vital use of symbols seems to display an invitation to, or demand, on the mind of the believer such that in the very moment of adverting to one symbol he has to move on to another one."[20]

The term *prescriptive* connotes the cohesive power of ritual language for the life of the ritual community. The content of the discourse and the action it accompanies has a decisive effect on the continued life of the community. Dependency on the ritual community is one of the most powerful features which affects religious ritual behavior and language. The prescriptive character leads to the secondary characteristics of *promissory* and *performative*. Because, the meaning expressed in ritual is the basis for the continued stable existence of the community, the ritual's participants are motivated to commit themselves to the values of the community and to live out these values in their concrete existence. Therefore, prescription implies promise and performance. The five characteristics of religious ritual language suggest a direct relationship between ritual and the life and structure of a community. This relationship will be explored in the following two sections of this chapter. At this junction some summary remarks on language are in order.

From a "common sense" perspective, language and communication are rather simple, common place, and readily accepted phenomena. When they are examined with some attention and precision, their complex and powerful structures become evident.

Language is potent. It exerts tremendous influence and power. Whether language is religious or non-religious it resides close to the life-center of the human community. It not only tells of life, but, in a real sense, determines the possibilities of cultural life. Language has the capacity of evoking a distinctively human element in existence i.e., meaning. Moreover, religious language has the additional power of disclosing an inexhaustible, undefinable, yet undeniably experience of meaning which transcends the ordinary.

Language and ritual go hand in hand. They are mutually explanatory. In the past, too little attention has been directed to the role of religious language in religious ritual, especially sacramental rituals. To some extent, the descriptive character of language has been accounted for in religious rituals. The heuristic and prescriptive character, however, have not been attended to or specified. Yet, it is precisely in these aspects of language that the efficacy and directional force of religious language resides. Consequently, these elements are indispensable for an adequate understanding of religious ritual, and therefore Christian sacraments.

In the search for a theory of religious ritual language, the ancient principle *lex orandi-lex credendi*, what the Church prays, the Church believes, must not be overlooked. This principle needs to be applied and expanded in our present age. A new phrase needs to be added to this theorum i.e., *lex faciendi*. The communicatory power of language is not limited to the transmission of concepts, but leads to actions and patterns of behavior.

Language is no less indigenous and necessary to the attainment and maintainence of personal and social integration than the actions of ritual. Together, ritual action and ritual language intertwine to sustain a process of introduction, identification, and healthy survival in the world of the "pseudospecies." This becomes clear when ritual is examined in terms of a culture's patterns of behavior.

Patterns of Behavior

Anthropological and sociological investigations of various "pseudospecies" or cultural communities note a similarity in their *mode-of-living-in-the-world*. Observation of various peoples has revealed a consistent, repetitive, or, what is called, patterned behavior with cultural variations. What exactly is a pattern of behavior?

The term *behavior* simply refers to the observable response, activity, of an individual or group to the realities of life which impinge on them. A *pattern* "is nothing other that repetitive human activities that reduce the raw and seemingly random stuff of experience to manageable proportions on both the individual and public social level."[21] When the forces which stimulate human behavior are taken as a whole, they are in oppositions, binary-oppositions. Consequently, the patterned quality of behavior attempts to resolve, even if only temporarily, the oppositions and sustain individual and social survival.

Patterns of behavior control and nourish individual and communal response to reality in a triple fashion. They foster effective group communication. They reduce intra-group conflict which could potentially stifle the resolution of binary-oppositions by the community's specific world view. Finally, they strengthen group bonding, coherence and solidarity.[22]

Patterns of behavior exercise a significant and central role in all social communities. It should not be surprising to find their appearance in religious communities. Although Geertz's well-known definition of religion does not specifically employ the term pattern of hebavior, the thrust of the definition included this concept:

> Religion is a system of symbols which acts to establish powerful and long-lasting moods and motivations in man by formulating concepts of a general order of existence, and clothing these conceptions with such an aura of facticity that the moods and motivations seem uniquely realistic.[23]

Religion attains its goal in and through the context of ritual. Ritual "is not a power, something to which social events, behaviors, institutions, or processes can be causally attributed; it is a context. . . . "[24] Within this context, meaningful action becomes a possibility.

"Functional theorists" in sociology of religion generally concur with Geertz's claims. They link religion with the finite character and experience of the human condition. Religion, for them, supplies two relations within social existence. First, it points to a "transcendent," "other worldly," or "fuller dimension" of life which can contextualize finitude in its manifold expressions, so that a meaningful rather than a meaningless interpretation of the experience is possible. Second, religion provides "the ritual means for facilitating a relationship to the beyond which gives enough security and assurance to human beings to sustain their morale."[25]

Functional theory further specifies these relations in six functions of religion. Religion (1) supports, consoles, and reconciles; (2) offers a path to a transcendent through cult which in turn fosters social identity; (3) sacralizes the norms and values of the established society; (4) can offer a prophetic critique of the established order; (5) fosters social and personal identity by communicating to people who they are and what they are; (6) sustains individuals through maturation crises co-relational to age.[26]

Ritual, within the framework of our previous definition, is a pattern of behavior. Care must be taken not to limit ritual exclusively to a functional or *expressive* role. First and foremost, ritual is an *articulation*. It not only expresses humanness, but is active in bringing it into being. R. Delattre has clarified the relation between ritual as *expression* and ritual as *articulation*.

> To speak of ritual as an expression of our humanity, or of some aspect of it such as the life of feeling, tends artificially to separate form and content. It is to look for the meaning of ritual in something else which it ex-

presses—a content for which it is the symbol, a reality otherwise constituted for which it is the ritual expression. There is truth in this
perspective on ritual, but it is of a secondary and external order and it
obscures something more fundamental. What it misses is that ritual does
not merely express a humanity and reality otherwise constituted, but is
itself creative and constitutive of our humanity and of wider realities insofar as we are engaged with them. Even when the expressive function of
ritual is distinguished clearly from its instrumental functions, as it is by
some scholars, the perspective of functionalism prevails and ritual is
seen in too narrowly an instrumental way.[27]

Consequently, it is important to distinguish ritual "before" and "after" institutionalization so that neither its articulative nor expressive characteristics are confused, lost, or forgotten.

Before formal institutionalization, religious rituals are not primarily
directed to the establishment of social relations and social structures.
Rather, ritual is primarily an acting out of feelings, attitudes, and relationships with a "sacred object." It is only secondarily concerned with the relationships between members of the social unit, even though social relations are implicit in all ritual activity. Susan Langer has commented:

> Ritual is a symbolic transformation of experiences that no other medium
> can adequately express. Because it springs from a primary human need,
> it is a spontaneous activity, that is to say, it arises without intention,
> without adaptation to a conscious purpose; its growth is undesigned, its
> pattern purely natural, however intricate it may be.[28]

"What the ritual process yields—to extend her analysis a little—is not, in
the first place, conformity or social unity, but anchorage, orientation,
meaningfulness, a sense of order."[29]

As religions become institutionalized, the formalized expression of ritual in words, gestures, and patterns of behavior shift from articulating attitudes to eliciting them. In this situation, the socializing function of ritual
and the power it exerts over social structures and social institutions becomes more prevalent. This aspect of ritual will be studied in the final section of this chapter. Our present concern is to summarize some of the fundamental patterns which direct ritual behavior, patterns which reach down
to the very foundation of humanness.

The reflections of B. R. Brinkman will serve as a guide through the
vast maze of data on patterns of behavior. His investigation of "sacramental man" presents four poles around which the content of our discussion

can be clustered; the way of intimacy, the social operational way, the way of interiorization, and the way of sacramental operationalism. Brinkman's vantage point permits and encourages the addition of supporting data from the anthropological and sociological fields.

Before exploring the four paths Brinkman articulates, it is important to identify the source of a key element in his analysis. The role and function of the "structured imagination" weaves its way throughout Brinkman's scrutiny of "sacramental man." He is indebted to Gilbert Durand,[30] the noted philosopher-anthropologist for his general theory of the "structured imagination."

Durand's imagination theory is grounded in two fundamental insights or postulates. First, images or mental representations are not totally free-flowing or disjunctive, but group together to form image-clusters which represent the material component of the structured imagination. Second, there are lines of movement between the various image-clusters which represent the operation and dynamic element of the structured imagination.

A person's structured imagination arises from a reciprocal interplay between innate image formation and their animation in concrete historical events and culture of a particular "pseudospecies." Durand labels this process "anthropological trajectory."[31] Two fundamental divisions designate and categorize all mental images. First, all mental images are divided into *Diurnal* or *Nocturnal* regions i.e., light and dark. Second, all mental images are clustered in conformity to humankind's three primary reflexes: gaining an upright position, ingestion of food, and the release of the sexual drive. These three reflexes stimulate three corresponding directional forces which further differentiate the images: ascending, enclosing, and uniting.

> These two basic divisions eventually experience a certain convergence: images of life (*sic.*, light) assimilate as ascending dynamism; images of darkness incorporate the enclosing dynamism; and between these two composite groups, we find the cyclic dynamism operating as a unifying factor. In these convergences are located the fundamentals of the Structured Symbolic Imagination, and within this basic structure many other groups of images come to be fixed in a person's consciousness.[32]

Imagination functions within a person's consciousness as a balancing force in pursuit of equilibrium.[33] This is specified by the imagination's thrust toward intimacy, interiorization, and integration amid the appearance and experience of new, conflicting, juxtaposing, etc., images. This process can be either conscious or unconscious. In light of the above imagination theory, Brinkman investigates the function of the imagination in the ritual activity of "sacramental man."

The Way of Intimacy

Reflection on the manifold drives of human existence notices a remarkable thrust for union or intimacy. Brinkman commences his reflections on "sacramental man" by analyzing the faculties, powers, and activities the human person employs to attain intimacy in sacramental behavior.

Preceding sections of this work should have neutralized any false utopian description of human existence as a harmony of positive elements and forces totally integrated by the human person. Likewise, any pessimistic description of human existence as a total discord of negating elements and forces which are irresolvable should be rejected. Human existence is lived between identified bipolar oppositions which find their resolution in the world view of a particular community or "pseudospecies."

Distance is the opposite experiental pole of intimacy. In terms of its bipolar opposition, the "way of intimacy" could be restated as the "way of overcoming distance." Brinkman alludes to this in stating that his "concern is with the way sacraments try to overcome distancing effects."[34] He sees distance overcome in two ways: first, through the use of the imagination; and second, through the repetitiveness of religious rituals.

In religious situations, two differences must be narrowed: the vertical and the horizontal. In sacramental behavior, the human imagination projects a vertical dimension which identifies the sacred object (God) as being above i.e., in a position of power and transcendence. The imagination also projects a horizontal dimension or time line of past, present, and future, a looking backward and forward which creates a sense of continuity. In both cases, the projection of the imagination is purposeful:

> The upward looking seems to make the sacrament effective, and the backward look provides a form of guarantee, while, when we look forward, we think we can somehow see that our insufficient performance here and now will by and by be made good.[35]

The vertical and horizontal projections of the imagination are synthesized when the "sacraments" are envisioned as extensions of some type of "incarnation" which adds "proximity" as a dimension.

What lies behind the projection of the imagination? Why does the human person resort to these operations? Is this merely logical or psychological play? The answer to these questions has already been germinally offered. Through the use of the imagination, the human person attempts to cut the universe down to a manageable size and control the religiously interpreted forces which confront human experience. Through the use of the imagination, humankind can also identify with the sacred object (God) and even attain intimacy with him. Imagination assists the human person in relating to what can appear as overwhelming yet necessary elements of life.

In institutionalized religion, the repetitive character of ritual formalizes the behavior which is linked to the imagination. It achieves this by supplying two forms of contact which lead to intimacy. First, repetition offers the individual or the group contact with its original charter event, or the happening from which the community traces its origin and distinctiveness. Second, repetition affords contact between the participants' past experiences of the charter event's reenactment and their present reenactment. Polanyi points out:

> By fully participating in a ritual, the members of a group affirm the community of "their existence," and at the same time identify the life of their group with that of the antecedent groups, from whom the ritual has descended to them. Every ritual act of a group is to this extent a reconciliation with the group and a reestablishment of continuity with its own history as a group. It affirms the convivial existence of the group as transcending the individual, both in the present and in times past.[36]

The Christian celebration of the Eucharist serves as an example of this dual contact. The ritualization of the Eucharist always has as a referent the Christian charter event of the Last Supper and at the same time, the referent of all previous celebrations of the Eucharist i.e., between the participant's own past experiences of the Eucharist and his present repetition of a previous reenactment.

Why are rituals reenacted? Usually, it is thought that certain rituals are prescribed by legislation or rules which require periodic performance. This is certainly true. There is, however, a more basic and fundamental reason, the reason for the rule or legislation itself. Ritual legislation and the repetition of ritual arises from the prescriptive character of the "sacramental" situation i.e., the need for the individual and the community to perpetuate their existence and by necessity the directives and laws which will attain this goal. Repetition, therefore, arises from the need to cope with what Brinkman calls "unfinished business."[37] "Unfinished business"

refs to those elements or values which are yet to be attained or lived up
to by the individual or the community in terms of their world view. Unfinished business accumulates in terms of both the "charter event" and the
nexus of past and present reenactments of the "charter event" since the
"pseudo-species" world view is *articulated* and *expressed* in and through
these ritual activities.

The psychological need for consummation is the source of the drive
for intimacy in terms of the charter event. Brinkman calls this the consummative mode of sacraments in distinction to the instrumental mode. The
two modalities can be distinguished in terms of animal behavior.

> A consummatory act is one by which the innate behavior patterns are
> directed toward stimuli which act as rewards for the species concerned.
> Thus eating, drinking, copulation are consummatory acts, whereas the
> learnt forms of behavior which bring the animal into contact with food,
> water or sexual partners are "instrumental" responses.[38]

The consummative mode of sacramental behavior arises from and resembles the human need to be fondled. It corresponds to the need for mutual
recognition which appears in infancy and perdures throughout life. This
need is not an infantile nostalgia. It emerges from the experience of "unfinished business" evoked by ritual celebrations of the charter event. Brinkman explains:

> Objectively and out there, we accept the perfect *ephapax*. But we are still
> pre-occupied. Hence we re-enact, we are present, not once but again and
> again until we are ourselves consummatively absorbed in the process . . .
> as the desire and the image of the past remain present, they still have the
> power to envelop and to fondle. But the process has an aim: in the im-
> mediacy and the contact produced by repetition we cope with the unfin-
> ished business which as a community and as individuals, we live with.[39]

In the reenactment of the charter event, the opportunity is offered for
"catching up" with and beginning to embrace again the fullness aimed at
but yet to be completely attained. In moments of intuitive self-evaluation,
a sense of responsibility to the meaning of the charter event and one's self
emerges, a responsibility which the reenactment of the event calls the participants to fulfill and complete.

Brinkman is not suggesting that the reenactments which provide intimacy between former and present reenactments of the charter event transform "unfinished business" into "finished business." Rather, he is pointing

out that "there is here by intimacy or contact, a feeling of absorption in a transparent reality to which the 'unfinished business' itself calls us."[40]

In the Christian sacramental liturgy, the drive for intimacy is induced by imagery i.e., what is being done on earth is being done in heaven.[41] The mechanism employed in this drive for intimacy is *projection*. Projection produces a coalescence of temporal dimensions and a feeling of spacial contact with the primordial past. Brinkman is not making a truth claim i.e., that contact with the divine actually transpires. He is attempting a phenomenological description of what is transpiring in ritual celebrations. He writes:

> Whether or not we can solve the problems attached to such a mystery (anxiety of the past) one still has to live with it. Sacramental man through his feelings and verbalizing can come to terms with himself and his world. He may well be in a state that a logical guarantee attaching to his every experience of the kind may only be a luxury. At the same time, the stronger and more reassured he becomes, the more he can take up again the problems of his religious existence. Indeed he is offered the opportunity to do this every time he receives a sacrament.[42]

Both the body and the idea of sexual union are placed in the service of imagination to enhance the drive and attainment of intimacy. The religious imagination employs the body to manipulate the category of space. Through actions performed by the body or activities done to the body, space is incorporated into the total drive for unity.

The introduction of the body into the way of intimacy leads to a recognition of the place of sexual union in ritual, especially religious ritual. This may initially seem quite foreign. Sexuality is usually repressed in religious discourse or associated with negative values. In analysis of the writings of the mystics, however, one finds the summit and apogee of intimacy with the "divine other" described in sexual terms. God is the lover who comes in the night and seduces them into the act of perfect love. The mystic is consumed in his or her sexual union with the divine.

The body is not merely an instrument for union with the divine. As a constituative feature of the human person it participates fully in consummative union. It is interesting that the more ritual is understood as union with the divine, the more the symbolism attached to the body shifts from the function of ingestion to the ontological reality of sexual union.

In his discussion of the way of intimacy, Brinkman demonstrates that the drive for intimacy is potentially fulfilled in religious rituals through a creative use of the human imagination and repetition. He draws certain conclusions from his observations.

... (a) that even the way of intimacy is not one clearly heterogeneous to each other in many ways. Observation must always be renewed. But because intimacy, even in the sacramental dimension, arises from and is polarized to inescapable biological, as well as psychological energies and drives, there remains a human constant, and in that constant rather than in variation and overlap can sacramental man discover himself and his God; (b) vague phobias about the nature of intimacy in religion had best be exorcized in face of a vast historic religious approval of sacramental intimacy and in fact of an increased knowledge we have of ourselves. There is no reason why Church thinking should not be much more sensitive; (c) the situation here is so fundamental, its mode being the mode of the Eternal Being itself, namely that of love, that we must conlude: a Christianity without sacramental intimacy would be like a Christ without humanity—a phantom of the Docetis.[43]

Religious rituals pursue the path of intimacy.

The Socially Operational Way

An essential dimension of ritual is its communal or social nature. Ritual always involves two or more persons. The question can be posed: "What does the admitted factor of sociality in sacramental life tell us about sacramentality itself? Or to put it another way: How does human sociality tell us more about the claim that sacraments are salvationary events in the fully human mode?"[44] To answer these questions, Brinkman explores what he calls the *socially operational way*.

A social imprint appears throughout an investigation of religious ritual's mulitple dimensions. Its presence in sacramental rituals will disclose either intimacy, communion, or an intensified relationship to the ritual community or the numinal or divine. This presence is indisputable. The important question, however, is: How are they operational? "What we want to know in the long run is whether ritual and sacramental symbols do perform in their religious and theological sense in virtue of their societal element."[45] To answer this query, two steps are necessary. First, the societal influence on symbols must be established. Second, a demonstration of the social operation and its effect within concrete religious rituals must be demonstrated.

Previous sections of this work have highlighted the importance of the unconscious elements in culture. Durkeim and Casel can be added to the list of scholars who have identified these elements, especially in the area of collective representations which present themselves in ritual as symbols. Of what are these collective representations or *Kult eidos* symbols? One could immediately remark: symbols of God or the divine. This response, however, would reveal little concerning their social operation. There is another avenue to collective representations, however, which can elucidate their social operation. They can be envisioned under the category of heuristic symbols i.e., symbols which evoke other symbols. Their heuristic character arises partially from societies' socializing function.

> The presentation of symbolic material is partially a social function. Society is responsible for the sociality of the symbols, in virtue of which they are socially mediated and are socially accessible to the individual—in virtue of which, of course, they become socially operational and set up a society which causes the sociality in question.[46]

In a sense, this is a circular argument. Symbols are social. They are socially mediated to an individual and consequently operate through social life. But circular argument is not necessarily incorrect. To identify the social operations of symbols is not necessarily to claim a "truth status." It could simply be a phenomenological description of what is observable operationalism in ritual.[47] Victor Turner has alluded to the general acceptance of this interpretation by the social sciences.

> In the social sciences generally, it is, I think becoming widely recognized that religious beliefs and practices are something more than "grotesque" reflections or expressions of economic, political, and social relationships; rather, they are coming to be seen as decisive keys to the understanding of how people think and feel about those relationships, and about the natural and social environments in which they operate.[48]

Further support for the social operation of symbols is marshalled when one is conscious of the effect of symbols on social change. Humankind's world is a composite of "givens," the "raw stuff of life," and human symbolic activities. Through human symbolic activity, the chaos of life is molded into a culture which orders and interprets the meaning of both the world and human activity. Social change is fundamentally symbolic change and symbolic change affects social change.[49] The symbols of ritual men and women are social and the social character of ritual men and women is symbolic. This framework is a given. It is present upon examination of reality and life.

The social operation of symbols can be detected in concrete religious rituals. For example, each of the Christian sacraments focuses on aspects of existence which imply social relationships of a determinative and constitutive nature. There are sacraments of initiation into the community, sacraments of re-integration, and sacraments of leadership and order. The Christian community even proclaims a sacrament "in respect to the establishment of a person-to-person relationship in marriage."[50] Every symbolic action focused in the Christian sacraments is, moreover, envisioned as and interpreted in terms of the Church, the social unit.

Sociality is effective on the individuals within the community through the power of the imagination. "In the end, if we want to answer the question, 'how does sociality in sacrament or rite on the individual,' there will be no other recourse except to an intuitive and disciplined use of the imagination."[51] Imagination leads not only to a communion and consummation with the "divine," but also with the ritual community. This is especially clear in the sacraments of the Eucharist and marriage. In both instances, "the individual is invited to sink his individuality in the unitary experience of the group."[52]

The unity of social operationalism extends in two directions. It produces an organization of experienced symbols and an organization of the individuals who comprise the ritual community.

> . . . in the socializing polarities of the sacramental event we organize the symbols with which we have to deal, and by the same token we organize ourselves. The more we accept the socializing offer of sacramental life, the more we socialize our individuality.[53]

The unity attained in both directions, is mutually reinforcing.

Brinkman concludes to an indispensable truth from the way of social operationalism. Sociality in religious ritual is an opportunity to see in human nature an openness to the divine. "It should show us that human nature is unlikely to succeed, if it looks for a divine call under either realized conditions to a pure Yea or Nay to a Gospel message transmitted in an ideological vacuum."[54] God, and any claim to his existence, will be discovered within the operations of human existence, or not at all.

It will be fundamental to the remainder of this work to remember the social character of symbols and the symbolic activity which flows throughout ritual. The intimacy attained in ritual through imagination is not a private affair, but is itself social.

The Way of Interiorization

The intimacy and sociality within religious ritual behavior raises the issue of response or reaction. What happens or what demands are placed upon the ritual participant who attains communion with the divine and the community? Brinkman labels this response *interiorization*. He defines the term broadly as: "any reaction of the organism on presentation of a symbol. This can be taken to cover any psycho-physical response, or interest arousal, and should allow for reactions ranging from the merely sensory and motor-rhythmatic to intellectual comprehension itself."[55] Interioriztion is a response to the attraction of a given event or situation. It may or may not be accompanied by conceptualization.

Interiorization is a degreed reality. It has a potential measure i.e., the acceptance of responsibility for the meaning offered in the experienced situation. "The fuller, the more human, the interiorization, the more I will accept responsibility for the meaning, or the proffered commitment, indeed for the gift as I may think of it, which is now entrusted to me."[56] For example, in the celebration of the Christian Eucharist the participants are called to become like Christ. They are offered the possibility of embracing his life style and values. When the participants accept this responsibility, they are involved in interiorization at the level to which the responsibility is realized.

Interiorization as a human potential emulates the cognitional and volitional dimensions of the human person. The radical unity of the human person finds a parallel demand for a conformity of theory-action, role-behavior in interiorization. In fact, this is what interiorization is all about. It is evident in an analysis of lifestyles where a concrete role is expected to be interiorized by a form of commitment. There are social roles for doctors, lawyers, social workers, etc. Interiorization requires that those who assume these roles transform them into personal biographies. This is especially true in the expectations surrounding the Christian priesthood. There is a demand that the individual priest interiorize (become) the serving, consoling, warming individual. Other religious rituals follow a similar scheme of role-corresponding commitment—prescriptive process. The initiated neophite is to live in accord with the proclaimed lifestyle of the community. The married person is to live the vows embraced. The reconciled sinner is to leave behind former deviations and pursue the way of the Gospel.

Why must role be transformed into personal biography? What is the ground of foundation for the interiorization process? Brinkman believes that two ways offer a glimpse at the source of interiorization: Bro's embracing negativity and moving beyond it, and, binary oppositions.

Brinkman lists Bro's insight as decisive for understanding sacramental life.[57] The relativization of human self-destruction hinges on the negation of self-asserting egoisms which would eventually reduce the universe to a human possession or toy. This fantasy would eventually crumble by the sobering effect of reality. To avoid the trauma of eventually meaninglessness, the human person needs negativity, a negativity which will allow the real self to emerge in a real world. This negativity can be attained through the repetition of ritual and the consequent realization that there is "unfinished business" in our lives. Brinkman notes:

> In living our lives we need negativity, usually in the form of a contradiction of the pleasure principle, as a motive or drive. We find it most commonly in the form of repetition. In sacramental interiorization we have a sound parallel. Not only we, but the creative moment needs creativity. It comes partly from the prescriptiveness that belongs to the sacrament; or, as in life, it comes from repetition which can also fill the bill. . . . [58]

Unfinished business further elucidates the function of repetition in negating the ideal self. By participating in the ritual action, the dual challenge of the original charter event and its previous reenactments confront the human person with the reality that all has not been attained and furthermore, that the attainment of goals, values, lifestyles, etc., cannot arise exclusively from within himself or herself. With this admission, the unfinished business can be taken up again not solitarily but within the context of the divine and the members of the ritual community.

Binary oppositions also demonstrate the need and presence of interiorization. Opposition demands either acceptance or rejection. "So far as one can tell, these binary oppositions, even the crudest, exist because somehow the opposition is there crying to be resolved; and, I think (Brinkman) by a process of interiorization."[59] The plethora and complexity of these oppositions only intensifies and heightens the need for interiorization.

> . . . the more complicated the sets of classification, the more interiorization is needed, while the need to cope with binary oppositions is already a sign that soem interiorization takes place, if only by a process of rearranging the pattern or cluster of symbols.[60]

The attempted resolution of binary oppositions points out interiorization.

In addressing himself to the way of interiorization, Brinkman locates the response to intimacy and sociality. Interiorization seems to stress personal responsibility over community. This concept, however, should be understood as a correlative rather than a juxtaposition. The interiorization Brinkman refers to unfolds within the context of a community, a community which bears social symbols that require the response of interiorization. Interiorization itself will be measured by the responsibility of the individual in his or her social existence. It is, nonetheless, important to remember interiorization as a feature of patterns of behavior.

The Way of Sacramental Operationalism

If humankind is directed to intimacy, social operationalism and interiorization, what is the final product or goal of their power, force, or presence? What is the purposefulness of these patterned behaviors? Why do they appear in religious rituals?

Brinkman attempts to answer these questions in exploring *sacramental operationalism*. He tries to avoid a "transcendental leap" in proposing his answer by consciously refusing to employ words like "grace," "salvation," and "holiness." Rather, he prefers to utilize the descriptive term *presence* as the ultimate goal of religious patterns of behavior.[61]

Anthropological and sociological research has pointed out that rituals and therefore sacraments are highly structured. Brinkman believes that an examination of this structured characteristic reveals the purpose of patterned behavior. Traditionally, the structured character of religious rituals has been interpreted in two ways. The first orientation stressed the unity between and symbol and what it signified. It "decided that halfway between the symbol or sign and its interior referent there was a 'symbolic reality' known as the *sacramentum et res*."[62] The locuna in this position was its failure to demonstrate how the final effect or "divine" effect was attained. "A symbol which merely produced a halfway house was not clearly itself producing a supernatural effect. Where was the divine action?"[63] The second orientation attempted to overcome the deficiencies between cause and effect stated above by assuming a metaphysical stance. "In effect it alleges that when certain holy sacramental actions or gestures or words are performed, then the transcendent God produces in the believer an enabling effect we call grace."[64] This solution is also inadequate to explain sacramental cause and effect. Why is it that these words, gestures, etc., so move the transcendent God? Brinkman turns to the power of the structured imagination to expose his understanding of sacramental purposefulness.

Brinkman capitalizes on Durand's lead that the main purpose of the structured imagination is the attainment of balance or equilibrium. The structured imagination eliminates distortions, randomness, and the continued introduction of new elements which would prohibit an integrated understanding. Brinkman calls the force which permits this elimination *directionality*. It can best be understood through the example he offers of its operation.

A serving sailor boy may want to kiss the photo his girlfriend gave him. *Ex hypothesi* she is absent. He is kissing her picture only. It is a directional gesture. Nothing here is random or perverse. If he said, "I will kiss her photo because she is trapped in it," that would be a gross misplacement of her concrete presence because she is four thousand miles away. He cannot say, "I will now kiss my memory of her," because if he tried, he would find nothing to kiss. So he kisses her photo. Is he mad if he thinks of the photo he has fixed above his bunk as a *comforting presence*? Of course, in one crass sense it is a piece of photographic paper which is the comforting presence, not the girlfriend.

Nevertheless, it is *a* presence of *some* kind. This is the logic of the structured imagination that takes over. The photo is now its own kind of reality, a symbolic reality (*res et sacramentum*). It calls for an attention that is not merely cognitive. That piece of symbolic reality involves the emotions, perhaps even a mild form of cult, if he puts a ribbon or flowers near it. By the imagaination, the boy now symbolically recreates the situation between himself and his girl. The total result has the logic of sacraments. It is *prescriptive*: his commitment and loyalty are involved. It is also heuristic: does she still look like that? Does she still love him faithfully? All this is a sign of deep "directionality" of the photo as a symbolic reality. The total situation for the boy is also purposive. By this kiss he is contributing to bringing about an enhanced state of affairs between himself and his girl. He contributes, for though she may never know about this particular kiss, she will finally, we hope, be the recipient of better sustained expressions of his deeper love. Again in the situation the boy himself receives, for now he is accepting again within him this present symbolic reality as a personal gift and symbolic presence of his girl, and is more deeply moved to love her.[65]

Through directionality, the sailor seeks after and discovers the achievement of a presence. Ultimately, all functions of the imagination search for this goal.

Imagination should not be confused with the purely imaginary. Directionality does not terminate in fantasy. "The point is rather that because the imagination is at work with symbolic realities, therefore it is the element of presence which comes to mind. For imagination is concerned with presence, above all it is a concern which is personal. What is present is present there for me. Otherwise the structured personal imagination has no interest."[66] Again, presence is not imaginary, but the product of the structured imagination in a total anthropological complex. The function of the imagination is to bring about that presence for *me* and potentially for *us*. Without the operation of the imagination with the force of directionality,[0] the attainment of the feeling of presence would be impossible. For example, even in the situation where the other who is present to me is in the same room, talking with me, touching me, communicating to me, the power of my imagination is continually at work making this presence something that is real.

Brinkman's way of sacramental operationalism is a way of presence. Religious ritual behavior is purposeful. It has a goal i.e., presence. This goal is attained from within the human condition, a condition which has the potent power of the structured imagination and the focus of directionality.

With the introduction of presence and directionality into his analysis of the structured imagination in religious ritual, Brinkman's reflections reach a point of integration, synthesis, and unity. Intimacy creates a feeling of closeness and reassurance which removes noxious threats. Interiorization demands conformity to the embraced symbols. The two taken together constitute humankind's imaginative presence, a presence for me and for us. The complex of the imagination works within the context of the social unit or community.

This cycle of structured imagination activity constitutes the patterned behavior of ritual or "sacramental" man. By identifying presence as the end of sacramental operationalism, Brinkman has returned to the theme introduced in the way of intimacy i.e., consummation. The variety of symbols employed in ritual, be it secular or religious, terminate in personal and communal presnece i.e., the symbol is for me or for us.[67]

Patterns of Behavior and the Human Situation

This brief presentation of a few patterns of behavior operative in culture demonstrates that certain drives present in the individual and "pseudospecies" cry out for fulfillment. These drives are not the fabrication of religion, but materialize and express themselves from within the human condition.

At the center of human existence, there lies a series of binary oppositions, juxtaposing contraries. Matching these oppositions is the power of the imagination to attempt a creative yet tenuous integration of the opposing realities. Imagination is the key to the resolution of chaos into meaning. It is the condition and force which sustain intimacy, social operations, interiorization, and sacramental operationalism. The structure in which these powers, needs, and forces come face to face is ritual, be it secular or religious.

Our previous definition of ritual enumerated three elements: patterns of behavior, repetition, and purposiveness. It is possible to further flesh out these elements in view of Brinkman's theory of "sacramental man."

The purpose of ritual is essentially to cope with human existence, an existence composed of rewarding and threatening experiences. The ability to cope is not exclusively individual, but essentially social. It will unfold within the context of a "pseudospecies" or not at all.

The repetition in ritual reinforces the "belief system" or world view of a particular "pseudospecies" within the individual. It achieves this by offering a contact with the original charter event of the community and its past reenactments. Through the repetition of ritual, the unfinished business of the individual and the community can be taken up again with renewed enthusiasm and conviction.

The patterns of behavior present in ritual are the basic drives or roads which lead to the experience of communion or consummation. Ritual in this perspective is a continual invitation to becoming permeated with the presence of whatever is conceived as "ultimate reality" by the "pseudospecies."

Our previous investigations of language and psychology correlate with the conclusions reached in studying patterns of behavior. Ritual language expedites the drive toward presence. The various speech acts are rallied to work for the proper goal or effect or ritual. They exegete the ritual actions to identify communion or consummation. Psychology confirms the importance of communion. It underlines its primary role in the formation of a healthy personality and identifies it as a stimulating need throughout the process of maturation and adult existence.

One can only conclude from this data, that ritual is thoroughly human, in fact, a necessity of human existence. Before leaping into "God-talk," which gives the impression of looking outside human existence to explain what human beings do and what meaning human life has, a search of human existence itself can expose the operations and goals of human behavior. When the claims of ritual or "sacramental man" are examined, it is evident that the same drives and forces guide secular and religious rituals.

The meaning attributed to these symbolic communal activities may be different. Yet, the operations and goals are the same.

Social Structures

Ritual not only arituclates what it means to be human, but functions to bring about humanness. Ritual is instrumental. It effects a socialization of the individual within the "pseudospecies." This affirmation leads us to a discussion of the third element of ritualization, *social structures.*

Common sense tells us that culture is a given, a reality which is objectively "out-there." Closer scrutiny, however, suggests that culture is less objective and more the product of human creativity.

From an anthropological point of view, culture is "the grand total of all the objects, ideas, knowledge, ways of doing things, habits, values, and attitudes which each generation in a society passes on to the next."[68] It is mediated or transmitted rather than instinctively generated.

Cultures develop in a process. Groups cluster customs together to form social roles. As specialized and formalized roles emerge, individuals occupy different social positions and attain different social status. Roles aggregate and become social institutions which function as the building blocks of society. The relational net of social institutions comprises the social system.[69] Socialization is the result of the interaction of the individual with the social institutions which form the plausible structures of the community. Socialization yields increasing internal consistency to the lives of those in the social group.[70]

What is the relation of ritual to the social structure? What is the function of cult in the social system? Before these questions can be answered adequately, some brief remarks on the metatheoretical positions of the different "schools" within the sociology of religion and anthropology are necessary, both to avoid misconceptions and clarify the stance assumed in this text.

During the last three to four decades, Talcott Parsons' structural-functionalist model has dominated the interpretation of religion in sociology. "The basic perspective of the structural-functional point of view emerges in its prime emphasis on society, and on the interrelation of its institutions, rather than on individual groups such as the family."[71]

Religion is one of the institutions which sustains the social system. Its function could be defined as "the manipulation of non-empirical or superempirical means for non-empirical or superempirical ends. . . ."[72] Structural-functionalism positively evaluates religion to the extent that it con-

SOCIOLOGY-ANTHROPOLOGY 95

tributes to the maintenance and continuity of the social system. It is not interested, however, with either the truth or reality of religious claims. It claims to be "value free."

The influence of structural-functionalism cannot be underestimated. The majority of texts on the sociology of religion reflect its tenets. In the last decade, dissenting voices have been heard which are shaking its throne. It is not that one or another point of its theory is questioned, but the central principle or presupposition of its system. Charles Lemert[73] has summarized the factions of this revolt. He has categorized them according to their response to two major issues confronting sociology. First, what is the relation of the individual person to the social structure? Second, what is the nature and location of meaning in social relationships?[74]

Three typical responses are detected by Lemert to the challenge facing sociology. The *promethean* response, represented by Luckmann and Berger, proposes a new definition of sociology. The *jasonian* response, emulated by Bellah, returns to an exploration of religious symbols themselves. The *sisyphean* response, imaged by Fern, remains tied to the structural-functionalist rock, "but has been willing to persevere, rolling it over and over again to find some potentially useful crevice."[75]

Luckmann understands religion as functioning to provide meaning. Contrary to the structural-functionalists, he maintains that social structures cannot be the place of that meaning. Meaning's locus is to be discovered in the biological and social aspects of the human person. He notes:

> Religion is rooted in a basic anthropological fact: the transcendence of biological nature by human organisms. The individual human potential for transcendence is realized, originally, in social processes that rest on the reciprocity of face-to-face situations. These processes lead to the construction of a world view, the articulation of sacred universes and, under certain circumstances, to institutional specializations of religion.[76]

In effect, Luckmann replaces structural functionalism with social functionalism.

Berger's approach is harmonious with Luckmann's with one exception i.e., "his abiding uneasiness with the latter's functional definition of religion."[77] In his most recent works he withdraws totally from functionalism, either structural or social, and emphasizes meaning in contradistinction to social structures. Although Luckmann and Berger offer a new interpretive thrust to the sociology of religion, they neither escape nor add new insight to the fundamental questions confronting sociology in general and the sociology of religion in particular.

The "Jason" of the new approaches in the sociology of religion, Robert Bellah, was originally a disciple of Parsons. In 1964, however, he began an intellectual journey which allowed the influence of structural-functionalism to fade and the discovery of *symbolic realism* to emerge.

Symbolic realism affirms "that religious symbols are not primarily social or psychological projection systems. . .but the ways which societies express their sense of the fundamental nature of reality or the totality of experience."[78] This symbolism allows the resolution (real or unreal) of the manifold conflicts present in social life which would hinder healthy performance and continued existence of the community.

Lemert keenly perceives that Bellah has also failed to escape the web of metatheoretical issues. He comments:

> But there can be no doubt that the crisis is invoked by social structure; and, accordingly, the resolution stated in terms of sociological theory is, once again, to conceive of the person as the primary architect of religious meaning in a complex structured social world.[79]

Bellah's position faces the same fault as the *prometheans*.

Fenn continues to employ Parsons' framework in his sociological vision. He is "*sisyphus* working uncritically with the structural-functionalist model."[80] Without abandoning Parsons' model, he moves in the direction of neglecting social structures and advancing the person as the center of meaning in religion. In his attempt to outline a new sociology of religion, this ambivalence is clearly witnessed. He writes:

> While it is not necessary to abandon the longstanding recognition that ulterior motives affect religiosity, a shift in basic assumptions may help to overcome the intellectual aridity of much interpretation by making greater allowance for non-rational religious activity; activity which *is* an end in itself, and which is precisely what it appears to be i.e., a search for "truth" or "transcendence."[81]

It is difficult to pinpoint what is "new" in this perspective. The abnegation of social structures leads to the emphasis on the person as the center of meaning but without the destruction of the structural-functionalist modular design.

Lemert attempts his own solution to the metatheoretical issues of the sociology of religion by turning to French structuralism for assistance. He depicts two requirements for a new sociology of religion: a positive theory of social structures and a prohibition of any presumption that meaning is self-evident.[82] These two requirements will be maintained when social structures are understood as semiotic tools with the corollary implication that they cannot reveal *a* center of meaning in the social phenomenon which exist.

Semiotics is the science of signs. Within semiotics there is a general presupposition that language, the prototype of all sign-systems, is the human and social construction *par excellence*. Linguistics makes a fundamental distinction bweteen language and speech which are dialectically related. Language is a social object bearing a fixed structure. Speech is an individual act involving selection and free choice. Both realities are wedded to each other. The possibility of speech has as its a priori language, and nothing enters language unless it is attempted in speech.

Lemert asserts that it is possible to reinterpret social structures as semiotic tools and thereby understand them as sign-systems.

> Quite clearly, the language/speech distinction can be used as a way of rethinking the social structure problem. It requires only that we first understand social systems as sign-systems; that is, they have to do with communication and signification. Thus they contain the codes by which human beings have been ordered in social life. But before all else, they are *systems*, which is to say that they are not to be explained in terms of meaning as such.[83]

This sociological model differs from Parsons' in the following respect. For Parsons, the social structure is an agency of moral patterns. In the semiotic perspective, it is possible to maintain the free spontaneity of persons in a necessary dialectic with the social structure as a system of communication. Neither the person nor the social structure requires negation or subordination to convey religious meaning.

The identification of social structures as semiotic tools implies the negation of every attempt to discover a center of meaning within the social system. Sign-systems are systems of differential juxtaposition, not identification. The verb/noun, vowel/consonant of linguistic systems cannot be referred to as the "center" or "identity" of language. These "are only differences and it is only by the systematic juxtaposition of differences that the meaningful codes are produced."[84] Consequently, no one "division of labor" within the social system can be envisioned as *the* point of integration. All the various social institutions form a code based on a structured system of differences. No institution is more important than any other.

Lemert recognizes that this orientation implies a relativization of the supposed function of religion in society. This does not imply, however, the erradication of religious meaning. Positively, this perspective enhances the freedom of the person within the context of social structures.

> ... to conceive of society as a centerless system of differences is to encourage an infinite possibility of substitutions. Here we return to the social structure/person dichotomy. If that structure is not the center, then it is possible to see the person as substituting within a definite and finite system but retaining the possibility to create, modify, and innovate within the terms of the structure.[85]

Through the introduction of French structural motifs to the sociology of religion, Lemert appears to have attained a balance which restores freedom to the person, as a correction of structural-functionalism, while still affirming the existence and importance of social structures. This critical corrective is of the utmost importance in exploring the relation of ritual to the social structure.

Battle lines similar to those within the sociology of religion are drawn when anthropologists interpret the relationship between ritual and social structure. Anthropologists cluster around two main interpretations of ritual "as a statement in metaphoric terms about paradoxes of human existence:"[86] ritual as action and ritual as belief. The former tends to emphasize ritual as a power which forms status relations between persons within the social system.[87] The latter tends to underline the partial independence of ritual from social structures and identify ritual as an expression of actual or substantial reality.[88]

Victor Turner has raised the metatheoretical questions in anthropology which Lemert introduced into the sociology of religion. In *The Ritual Process* and *Dreams, Fields, and Metaphors*, he presented a theoretical framework which fosters a critical understanding of the relation between ritual and social structure.

In stating the goal of *Dreams, Fields, and Metaphors*, Turner places himself in opposition to any structural-functionalist interpretation of social action. He rejects any interpretation of social dynamics as a set of performances grounded in a program based on "processual structure of social action itself."[89] The process of social action includes an escape from the normative value of structural elements, or *liminality*. "Without liminality, program might indeed determine performance. But, given liminality, prestigious programs can be undermined and multiple alternative programs generated."[90]

If programs are not the exclusive determinants of social performance, what is/are the element(s) generating social action? Turner finds his answer in the dialectic of structure-anti-structure expressing the social drama. He writes:

> When one surveys large spans of social processes, one sees an almost endless variety of limited and provisional outcomes. Some seem to fall on the programmatic side of the scale, others eschew precise structural articulation. But the besetting quality of human society, seen processually, is the capacity of individuals to stand at times aside from the models, patterns, and paradigms for behavior and thinking, which as children they are conditioned into accepting, and in rare cases, to innovate new patterns themselves or to assent to innovation.[91]

Turner situates social dramas in the constellation of fields, paradigms, and arenas. Fields are the abstract cultural domains where paradigms are formulated, fixed, and enter conflict. Paradigms are the sets of rules which exclude or include sequences of social action. Arenas are the concrete settings where paradigms are transformed into metaphors and symbols, and vie for power within the total paradigmatic cluster of social institutions and structures. "'Social Dramas' represent the phased process of their consternation."[92] Behind Turner's analysis of social dramas lies one pervasive idea: "that social life is the producer and product of time, which becomes its measure. . . ."[93]

In stressing the "becoming" character of the social world, Turner takes seriously the monition that such language is metaphoric. He relates his understanding of the term *root metaphor* to Stephen Pepper's and Max Black's "conceptual archetype." For Pepper, a root metaphor is the product arising from the attempt to understand the world in terms of an analogy with some common-sense fact. "A man desiring to understand the world looks about for some clue to its comprehension. He pitches upon some area of common-sense fact and tries if he cannot understand other areas in terms of this one. The original area then becomes his *basic analogy* or *root metaphor*."[94] Black defines a "conceptual archetype" as a "systematic repertoire of ideas by means of which a given thinker describes, by *analogical extension*, some domain to which those ideas do not immediately and literally apply."[95]

Turner does not present the structure of a metaphor as a juxtaposition of unrelated elements. He prefers to align himself with I. A. Richards' "interactional view." "This view emphasizes the dynamics inherent in the metaphor, rather than simply comparing the two thoughts in it, or regarding one as 'substituting' for the other. The two thoughts are active together, they 'engender' thought in their co-activity."[96]

Personal field research led Turner to entitle his metaphor as *dramatic* and to understand it as a product of culture rather than nature. He strove to include the "human co-efficient" in his metaphor. He commented:

> I felt I had to bring the "human co-efficient" into my model if I was to make sense of human social process. One of the most arresting properties of Ndembu social life in villages was its propensity toward conflict. Conflict was rife in the groups of two dozen or so kinsfolk who made up a village community. It manifested itself in public episodes of tension eruption which I call "social dramas."[97]

Not all structures are dramatic or involved in conflict. Some are organizational and harmonic. The investigation of social dramas and conflict may, however, be more revelatory of the "normal" social network than a study of the "normal" itself. "Conflict seems to bring fundamental aspects of society, normally overlaid by customs and habits of daily intercourse, into frightening prominence."[98]

Social dramas consist of four observable phases: breach, crisis, redressive action, and reintegration. In breach, the patterns of social interaction breakdown. Actions contrary to or not fulfilling a crucial norm regulating social interaction appear. If the breach remains unhealed, it widens and extends. An escalating crisis ensues. This second phase has a liminal character:

> Each public crisis has what I call liminal characteristics, since it is a threshold between more or less stable phases of the social process, but it is not a sacred limen, hedged around by taboos and thrust away from the centers of public life. On the contrary, it takes up its meaning stance in the forum itself and, as it were, dares the representatives of order to grapple with it. It cannot be ignored or wished away.[99]

Breach, intensified into crisis, calls forth redressive action. Redressive machinery is enlisted to limit the crisis. "It is in the redressive phase that both pragmatic techniques and symbolic action reach their fullest expression."[100] The social unit is fighting for survival and draws upon all its resources to halt the crisis.

The final phase of the social drama is reintegration. It can consist of either a reintegration of the breached group or a legitimatization and recognition of the alienated parties as a social entity unto itself. From this culminating phase of the social drama, the researcher can take stock of the whole social drama.

Turner argues for both change and continuity throughout the social drama. In his opinion, the basis for both change and consistency can only "be found by systematic analysis of processual units and temporal structures, by looking at phases as well as atemporal systems."[101] Any invesitgation of social structures *per se*, without a similar investigation of the process or processual units in which they emerge, is insufficient. More importantly, only an investigation of what Turner calls the social anti-structure as a theoretical operator allows positive structuralism to become a processualism and thereby more adequately reflect what is actually taking place in the social drama.[102]

Anti-structure is the theoretical concept sustaining Turner's rejection of structural-functionalism. It draws together his ideas of communitas, liminality, and religious symbols and rituals. At first glance, anti-structure connotes a negative term. The negative tone only arises, however, when it is seen from the vantage point of structure. "It is no more 'anti' in its essence that the American 'Counter-culture' is merely 'counter'."[103] Anti-structure is really a generative center, a positive reality.[104]

Liminality and communitas are the components which define the social anti-structure.[105] Liminality refers to the condition of being "betwixt and between the positions assigned and arrayed by law, customs, and ceremonial."[106] The liminal persons or principles share the common characteristics of falling in the interstices of the social structure, existing on its margins, and occupying its lowest positions.[107] Communitas refers to the type or form of social relationships existing in the liminal condition. Communitas is a bond uniting people over and above any formal bond of the social structure (as opposed to the social anti-structure).

The bond of communitas is especially clear at times of crisis. "When the turn of events breaks open the habitual patterns of interaction, shaped by societies' conditioning of its members, we find that we fall back on more primitive patterns of interaction."[108] The spontaneous communitas spawned in crisis is usually short lived. Communitas quickly develops into a structure with social norms. Consequently, Turner distinguishes three forms of communitas: the existential or spontaneous; normative communitas; and ideological communitas.[109] "Both normative and ideological communitas are already within the domain of structure, and it is the fate of all spontaneous communitas in history to undergo what most people see as a 'decline and fall' into structure and law."[110]

The bonds of the liminal *persona* in the communitas social relations are anti-structural "in the sense that they are undifferentiated, equalitarian, direct, extant, nonrational, existential, I-Thou . . . relationships."[111] Root metaphors, conceptual archetypes, and paradigms arise from liminality and communitas as components of the social anti-structure.[112] This anti-structure is the fertile source for human imagination and creativity, the arena of symbol and ritual, elements which will later appear in the social structure.

Turner portrays a dynamic tension and interplay between social structure and social anti-structure.

> In human history, I see a continuous tension between structure and communitas, at all levels of scale and complexity. Structure, or all that holds people apart, defines their differences, and constrains their actions, is one pole of a charged field, for which the opposite pole is communitas, or anti-structure, the egalitarian "sentiment for humanity" of which David Hume speaks, representing the desire for a total, unmediated relationship bwtween person and person, a relationship which nevertheless does not submerge one act of realizing their commonness. Communitas does not merge identities; it liberates them from conformity to general norms, though this is necessarily a transient condition if society is to continue to operate in an orderly fashion.[113]

Neither structure nor anti-structure has exclusive claims to social life. It is *together* that they form processual, historical, temporal realities of cultural existence, and the social drama. "When a social structure acquires a certain stability . . . there tends to develop in the temporal relation between structure and communitas a process to which it is hard to deny the epithet 'dialectical'."[114]

Turner's insistence that social relations are temporal and cultural products also applies to his understanding of ritual and symbol.[115] In fact, ritual symbols are intimately involved in temporal processual units by instigating social action. Ritual symbols work in social action by condensing many references, uniting them in a cognitive and effective field.

Although ritual symbols are multivalent, they polarize between two posts: the oretic pole of physiological phenomenon e.g., sexual intercourse, death, blood etc.; and normative social values e.g., respect for elders, generosity to the poor, kindness to kin etc. The drama of ritual action "causes an exchange between these two poles in which the biological referents are enobled and the normative referents are charged with emotional significance."[116] This interchange presupposes social structure and, even more so, communitas in the ritual community, enhancing the creative tension within the social unit. The ritual action mediates the relation between the individual and the exigencies of the social group, including both structure and communitas, freedom and norms.

> The exchange of qualities makes desirable what is socially necessary by establishing a right relationship between involuntary sentiments and the requirements of social structure. People are induced to do what they must do. In this sense ritual action is akin to a sublimation process, and one would not be stretching language unduly to say that its symbolic behavior actually "creates" society for pragmatic purposes—including in society both structure and communitas.[117]

Turner suggests that the level, depth, or intensity of communitas within the ritual community is correlational to the effectiveness of the ritual symbolic behavior. ". . . if the cultural form of communitas—as found in liminality—can correspond with the actual experience of communitas, the symbols there presented may be experienced more deeply, than in any other context, if the ritual subject has what theologians would call the proper disposition."[118] Turner agrees with Brinkman's and Polyani's insight into ritual. All three authors focus on the potency of ritual behavior to create a deep, foundational, and fundamental bond among members of the ritual community, a bond which is trans-temporal and trans-spacial, yet operating and originating within both. Dupré characterizes this function of ritual well:

> . . . its structuring activity is always for the group, never for the isolated individual. Whenever an individual starts developing strictly private rites, we usually interpret his behavior as neurotic. The activity of the "ritualist" isolates rather than integrates, while rites are normally the cement of social life. Through participation in the same structuring activities men become more aware of their essential togetherness. Moreover, the rites surrounding birth, adulthood, marriage, and death incorporate the individual into the group by giving the private events of his life a public character.[119]

Urban Holmes has collected the disparate reflections of Turner on anti-structure, root metaphor, and ritual symbolism in a fashion which will allow a summary of his thought while pinpointing the relation of ritual and social structure. Turner alluded to anti-structure as the spawning ground of root metaphors and the place were symbols are discovered.

Holmes suggests that "ritual is endemic to anti-structure, to liminality, and to communitas, and becomes the source for the discovery and development of certain primordial experience."[120]

Although root metaphors are one step removed from symbols, they are still "essentially primordial, that is, not necessarily a part of the common sense or thinking reality of a given society and its socialization."[121] Root metaphors, arising within the anti-structure, are shaped by and in turn shape ritual at its deepest level. "These archetypes become in turn the nodal images about which a community constitutes what Turner describes as social drama, a kind of world hypothesis."[122]

The central role of ritual in the social drama implies that participation in ritual becomes "the key to the corporate intentionality of the community"[123] existing in the creative tension of social structure—communitas, freedom and norms. Ritual reveals the text of the social drama vibrating between continuity and change as a processual unit.

Ritual both shapes and is shaped by social relationships. In a social system understood as a tension of continuity and change ritual can be interpreted in two manners relating dynamically and creatively, cognitively and affectively. Ritual can sustain a social system by reaffirming the root metaphor(s) which is its primordial ground. Ritual can also create a new social system and relations by reaching down to the primordial level of human experience and devising new root metaphors as the social drama demands them. Ritual is the expression of symbolism in the unending processual journey of societies through time, supplying the creativity indispensable for communitas which is in turn destined to become social structure. Ritual is the source for both stability and freedom in society. For individuals, it is a vehicle of identification and passage.

Conclusion

An exploration of the sociological-theological research leads to a general conviction. Ritual is a "given" of human existence. It is an a priori necessity for the very existence and sustenance of a cultural group's or social unit's life. Without ritual, a "pseudospecies" is doomed to perish.

Ritual permeates the three dimensions of culture: language, patterns of behavior, and social structures. Ritual language and gesture disclose meaning for the "odd" situations of life. Ritualized patterns of behavior evoke intimacy, interiorization, sociality, and presence. Ritual is at the same time the building block for social structure and the locus for culture's alternative i.e., the social anti-structure.

If psychological research attests to the absolute necessity of ritual for personality development and mature integration, sociology and anthropology issue an equal claim for ritual's indisputable role in cultural and social existence. Communal health and stability parallel individual development and wholeness. Even a superficial glance at the data presented in this and the preceding chapter calls for a rejection of any interpretation of ritual as a secondary or insignificant feature within human existence. Without ritual, there would be no human society. With impoverished ritual, human community becomes weakened, fragile, and disarrayed.

Ritual is a commentator explaining the meaning of life as lived by various "pseudospecies" in their dialogue with time, space, and history. Ritual speaks of humanity. It preserves its origins, expresses its stability, and affirms its creativity and dynamism for change and development.

NOTES

1. J. L. Autin, *How to Do Things with Words*, J. O. Urmson (ed.), (Oxford: Clarendon Press, 1962). For an analysis of the multiple dimensions of Austin's thought, cf. K. T. Fann (ed.), *Symposium on J. L. Austin*. (London: Routledge and Kegan Paul, 1969); *Essays on J. L. Austin*, (Oxford: Clarendon Press, 1973). On the general category of language, cf. Jean Ladrière, *L'articulation du sens, Discours scientifique et parole de la foi*. (Aubier Montaigne: Editions du Cerf, 1970); John Macquarrie, *God-Talk: An Examination of the Language and the Logic of Theology*. (London: SCM Press, 1967), pp. 55-78; E. L. Mascall, *Words and Images*. (London: Darton, Longmann and Todd, 1957); Tracy, pp. 120-124; Wolfhard Pannenburg, *Theology and the Philosophy of Science*. (London: Darton, Longmann and Todd, 1976), pp. 29-57.

2. A. P. Martinich, "Sacraments and Speech Acts, I," *Heythrop Journal* XVI (1975), p. 298.

3. Austin, p. 108; also cf. A.P. Martinich p. 291. "Locutionary acts, which themselves are complex and sophisticated acts, are constructed from words, which in turn are formed from morphemes. A locutionary act is any utterance of a meaningful sentence, e.g., 'The cat is on the mat.'"

4. *Ibid.*; also Martinich, p. 291: "An illocutionary act is an act performed in putting a sentence to use. It is more complex than a locutionary act, for it builds on a locutionary act."

5. *Ibid.*

6. Cf. John Searle, *Speech Acts*. (London: Cambridge, 1969).

7. Martinich, p. 410; also, cf. N. Fotion, "Master Speech Acts," *Philosophical Quarterly* 21 (1971), pp. 234-243.

8. Austin, p. 150.

9. Martinich, p. 410; also, cf. N. Fotion, "Master Speech Acts," *Philosophical Quarterly* 21 (1971), pp. 234-243.

10. William Shea, "Sacraments and Meaning," *American Ecclesiastical Review* 169 (1975), p. 404.

11. Ian Ramsey, *Religious Language: An Empirical Placing of Theological Phrases.* (New York: Macmillan, 1967); *Models and Mystery.* (London: Oxford University Press, 1964).

12. Frederick Ferré, Language, *Logic and God.* (New York: Harper and Rowe, 1961); "Metaphors, Models and Religion", *Soundings* 51 (1968), pp. 327-345; "Mapping the Logic of Models in Science and Theology," in *New Essays on Religious Language*, D. M. High (ed.), (New York: Oxford University Press, 1969), pp. 54-97.

13. Tracy, p. 121.

14. II Samuel 12: 1-7.

15. Daniel Stenik, "The Language of Prayer," *Worship* 52 (1978), p. 546.

16. *Ibid.*, p. 547.

17. B. R. Brinkman, "On Sacramental Man: I Language Patterning," *Heythrop Journal* XIII (1972), p. 377.

18. *Ibid.*, pp. 383-401.

19. *Ibid.*, p. 387.

20. *Ibid.*

21. A Kavanagh, "The Role of Ritual in Personal Development," in *The Roots of Ritual.* p. 153.

22. Cf. *Ibid.*, p. 154.

23. C. Geertz, "Religion as a Cultural System," in *Religious Situation.*

24. *Ibid.*, p. 14.

25. O'Dea, p. 14.

26. *Ibid.*, pp. 13-16.

27. Roland Delattre, "Ritual Resourcefulness and Cultural Pluralism," *Soundings* LXI (1978), p. 285.

28. Susan Langer, *Philosophy in a New Key,* p. 40.

29. Delattre, p. 283.

30. Cf. Gilbert Durand, *Les Structures Anthropologiques de l'Imaginaire. Introduction a l'Archétypologie géneral.* Zeme, (ed.) (Paris: Bordas, 1969); *L'Imagination Symbolique.* (Paris: P.U.F., 1968); "Les Structures Polarisantes de la Conscience psychique et de la Culture," *Eranos-Jahrbuch.* (Zurich: Rhein-Verlag 1967.)

31. *Ibid.*, p. 21.

32. Matthias Neuman, O.S.B., *The Imagination in Theology: Some Contemporary American and British Perspectives.* (Rome: Pontificium) *Athenaeum Anselmianum,* (1975), p. 53.

33. Durand, *L'Imagination Symbolique*, pp. 111-112.

34. B. R. Brinkman, "On Sacramental Man: II The Way of Intimacy," *The Heythrop Journal,* XIV (1974), p. 6.

35. *Ibid.*, p. 5.

36. Michael Polanyi, *Personal Knowledge: Towards a Post-Critical Philosophy* (corrected ed.), (Chicago: University of Chicago Press, 1962), p. 211; also, cf. Holmes p. 198: "I would define ritual . . . as the repetition of those symbols which evoke the feeling of that primordial event which initally called the community into being with such power that it affects our presence at that event—in other words, represents the primordial event."

37. Brinkman, "On Sacramental Man: II," p. 9: "It is not the rules we have about the repetition of sacraments which explain the phenomenon. They merely express what I have already called the *prescriptive element* in the sacramental situation. Behind the fact of these varied imperatives lie the needs of sacramental man. As sacramental man changes and develops amid the vicissitudes of his own and his community life, his needs build up, and it is repetition which helps him to cope with the "unfinished business of earlier personal experiences."

38. Jeffrey Gray, *The Psychology of Fear and Stress.* (London: 1971), p. 128.

39. Brinkman, "On Sacramental Man: II," p. 10.

40. *Ibid.*, p. 11.

41. Cf. Eric Peterson, *The Angels and the Liturgy.* (London: 1964).

42. Brinkman, "On Sacramental Man: II," p. 16.

43. *Ibid.*, p. 34.

44. Brinkman, "On Sacramental Man: III The Socially Operational Way," *Heythrop Journal* XVI (1973), p. 162.

45. *Ibid.*, p. 165.

46. *Ibid.*, p. 167.

47. *Ibid.*, "I think we can answer in only one way, namely that these symbols are directly or indirectly symbols of other symbols. There is nothing else, if we exclude the 'divine realities.' There is no reason why we should not say that. This is curious logic! . . . Yet . . . my purpose in pointing to a socially operational way of sacramental behavior was precisely to avoid being caught up in the process of going or getting beyond. It is enough if we can say: 'Look, it's operational; it works.'"

48. Victor Turner, *The Ritual Process.* (Chicago: Aldine Publ. Co., 1969), p. 6.

49. Cf. John Smith, "The Influence of Symbols upon Social Change: A Place in Which to Stand," in *The Roots of Ritual,* pp. 121-143.

50. Brinkman, "On Sacramental Man III," p. 174.

51. *Ibid.*, p. 170-171.

52. *Ibid.*, p. 176.

53. *Ibid.*, p. 183.

54. *Ibid.*, p. 174-175.

55. Brinkman, "On Sacramental Man: IV The Way of Interiorization," *Heythrop Journal* XIV (1973), p. 281.

56. *Ibid.*

57. *Ibid.*, p. 286-287.

58. *Ibid.*, p. 287.

59. Brinkman, "On Sacramental Man: IV . . .," p. 289.

60. *Ibid.*, p. 290.

61. Brinkman, "On Sacramental Man: V The Way of Sacramental Operationalism," *Heythrop Journal* XIV, p. 396.

62. *Ibid.*, p. 397.

63. *Ibid.*, p. 398.

64. *Ibid.*

65. *Ibid.*, pp. 400-401.

66. *Ibid.*, p. 402.

67. *Ibid.*, p. 406.

68. Inkles, p. 66.

69. O'Dea, p. 73.

70. Cf. David B. Burrell, "Ritual and Conceptual Systems: Primitive Myth to Modern Ideology, in *The Roots of Ritual*, p. 199; also, Judson R. Lawdis, *Sociology: Concepts and Characteristics.* (Belmont, California: Wadsworth Publ. Co., 1971), pp. 6-12.

71. Inkles, p. 34. For an excellent overview of Parsons, cf. Alvin W. Gouldner, *The Coming Crisis of Western Sociology.* (New York: Avon Books, 1971).

72. O'Dea, p. 7.

73. Charles C. Lemert, "Social Structure and the Absent Center: An Alternative to New Sociologies of Religion," *Sociological Analysis* 36 (1975), pp. 95-102.

74. Thomas Luckman, *Invisible Religion.* (New York: Macmillan, 1972), p. 12.

75. Lemert, p. 98.

76. Luckman, p. 69, on face-to-face relations or primary groups as distinct from secondary groups. Cf. Kingsley Davis, *Human Society.* (New York: Macmillan, 1957), p. 306, and the classical study by Ferdinand Tönnies, *Gemeinschaft und Gesellschlaft.* Translated by Charles P. Loomis in *Fundamental Concepts of Sociology.* (New York: American Book Company, 1940). On "Symbolic Universe," cf. Peter Berger and Thomas Luckmann, *The Social Construction of Reality.* (New York: Doubleday, 1966); P. Berger *The Sacred Canopy*, p. 175-177.

77. Lemert, p. 99; cf. The Sacred Canopy, p. 175-177.

78. Robert Bellah, "Response to Comments," *Journal for the Scientific Study of Religion* 9 (1970), p. 113. Bellah's position does not imply a rejection of the function of the imagination in Brinkman's theory. They are treating two different realities.

79. Lemert, p. 100.

80. *Ibid.*, p. 101.

81. Richard Fenn, "Toward a New Sociology of Religion," *Journal for the Scientific Study of Religion*, II (1972), p. 31.

82. Lemert, p. 102: "So what is at stake is whether or not we can specify a new sociological approach to religion that makes some positive accounting for *so-*

cial structure, and does so without centering its conception of social reality or of religion in *meaning* taken as a necessary and primary metatheoretical category."

83. *Ibid.*, p. 104.

84. *Ibid.*, p. 105.

85. *Ibid.*

86. Christopher Crocker, "Ritual and the Development of Social Structure: Liminality and Inversion," *The Roots of Ritual*, p. 47.

87. Cf. *Ibid.*, p. 48: "The ritual-as-action theorists assert that certain culturally stereotyped behaviors, depite their ostensible reference to various cosmological esoteria, are but statements about the status of persons relative to one another." The proximity to a structural-functionalist theoretical paradigm is evident here.

88. Cf. *Ibid.*: "The ritual-as-belief theorists maintain that the understanding of a given rite must derive from knowledge of the entire conceptual system of the society; ceremonies must be analyzed in terms of the categories by which the society attempts to order the inchoate world of experience of action. This approach emphasizes the partial independence of belief from social structure, the last of causal relationships between the two. . . . "

89. Victor Turner, *Dreams, Fields and Metaphors*. (Ithaca: Cornell University Press, 1974), p. 13.

90. *Ibid.*, p. 14.

91. *Ibid.*, p. 14-15.

92. *Ibid.*, p. 17.

93. *Ibid.*, p. 23.

94. Stephen C. Pepper, *World Hypotheses*. (Berkeley: University of California Press, 1942), pp. 38-39.

95. Max Black, *Models and Metaphors: Studies in Language and Philosophy*. (Ithaca: Cornell University Press, 1962), p. 241.

96. Turner, *Dreams. . .*, p. 29.

97. *Ibid.*, p. 33.

98. *Ibid.*, p. 35.

99. *Ibid.*, p. 39.

100. *Ibid.*, p. 41.

101. *Ibid.*, p. 43.

102. *Ibid.*, p. 45.

103. *Ibid.*, p. 50.

104. *Ibid.*, p. 273.

105. *Ibid.*, p. 50, 273.

106. Turner, *The Ritual Process*, p. 95.

107. *Ibid.*, p. 125. Turner sees two main types of liminality: rituals of status election and rituals of status renewal; *ibid.*, p. 167-168.

108. Holmes, p. 203.

109. Turner, *The Ritual Process*, p. 132.

110. *Ibid.*

111. Turner, *Dreams. . ., p. 274.*

112. *Ibid.,* p. 50.

113. *Ibid.,* p. 274.

114. *Ibid.,* p. 252.

115. *Ibid.,* p. 55: "Since I regard cultural symbols including ritual symbols as originating in and sustaining processes involving temporal changes in social relationships, and not as timeless entities, I have tried to treat the crucial properties of ritual symbols as being involved in these dynamic developments."

116. *Ibid.*

117. *Ibid.,* p. 56.

118. *Ibid.,* p. 258.

119. Dupré, p. 177; also, O'Dea, p. 41.

120. Holmes, P. 204.

121. *Ibid.,* p. 205.

122. *Ibid.*

123. *Ibid.,* p. 208.

6 A PHILOSOPHICAL NOTE

The "purely" behavioral sciences are not alone in providing a perspective and content for the anthropological dimensions of sacraments. Contemporary philosophical reflection renders additional support and insight to the importance of ritual and symbolism in the unfolding of individual and collective existence.

Since the beginning of the nineteenth century, various philosophical traditions have broken free of a narrow "objectivism" and returned to an investigation of the dynamic forces and realities operative in the drama of human history.[1] Whether the fundamental orientation be phenomenology, existentialism, or process thought, the philosophical milieu appears to have rediscovered and accepted the challenge presented by the complex web and intricacies of "being."

Previous discussion has pointed out the presence of unconscious presuppositions, root metaphors, or world views present in culture which sustain and express its participants' resolution of experienced binary oppositions. It is philosophical reflection's domain to make these presuppositions conscious and articulated, to the extent that this is a real possibility.

Since the time of Kant, philosophy has turned to an investigation of the subject and transcendence. Both elements pervade and underpin our prior description of symbol and ritual. Space makes it impossible to fully work out how these areas correlate with all the psychological, anthropological, and sociological data. But some notation on two areas is important: the recognition that human existence is a co-existence; and a discernment of the origin or basis of human transcendence. It is here that our philosophical note touches the content of ritual and symbolism both anthropologically and, as we will see, theologically. Co-existence

Co-Existence

Sociology and anthropology as sciences are only possible if human existence is relational. These sciences investigate the *fact* of human commu-

111

nities. This fact has been affirmed on the philosophical level by the work of Husserl, Heidegger, Camus, Marcel, Buber, and a host of others. Emmanuel Levinas has most clearly exposed this "doctrine" in his work, *Totality and Infinity*.[2]

Levinas' title contains the key to his insight. Totality refers to the attitude of the self-centered person (child) who relates all things to himself. His ego is the center of the meaningful universe. When this attitude is taken to an extreme, this individual becomes a closed entity, impenetrable by any entity. His ideal ego becomes an encased center of life.

For Levinas, the barriers imposed by the totalizing self must be torn down. Yet, the only reality that can attain this task is another person who shares in the uniqueness of human existence. Totality can only be broken in an encounter with the "face of the other," the *visage significant*. In the face of the other, the tendency to absolutize all reality around my individual ego is destroyed. The other opens my closed world by making me recognize him. My action of recognition causes me to shift from focusing on how reality is related to me to seeking an understanding of how things and persons relate among themselves and my place in these relations.

In turning from self-centeredness to interrelatedness, a valuable lesson is learned. Life is richer than the individual self. To turn from egoism to relations does not diminish my meaning. Rather it invites me to participate in a richness greater than myself. Negation of my ideal self is not a dimunition but an enhancement.

> As long as the possibility of encounter has not occurred for a man, he lives, serenely innocent, in his "element," wherein he feels at home. Thus sheltered in his human dwelling place, he makes of the surrounding world a domain of which he is the center. He takes all things unto himself as food for his enjoyment. Whatever remains outside of him is referred to himself as an object for viewing. Thus he becomes a totalizing subject looking on all other things and persons as objects and brings them into the totality of his world. His philosophy will be egology.[3]

In Satre's terminology, the totalizing subject makes all other realities *en soi pour moi*.

A radical transformation occurs when another person enters into the world of the individual as a different subject.

> . . . this totalization is shattered as soon as another man addresses me . . . thus becoming for me a *visage significant* (a meaningful, a speaking face). This other comes to me not as some object of thought which I may interpret and introduce into my totality . . . he comes with "naked" face

as an "other" as a subject, who can be interpreted neither in terms of my totality nor reduced to it. It is a totally new, pure and absolute experience, not a phenomenological and thus subjective unveiling, but a revelation. The other confronts me with the demand that I acknowledge him—that is that I unconditionally abandon any effort to introduce him into my totality, that I step out into pure disinterestedness from my totalizing self-centeredness towards his otherness. What is revealed to me by his naked face is an absolute, unconditional demand which wrests my whole existence out of totality and throws it open for the totally unforeseen, for the infinite.[4]

The encounter with the other as a co-existing subject affirms his and my freedom. It initiates a drive to recognize the infinite richness of reality. Infinity is the opposite pole of totality. Infinity represents the total potential for meaning in the universe. It is addressed to me in the face of the other.

Levinas is not alone in his philosophical orientation. Buber, Marcel, and Heschel have developed similar orientations. Buber's *I and Thou* stressed the relational, dialogical character of human existence in a vein which concurs with Levinas' option for either the limitations of totality or the possibilities of infinity.

Buber foresees the possibility of a human subject relating to others as either things or fellow subjects. Consequently he distinguished *I-It* and *I-Thou* relationships. To relate to the other as a *thou* is to affirm his or her value and uniqueness. It is to affirm a bond among all who share existence as human, an existence which is a radical co-existence.

The thou unfolds for me a meaning of life which is different but not contradictory to the meaning I experience. By participation in the unique difference of the thou, through dialogue, I am opened to a fuller and deeper meaning of life in general and my life in particular. In communion with the other I can perceive and experience a greater depth to life.

Buber explores one further dimension. The co-existential relation of the I-Thou can grow to become a *We*. My dialogical existence with others can mature into human community. This only increases the possibility for growth in understanding the meaning of human life. It also expresses the enigma of human existence. Individual meaning is dependent on the interrelatedness of persons. My individual meaning is discovered in and flows from correlational and coexistential life. Yet, nothing of selfhood or individuality is lost in community.

It is important to note that the interrelational or coexistential character of human existence is not an isolated element of life, but pervades all domains. Knowledge, choice, conceptualization, actions, and every other potential faculty of the human person are shaped and expressed in community, in co-existence. This has been reflected in our anthropological-socio-logical data. The process of personality integration, socialization, language performance, and ritual expression reflect the foundational co-existence which defines humankind.

Transcendence

The very possibility of a person moving from totality to infinity brings us to the issue of human transcendence. Interest in transcendence is not directed to the question of the object of transcendence i.e., and infinite being, the "Other," or God. Rather, our interest is in the act of transcending or the power identified as or labeled transcendence. Therefore, our goal is to try and locate the origin of human transcendence, its basis. This task is necessary to understand more completely the term "symbol" which is operative in the process of human transcendence.

Dupré has noted that philosophical traditions which lead to transcendence assume one of two models or approaches: either a metaphysics of being or a metaphysics of consciousness.[5] In a metaphysics of being, any particular actual being is only conceivable within an implicit horizon of unlimited or infinite being. By a participation in finite being, there is a quasi-participation in infinite being and consequently an expansive movement or dynamism called transcendence i.e., moving beyond the limits of finite space and time.

In the metaphysics of consciousness model, transcendence is affirmed as the power of cognition and volition evident in the human person continually thrust him or her toward a greater depth and realization of potential knowledge and decision. This model has representative thinkers. Husserl investigates intentionality. Blondel studies the willing will. Bergson isolates the *elan vital*. Newman explores the "illative sense." All these authors have in common an analysis of one or another human faculty which is operative in transcendence.

To elucidate the meaning and source of human transcendence, the thinking of Heideggar and Rahner is seminal. In his magisterial work, *Being and Time*, Heideggar presents man as the being who in his being is concerned with being. This type of existence is termed *Dasein* i.e., being there or there being. *Dasein*, and all other beings, participate in *Being* or all that is. *Dasein's* participation, however, is unique. It is the place or location where *Being* discloses itself. *Dasein* is the center where *Being* reveals itself. By knowing a particular being, it partially knows all *Being*. It has a special role in existence i.e., the place of transcendence. The power to transcend the limits of existence is not something which is added to *Dasein*. Rather, it is characteristic and constitutive of *Dasein's* particular form of existence.

Karl Rahner has assumed Heideggar's fundamental scheme to develop a "doctrine of intrinsic symbolism."[6] He commences his explanation of transcendence and symbolism with a reflection on the unity and multiplicity of being. It is the key to his insight into the origin of human transcendence.

Being is a unity, a oneness. Being is also a multiplicity. Being is symbolic in that the unity expresses or discloses itself in multiple expressions which are symbols of the unity. The richness of reality is the unity of being. This richness, however, is only expressed and perceived through the prism of individual beings, individual expressions or beings multiplicity. When the multiple refractions of being are taken together and reconstituted into the wholeness of their origin, they are the perfection of the original unity. The unity is enriched by its multiple expressions in that its multiple expressions are revealed as interrelated.

The ebb and flow of *Being* take place in all individual beings. Rahner calls this *selbstvollzung*, self-actualization. He writes:

> All things strive to return to themselves, want to come to themselves, to take possession of themselves, because the "having being" which they desire comes to be in the measure in which they take possession of themselves. All activities, from the sheer material to the innermost life of the Blessed Trinity, are but modulations of this one metaphysical theme, of the one meaning of being: self-possession, subjectivity. "Self-possession," however, is itself realized in a double phase: a flowing outwards, as exposition of its own essence from its cause, an *eminatio*, a withdrawing into itself of this essence, which has expressed itself in terms of its specific cause which has, as it were, revealed itself.[7]

Self-actualization constitutes Being as such "so that the moments of realization are rooted in a dynamic unity which is prior to the resolution into multiplicity."[8] On the other hand, the multiple expressions of being are an attestation to the unity of Being insofar as these expressions become self-actualized.

For Rahner, the ontological foundation for symbolism and transcendence lies in the unity and multiplicity of Being. Symbolism is possible because Being is symbolic. The multiple expressions of being are symbols of Being i.e., they participate in the fundamental unity of Being without being absolutely identical to that unity. Insofar as they move toward that unity, they exercise the power of transcendence.

The human person stands in a unique place among the multiple expressions of Being. It is within the human drama that the meaning of the unity of Being is expressed in its multiplicity. The human person as an existent, who possesses the type of existence characterizing *Dasein*, is the locus where the symbolism of the unity of Being reveals itself and is comprehended. Since this characteristic of the human person is not an addition to his or her nature, but constitutive of nature, human existence should be expected to be a symbolic existence.

Men and women are symbolic in their constitution i.e., they are embodied spirits who are at the same time receivers and interpreters of symbols. This is the source of their transcendence. It was previously noted that symbols are not the creation of humankind. Humankind discovers them in existence. Yet, humankind comprehends, interprets, and understands the meaning and significance of symbols. Hence, humankind is entwined in meaning. Through its unique role in reality, humankind's type of existence is the a priori condition for the possibility of meaning, not by creating meaning *ex nihilo* but by receiving and employing its significance.

By relating and employing the symbols offered to them, humankind works for the full realization of the unity of Being. In order to attain this goal, humankind must transcend any particular expression of Being. Humankind can never cease to transcend until all knowledge and choice are achieved. This continuing power of transcendence is the ontological basis for the particular transcendence which is expressed through ritual in individual and social life. It is transcendence which empowers ritual to attain its social role as discerned through psychology, anthropology, and sociology.

Conclusion

Philosophical traditions in our present age have explored the dual dimensions of co-existence and human transcendence. Both realities have been highlighted as key operatives in the process of human life. They are not secondary to human existence, but constitutive and essential. They are the ground work for a complete vision of the function of ritual and symbol for the individual and the human community.

Our "Philosophical Note" is not in any way an attempt to expose and defend a philosophy of co-existence or a philosophy of human transcendence. It is a quick look at a line of thought which has been worked out by the authors cited, a glance which takes note of the compatability of a certain philosophical position with the data more thoroughly explored in our exposition of ritual in the behavioral sciences. To this extent it should, even if only in a small way, add credence to the path previously pursued.

Looking forward, coexistence and transcendence will be major themes in our attempt to reconstruct a theology of sacraments commensurate with our anthropological data. To appreciate them as intrinsic to human existence only enhances the possibility of developing a theology of sacraments which is true to life as lived in our own days.

NOTES

1. Lonergan, *The Subject*.

2. Emmanuel Levinas, *Totality and Infinity*. (Pittsburgh: Dusquene University Press, 1969).

3. Louis Monden, *Faith, Can Man Still Believe?* (New York: Sheed and Ward, 1970), p. 28.

4. *Ibid.*, pp. 28–29.

5. Dupré, pp. 135–138; also, *Transcendental Selfhood: The Rediscovery of the Inner Life*. (New York: Seabury Press, 1976).

6. Karl Rahner, "The Theology of Symbol," *Theological Investigations*. Vol. 4, (Baltimore: Helicon Press, 1966), pp. 221–252.

7. Karl Rahner, *Hearers of the Word*. (New York: Herder and Herder, 1969), p. 49.

8. John O'Grady, *Jesus, Lord and Christ*. (New York: Paulist Press, 1973), p. 108.

SUMMARY: PART TWO

In examining the sciences of psychology, sociology and anthropology, clear lines of convergence are noticeable on the function and significance of ritual for personal and communal life. All the behavioral sciences identify a drive in human existence for meaning in the face of an inconsistent world. Be it the ideal self which requires negation, the drive of the human spirit for intimacy within the experience of distance, or a culture's search for a unified world view amid binary oppositions, the quest for identity, harmony, and wholeness is a constant. Ritual is ever present in this context as a medium, tool, and potential cause of these life sustaining goals.

The drives articulated in these chapters on the role of ritual in the vision of the behavioral sciences cross cultural boundaries. The actual answers to life's exigencies will vary from culture to culture. But, the actual operation and function of ritual within different cultures' answers appear to be invariable. Ritual is indigenous to everyone and every culture. At the same time, it is adaptable and flexible so that it can function in different cultures.

Each science we have explored has unmasked a different dimension of ritual. At the same time, these differing ritual dimensions have been complementary and not contradictory. Psychological analysis understands ritual as an integral feature in the development of the human personality and the maintenance of this mature personality in adulthood. During the various stages of personality emergence and development, different elements are introduced to the individual through ritual which opens the possibility for the next advancement. Once the process is begun, the individual person hungers for further validation and reinforcement throughout his or her life. Ritual is every ready to supply this need.

Anthropological-sociological analysis of culture and social groups also speaks of the importance of ritual, not only for the individual, but for the very existence of these social units. Ritual permeates the three main components of culture. Language, patterns of behavior, and social struc-

118

tures employ, rely upon, and sustain ritual. In turn, ritual makes these features of culture productive and effective. Ritual both preserves culture and can be a creative source for change in culture.

Our brief philosophical note collaborated the essential features of our behavioral conclusions. Philosophy has turned to the two basic elements which ground ritual: the coexistential character of human life and the human power for transcendence. Humankind has an exaulted place in creation, in the order of existence. It is the locus where meaning is revealed. Ritual is the key vehicle that allows both human coexistence and transcendence to be transformed from ideas to reality, from potential to actualization.

Psychology, anthropology, sociology and philosophy are laiden with further questions on ritual and its relation to reality. Is the numinous of Erikson's theory merely a sense, feeling, description, projection, or a reality? Psychology leads us to the question, but not the answer. Anthropology and sociology speak of a meaningful network within culture, a resolution of binary oppositions and the discovery of an ordered world view. Is this reality or social fantasy? Anthropological-sociological reflection can describe what is happening in the dimensions of a particular culture or social group, but cannot answer the question of their real or imaginary status. Likewise, philosophical reflection takes humankind to the brink of experience by isolating the drive for human transcendence as directed toward the fullness of *Being*. Again the question is faced: Is absolute *Being* fact or fancy?

Our purpose is not to answer the above questions. This task falls to what is called fundamental theology, formerly apologetics. Our concern is to demonstrate that the person who believes, who is a Christian, performs the behavior described as normal by the behavioral sciences in their sacraments, their rituals. Religious ritual behavior is as normal for the Christian as ritual behavior is for everyone.

We should expect that Christian culture will follow the same psychological, anthropological and sociological lines as any culture. The difference between Christian culture and any other will not be whether or not ritual is present. The difference will be in the truth status claimed for its interpretation of the meaning and style of life. In Christian culture the numinous is a reality. In Christian culture human coexistence is not an option but a divine dictate. In Christian culture transcendence is a divine call to blessed union with the personal absolute.

The anthropological data on ritual is more than an overture to the theology of sacraments. This data supplies the insights through which the religious rituals of Christianity can be adequately understood and explained. Sacraments, as Christian religious rituals, follow the norms, structures, and functions of ritual in general as specified within the peculiarly Christian world view. A theology of sacraments, constructed without reference and docility to the behavioral sciences, is blind to a source of great insight and nourishment.

In the next part of this work, we will analyze what Christians claim of the ritual behavior they call sacraments. We will not attempt to defend the truth claims of this world view, but try to demonstrate that it is a possible valid interpretation of human existence and behavior which meets the exigencies of the anthropological dimensions we have witnessed in this section.

PART THREE
THE THEOLOGICAL DIMENSION
OF SACRAMENTS

Investigation of the human sciences yields cumulative and progressive insight into the function and importance of ritual for all phases and modalities of human life. Ritual is the unspoken creed interpreting human experience. To understand a people's ritual and the symbols which comprise it is to enter into the people themselves, to see their world through their eyes, to participate in their interpretive meaning system. In Part Three, our goal is to understand Christian ritual as it is manifested in sacraments. Our task is to outline the elements which comprise a theology of sacraments as confessed by Christianity in view of the enlightenment afforded by research into ritual in general. This orientation serves the purpose of unfolding the main dimensions of the Christian root metaphor and demonstrating the resonableness of Christian sacraments within Christianity's world view.

As far as possible, our data will follow the pattern presented in Part Two. First, the general meaning of the term "sacrament" will be recorded. This general orientation will lead to an analysis of the relation of "word" and sacrament, sacramental behavior, and sacraments and grace. In a final chapter, a summary of sacraments as ecclesial root metaphors will be attempted.

7   REDEFINING THE TERM "SACRAMENT"

There are a variety of definitions for the term *sacrament*. A cursory glance at catechetical texts from the Protestant and Catholic traditions reveals the different meanings attributed to this word.[1] This text operates from a particular definition of sacrament which is important to explain. Its elucidation can be accomplished by comparing and contrasting it with the definition most familiar to members of the American Catholic tradition, the *Baltimore Catechism*.

The *Baltimore Catechism* portrayed a sacrament as "an outward sign instituted by Christ to give grace." In our perspective sacraments are *symbols arising from the ministry of Christ and continued in and through the Church, which when received in faith, are encounters with God, Father, Son and Holy Spirit*. In both definitions, four key elements can be identified: sign-symbol, relation to Christ, effectiveness or power, and what is effected, brought about or produced.

Sign-Symbol

The *Baltimore Catechism* employs the term *sign* for a sacrament. Our definition prefers *symbol*. As noted in our chapter on terms, all symbols are signs. A symbol, however, is more potent than other signs. It is supercharged with a meaning which is not created, but discovered by humankind. Symbols reach down to the depths of reality. They are ontological in character.

By designating the sacraments as symbols, any possibility of relegating them to the category of the conventional is precluded. Furthermore, to speak of sacraments as symbols is to envision them as dynamic rather than static realities. It is to honor their potency. Symbols have the power to point to a reality different from themselves and make it present, without

123

being identical to it. Symbols have a direct and intrinsic relation to the reality they symbolize.

To refer to the sacraments as symbols, therefore, is in no way to weaken their reality. On the contrary, it is to argue for a greater depth of reality and power for sacraments. Sacraments are not merely signs, but symbolic signs.

Institution

In both the *Baltimore Catechism* and our definition, a link is made between the sacraments and Jesus. Both definitions claim an essential bond between the activity of the historical Jesus and the sacramental actions of the Church. The difference between the two definitions lies in the meaning of the word "instituted."

When one reads the *Baltimore Catechism*, the impression is created that Christ specifically and exactly established each of the seven sacraments. Institution in this case can only mean that every phase, step, and form of action, organization, and program is definitively placed in motion by an individual or a group. Institution, however, can have an alternate meaning. It can refer to the establishment of guidelines or open-ended principles, while leaving the exact form or expression of what is established to historical development and evolution.

An example of this second type of "institution is found in comparing the present political, legal and social situation of any nation with the original vision of the founding fathers of that nation. In a real sense the founding fathers "instituted" the nation, even though in many, if not all, situations, they would not recognize their nation in its present form.

Our definition of sacraments assumes this broad meaning of "institution," whereas the *Baltimore Catechism* reflects the first or literal meaning of "institution." The main reason for choosing this broad interpretation of institution is critical biblical and historical scholarship.

From the data available, contemporary scholarship disallows a literal institution by Christ for each of the seven sacraments. At most, biblical scholars see a Scriptural foundation for four specific sacraments: baptism, Eucharist, reconciliation, and holy orders. More conservatively, scholars will claim foundation for two: baptism and the Eucharist. Most scholars go further, and point out that if one is going to speak of Jesus "instituting" anything it was the community of his followers which became his Church after the resurrection. The Church then evolved specific ritual celebrations in their living out of Christ's commands which evolved into the sacraments as we know them.

If sacraments have an ecclesial origin, what exactly is their relation to the historical Jesus? Did the Church have free reign to decide what would be sacraments and what would not? Was the Church faithful to even the general guidelines issued by its founder? These questions are quite normal once a literal understanding of institution is abandoned in sacramental theology. They can be answered.

Sacraments are not isolated entities. Each sacrament is not encased in a little box that is opened at the right occasion. All the sacraments are essentially related to each other by their power to unfold aspects of Jesus' ministry. The relationship of the sacraments to Jesus' ministry is the key to understanding the continuity between Jesus' intention in forming a community, and the communities faithfulness to Jesus in evolving and celebrating the sacraments.

Jesus had gathered disciples to himself so that his mission of proclaiming the kingdom of God might be realized in human history. After his death and resurrection, his Church continued this vocation in his name. Those who heard and believed the Jesus story inherited the mission of continuing Jesus' work of redemption. Gradually, the Church came to realize that particular communal activities expressed in a heightened form Jesus' saving work. These eventually became known as sacraments. At the Fourth Lateran Council in 1215, the number of these activities became fixed at seven.

Although attempts have been made to link the various sacraments according to a person's age and need, the real intrasacramental bond lies in their unfolding aspects of Jesus' ministry. The Eucharist, the central Christian sacrament, celebrates the central saving activity of Christ and the center of Christian faith i.e., Jesus' death-resurrection. Baptism and confirmation celebrate the initiation of new members into the Christian community. Reconciliation celebrates Jesus' forgiveness of sins. Matrimony celebrates the intimacy of human love mirroring the love of Christ for his community of followers, the Church. Holy Orders celebrates the ministry of service which Jesus demanded of those who would lead his community. Anointing of the Sick celebrates the healing power of Christ. Clearly, each sacrament expresses a vital activity of Jesus as the redeemer and savior sent by the Father to bring about the kingdom of God in the world. Consequently,

> Each of the sacraments is tied to Jesus, the basic and primordial sacrament. All the sacraments, and the Church itself, arise and flow from the one sacrament of the Father, his only Son. The Church, in celebrating the seven sacraments, continues Jesus' ministry. We can then say that in

drawing a people to himself, Jesus implicitly "institutes" the sacraments of that people, the Church. The Church in turn celebrates various aspects of Jesus' ministry in the various sacraments.[2]

In order to avoid any over-literal understanding of the origin of the sacraments in Christ, the terminology *arising from the ministry of Jesus* is employed over "institution." This choice still permits and insists on Christ as the originator and final reference of the sacraments, while maintaining the nuances demanded by contemporary biblical, historical, and theological research.

Effectiveness

Both the *Baltimore Catechism* and our definition suggest an effectiveness to sacraments. The sacraments *do* something. The *doing* of sacraments can only be understood, however, with reference to the continuation of Christ's ministry in the community of faith, the fellowship of those who believe in him. Sacraments demand faith, if they are to be effective.

External rites and rituals void of personal faith and actions are hollow. The great scholastic theologians of the thirteenth and fourteenth centuries were well aware of this. They distinguished two essential and inseparable elements in sacraments: the action performed and the action of faith in the recipient of the sacrament. Sacramental *ex opere operato* and *ex opere operantis* formed one whole reality. Faith is a *sine qua non* of sacramental life and performance. Our definition explicitly adheres to this principle. Sacraments are encounters with God only when they are *received in faith*. Without faith, sacraments become masked symbols and empty actions.

Unfortunately, the *Baltimore Catechism* fails to emphasize the faith dimension of sacraments. One can discover a reference to a proper disposition in the recipient for a valid and fruitful participation in the sacraments in the *Baltimore Catechism's* text. The disposition, however, is stated negatively i.e., no *obex* (obstacle) is to be placed in the way of the sacraments. This approach can lead to a purely passive understanding of faith. Sacramental faith, however, is active. It is a personal, total commitment to the living God. It involves all the dimensions of the human person. Faith is not disinterested observation, but attentive involvement.

Why are the sacraments effective? How are they effective? Sacramental causality is closely linked with the issue of faith and the sacraments. This question will be dealt with at greater length in following chapters.

But, it is important to demonstrate the general difference between our understanding and the *Baltimore Catechism's*.

The *Baltimore Catechism* employs the word *give* to explain the causality of the sacraments. This word often leads to an image of "mechanistic production" in the popular mentality. The sacraments are commonly taken to work automatically and instantaneously, like a gas pump or slot machine. The causality of the sacraments is impersonal and individual. It is important to see that this vision is only possible when personal active faith is absent or really insignificant in one's definition of sacraments.

In our definition, the causality of sacraments is qualified by the term *encounter*. Our image shifts from a physical-mechanistic paradigm to a humanistic-personalistic paradigm. In an encounter, there is a real involvement and exchange of persons. Encounter suggests self gift, active involvement, and creative love.

In the sacraments, the risen Lord offers himself and the Father's love through the power of the Holy Spirit. Causality does not refer to a transfer of matter. Sacramental causality refers to the dynamic interchange between the living Christ and the ritual participants who believe in him. Faith, which is a gift of the risen Lord, is ultimately the basis for sacramental causality.

Final Effect

Closely associated with the issue of sacramental causality is the effect of sacraments, or what they cause. In the *Baltimore Catechism*, sacraments are said to give *grace*. In itself, this claim is absolutely correct. Due to its dimunition of the role of faith and its mechanistic model of causality, the term *grace* has been misconstrued. Physical examples reinforced in catechetical texts and homilies have led the faithful to conceive of grace as some*thing*.

A brief reflection on one's childhood religious education should substantiate this judgment. Frequently, grace was described in quantitative terms. One accumulated grace. Perfect happiness consisted in having your soul filled to the brim with grace. When one sinned he or she lost some or all grace.

Our definition prefers to present grace as God himself, Father, Son, and Holy Spirit. Grace is not a physical or quantitative reality. It is not a substance. Grace is the presence of a living person. It is a relational, qualitative reality.

The biblical and patristic traditions clearly speak of grace as God himself. The Fathers knew well that when the Scriptures spoke of eternal life, they were referring to the indwelling of the Trinity i.e., the relation between God and the person who accepts him in faith. This relationship is deepened and intensified in and through the celebration of the sacraments. To speak of an "increase of grace" is to refer to a growing communion of mind, heart, and will between and individual and God.

Conclusion

In redefining the term *sacrament*, the central elements of the Christian tradition have in no way been abandoned. Rather, the key dimensions of sacraments have been presented in a personalistic paradigm which appears more faithful to Scripture, the Fathers of the Church, and human experience. Our definition of sacraments as *symbols arising from the ministry of Christ and continued in and through the Church, which when received in faith, are encounters with God, Father, Son, and Holy Spirit* also offers a glimpse at some of the areas which require exposition in the following chapters.

In a sense, to offer a definition of a sacrament at this point is to place the cart before the horse. Yet, this procedure proves valuable in hinting at the fundamental orientation or intuition guiding our task of reconstructing a sacramental theology which will focus on human experience, Christ, and the Church.

In the brief comparison of our definition with the *Baltimore Catechism's*, attention should be called to the importance of *models* in sacramental theology and theology in general. Models can beneficially elucidate the truth of a theological statement or distort these statements and lead to misinterpretations. Theological statements and models go hand in hand in any attempt to expose Christian faith.

NOTES

1. Cf. George S. Worgul Jr., "The Sacraments in Catholic and Protestant Catechisms," *The Living Light* 15 (1978), pp. 529–548.

2. George S. Worgul Jr., "What Is A Sacrament?," *U.S. Catholic* 42 (1977), p. 30.

8 WORD AND SACRAMENT

Historical, anthropological, and theological data suggest an exploration of the relation between word and sacrament as a starting point for a contemporary theology of sacraments in general. The historical variance between Protestant and Catholic traditions was sharply drawn precisely on this issue. In the Protestant traditions, the *word* as proclamation of the Gospel predominated over symbolic action. In the Catholic tradition, the relevance of the word within sacramentology found little recognition. The Scriptures had a value for apologetics i.e., to defend the number and institution of the sacraments by Christ, but were minimally involved in sacramental theology *per se*. A correct understanding of the relationship between word and sacrament can dissipate denominational tensions and embellish the theological perception of sacraments in each tradition.

Our previous anthropological data underscored the significance of language in ritual performance. Language, as an explanatory narrative, both unfolds and intensifies the meaning of symbolic gesture and symbolic activity, which in turn express the root metaphor of a people. Language is charged with a potency or force that is potentially disclosive and/or controlling to those who "hear." As a constitutive anthropological fact of ritual, language is indispensable in understanding the religious rituals Christians call sacraments.

The stimulus for attending to the relation between word and sacrament does not emerge purely from the "secular" sciences. Theological research, especially in Christology and ecclesiology, calls attention to the significance of language and a theology of the "*word*" of God.

Christian revelation, and therefore Christian theology originates in the revelation of God as Father in his word, Jesus the Christ. Jesus is the word spoken by the Father throughout all eternity. At the same time, Jesus is the word proclaimed by the Church. The ecclesial community proclaims the Word of God in the words of men. Since sacraments arise from the ministry of Jesus, the word continued in the Church, they are constitutively bound to the word of God expressed in the words of people. It is the special character of God's word proclaimed in and through the Church that is the contemporary point of departure for a theology of sacraments.[1]

This chapter will focus on three dimensions. First it will reflect on Jesus as the word of God. Second, it will outline the relationship between Church and the word of God. Finally, it will examine the relationship between the word of God and sacraments.

Jesus as the Word of God

To understand properly Jesus as the word of God, one must turn to the rich biblical tradition of the term *dabar*. In the Old Testament, *dabar* concurrently means *word* and *event*. The unity to these two elements reaches its climax in the divine *dabar*, the divine proclamation and deed. When God speaks his word, what is spoken transpires. Divine utterance is, at the same time, a divine happening. In a real sense the divine *dabar* is a creative reality.

As a creative reality, the word of God is both "sacramental" and historical. To the extent that the word accomplishes what was spoken, it is efficacious of what it symbolizes i.e., it is sacramental. The word, however, is not segmented into disconnected events or time-frames. On the contrary, the word is the one continuous reality which permeates and unifies time. "History is a process which is governed by the word of Yahweh; rather, history is the word of Yahweh, the reality which fulfills his utterance."[2]

It is precisely in the word of God as history that the self-communication of God to humankind is to be located. By speaking his word, God identifies who he is to humankind. In the Old Testament, this process is enshrined in a covenant expressed through the law and the prophets.

The word of God is always a mediated word. Whether the word is communicated by event or speech, it is always transmitted through humanity. This implies that there will always be a distance between the expression of God's word and the reality of that word. This limitation applies not only to the medium of the law, but also to the medium of prophecy.

> The prophetic communication of God is not a revelation of God independent of the relation with man that God has sustained in history. God is present in his Word, but the words of man are never adequate to express the Word of God. God is far beyond all words. The Old Testament reveals the Word of God, but in a limited fashion.[3]

In the New Testament, the word of God is also expressed through the words of men. This testament, however, claims the existence of a unique expression of the word of God, an unrepeatable and insurpassable concurrence of word-event in the person of Jesus, the Christ. Jesus, fully man, is the lawgiver and a prophet par excellence. He surpasses all who preceded him and all who follow. Jesus is the expression of the word of God as the enfleshment, the Incarnation of the word. Jesus not only speaks and lives the word, he *is* the word in the totality of his person.

Once the Incarnation became fact, to speak of the word of God was not to refer primarily to the Hebrew Scriptures or the proclamation about God in the language of men, but to speak of a person, Jesus the Christ. In its fullest expression, the word of God is not a "what" but a "who," not a "thing" but a "person."

If Jesus is the final and full expression of the word of God in human history, the traits of the word previously revealed should be present in a heightened form in this unique person. Jesus should be sacramental and historical. As such, he should be the medium for the Father's self-communication to humankind.

Jesus is sacramental. He is the sacrament of the Father. He makes the Father present without being identical to the Father. Any explanation of Jesus' sacramentality is inadequate, however, if it fails to include the Incarnation of the word as its foundation.

The Council of Chalcedon defined the position that Jesus is truly God and man in the unity of one person. The Son of God is a man and this man in personally God's Son. He is God in a human way and man in a divine way. Everything that the God-man did was a divine act in human expression. Herein lies the radical sacramentality of the word, Jesus.

> Because the saving acts of the man Jesus are performed by a divine person, they have a divine power to save, but because this divine power to save appears to us in human form, the saving activity of Jesus is sacramental.[4]

The word of the Father was not merely audible. It was visibly enfleshed in the bodiliness of the person Jesus. Jesus' saving activity included his bodiliness or corporeality. It was in and through the visibility and tangibility of his real body that Christ was the salvation of God for humankind. Consequently, to encounter the man Jesus as he lived in our world was to be in the locus of God's gift of salvation in its fullest realization.

The man Jesus, as the personal visible realization of the divine grace of redemption, is *the* sacrament, the primordial sacrament, because this man, the Son of God himself, is intended by the Father to be in his humanity the only way to the actuality of redemption. "For there is one God, and one mediator of God and man, the man Christ Jesus."[5]

The unique sacramentality of Jesus is not a discontinuous event in the history of salvation. As *the* sacrament of God, Jesus continues and perfects the sacramentality of Israel. Israel was to have been the locus for the self-communication of God. It was for this purpose that Israel was chosen and charged with responsibilities. Israel's election as the people of God required that they be a sign among the nations of God's faithful mercy, that they offer true worship i.e., obedience to God, and that they show a profound care for the poor. In fulfilling this mission, all would come to know that Yahweh the Lord was God alone. Israel, however, was only partially successful in its task.

The New Testament writers portray Jesus as fulfilling and completing the mission of Israel. He is the perfect response to the Father and consequently the great symbol of the Father. Jesus is *the* sign raised among the nations demonstrating the love of God for humanity. He offers true worship to the Father by placing his total being in the service of proclaiming by word and deed the love of God for everyone. This obedience leads him to his death. Finally, Jesus manifests a profound concern for the poor, a radical love which permeates and colors all his activity. Jesus was the living symbol of God.

Jesus "is the historically real and actual presence of the eschatologically victorious mercy of God."[6] The God-man who entered our history was the offer of salvation to humankind. This offer received a definitive and final permanence in his death and resurrection. In principle, humankind's acceptance of this offer is irreversibly established in the person of Christ, even though the actual acceptance needs to be personalized in each human life. In Christ,

... the whole of mankind is in principle already accepted for salvation in this member and head of mankind who is irrevocably united with God in the unity of person. From the moment the Logos assumed this human nature from out of the unity of mankind, and as a part of it, redemption cannot be arrested or cancelled. The fate of the world has been finally decided, and in the sense of divine mercy.[7]

Before Christ, the question of human salvation was open-ended. The history of the world could have led to unity with God or rejection. After Christ, humankind's global salvation is positively sealed.

As the symbol of God for humankind, Jesus is both the sign and cause of God's saving love. The person of Jesus is not a welding together of sign and cause conceived as disjunctive realities. Rather, in Jesus, there is a concurrence of sign and cause in the elements which compose his person i.e., his interiority and bodiliness. The Incarnation, life, death, and resurrection of the enfleshed word is simultaneously the sign of the Father's love and the actualizing cause of this love by being God's acceptance of humankind. Jesus, therefore, represents the dual movement of God reaching out to humankind, and humankind responding to God's offer. This paradigm is especially clear in Jesus' worship of the Father.

> Jesus became the redeemer in actual fact by freely living his human life in religious worship of and attainment to the Father. In Christ, not only were God and his love for man revealed, but God also showed us in him what it is for man to commit himself unconditionally to God the invisible Father.[8]

Jesus is the Incarnation of divine love and the prototype of how humankind is to respond to the divine gift of love.

The signification and causality of Jesus are historical. They involve a processual unfolding. The main demarcations in this process were the Incarnation, the life-events, the death-resurrection, and the glorification. In the Incarnation, the very possibility of Jesus being the sign and cause of salvation was established. The life of Jesus is the story of a continual concrete dialogue of offer-acceptance of his Father. Christ's death summarized his life and definitively established salvation for humanity to which his resurrection is a testimony. In his glorification, Jesus becomes *Kurios*, Lord of history, and returns to his place of power at the right hand of the Father from which he sends his Spirit upon the world.

As sacramental and historical, Jesus is revelatory. He makes the Father known by being his image. "Jesus is the revealer and is such because he is the word of God."[9] Jesus is the medium of the Father's love, a love humankind always experiences through mediation.

An anthropological investigation of language identifies its general disclosive character and its specific narrative/descriptive, heuristic, prescriptive, promissory and performative features. Jesus as the *word* exemplifies these qualities.

Jesus as the word of God is the ultimate disclosure of God in human history. Jesus discloses that God is a personal Father. The unique character of this disclosure is not merely in the words spoken by Jesus or in his life-actions, but in *who he is*. Because he is personally the Son of God, God is known as Father. All previous disclosures of God are relativized by this unique unrepeatable disclosure. There is no doubt as to the indentity or character of God after Jesus the word.

Jesus as the word of God is a narrative/description. In his personal unity, he is an exegesis of the activity of God in human history and a simultaneous exegesis of humankind in that same history. It is against the horizon of Jesus that the particular events and whole continuity of history are comprehensible, although this may not be immediately apparent at every particular moment. The story or narrative of Jesus is not only a dictionary for interpreting the past, but also a norm for the future. In Christ, the final destiny of humanity has been decided vis-à-vis humankind's acceptance or rejection of God.

Jesus as the word of God is heuristic. He evokes discovery. There is a binary structure to the heuristic character of Jesus. He evokes discovery of the Father. He also evokes discovery of man's and woman's meaning. Both heuristic components are wedded in Jesus' person.

Jesus as the word of God is prescriptive. As the final revelation of the Father, he is paradigmatic both for the Godhead and the relation of humankind to God. God can never be revealed in a way contradictory to his self-revelation in his word, Jesus. Likewise, there is no other way for a man or woman to come to the Father except *the Way*, Jesus.

Finally, Jesus as the word of God is promissory and performative. He is the basis for living as a human person in the world. Jesus is not a "dead" word but a "living" word. In him, locution and audibility blossom in action. In Jesus practice and theory are one. So must it be with those who follow him.

Church and the Word

In his death and resurrection, Jesus leaves history. Yet, the paradigmatic model of God's self-communication and love established in him as *the* word of God is not negated. Consequently, the departure of the visible manifestation of God demands a "replacement."

Jesus does not leave his followers orphaned in his exodus from history. He promises and bestows on them his Spirit. This Spirit will be his abiding presence "until he comes again." This Spirit binds the scattered followers of Jesus together as the nucleus of the Church. Spirit and Church together are the continuing presence of the sacramental historical Jesus in the world. The spirited Church is to be the visible sign of the invisible Christ i.e., the sacrament of Christ.

There can be no more valid theological starting point for ecclesiology than an examination of its starting point in the word of God. Before all other images and explanations of its nature, the Church is fundamentally the community formed in the word of God. The Church originates in the word, prolongates the word, and realizes the mission of the word. The Church is the *Ursakrament* of the word. There would be no Church unless men and women heard and believed the word.

The constitutive character of the word of God for the Church can be described in six theses.[10] First, the Church is the locus of God's word in history. The Church utters the word of God, so that it is preserved in its entirety. Second, the power which sustains and preserves the ecclesial community is the inner movement of God's word. As the divine offer of salvation was made fact in the historical Jesus, it is also continued presently in the Church through the inner movement of the same word of God. Third, the Church participates in the special, unique, and paradigmatic character of the salvific action of God in Christ because he moves within the Church as *the* word of God. Fourth, the Church is symbolic. Through the power of the word of God, the ecclesial community makes present the divine offer of salvation which it signifies. Fifth, the presence of the word within the whole life of the Church varies in degrees of concentration and intensity. Finally, "the supreme realization of the efficacious word of God, as the coming of God's salvific action (that is, as the Church's own, full realization) in the situations decisive for an individual's salvation, is the sacrament and the only sacrament."[11]

In these theses, the Church is portrayed as founded on God's word, Jesus, and, at the same time, a continued speaking of that word in history. The word proclaimed in the Church is not only the offer of salvation, but, as heard and accepted word, the actualization of salvation. When the Church proclaims the word, it is realizing its inner most nature i.e., being the presence of the risen Lord in history.

Like Christ, the Church as herald of God's word is sacramental and historical. The Church, as proclaimer of God's word, Jesus, is the abiding presence of the offer and definitive establishment of salvation in the continual unfolding of history. The Church continues to effect what has been uttered by the Father in Christ by being what it is i.e., the community of persons gathered together with Christ as its head and his Spirit as its dynamic life-force.[12] The Church is sacramental because it realizes salvation in signifying Christ, God's word. The Church is the sacrament of Christ, the sacrament of the Father.

To refer to the Church as sacramental is not to tag another title on to its many titles and descriptions. It is to pinpoint the ecclesial essence.

> This designation of the Church as the "primordial sacrament" (*Ursakrament*) is not simply another "notion of the Church," but is the meaning and ontological sense of the mystery expressed in the statements found in revelation regarding the Church. To see the Church as a sacrament is to grasp the connection between the various partial aspects of the Church, particularly those of her mysterious, divine interior and her social, human exterior. For as the Church has taught throughout the centuries, the essence of a sacrament is to bind together a complex of realities, interior and exterior, human and divine, in the relation of sign to signified, of cause to effect.[13]

When the New Testament is searched for images of the Church, three are discovered which facilitate a comprehension of its sacramentality. As the *people of God*, the Church is an outward physical reality pointing to the offer of God's salvation. As the *Mystical Body*, the Church is an invisible spiritual reality. As the *Bride of Christ*, the Church is a witness to the personal disposition and choice involved in accepting God's offer of salvation.[14]

As *Ursakrament*, the Church is an effective sign. It not only points to salvation, but brings it about. The realization of the Church's purpose happens in concrete history. Ecclesial sacramentality is historical. "The Church exists in the fullest sense, in the highest degree of actual fulfillment of her nature, by teaching, bearing witness to Christ's truth, bearing the cross of Christ throughout the ages, loving God in her members, rendering present in rite in the sacrifice of the Mass, the saving grace that is hers."[15]

In a general sense, all the various historical activities of the Church could be called sacraments. In the technical sense, however, the Church is sacramental when it acts in a concrete situation for the salvation of a person in its official capacity as a source of redemption. As Rahner notes:

> . . . when the Church in her official, organized public capacity precisely as the source of redemptive grace meets the individual in the actual ultimate accomplishment of her nature, there we have sacraments in the proper sense; and they can then be seen to be the essential functions that bring into activity the very essence of the Church herself. For in them

she attains the highest degree of actualization of what she always is: the presence of redemptive grace for men, historically visible and manifest as the sign of the eschatologically victorious grace of God in the world.[16]

For the Church to attain her nature, she must incorporate individuals within her community. It is insufficient for an individual to assent intellectually to the Church's existence for salvation to be actualized. Likewise, the Church can never remain indifferent to the existence of any individual person. A mutual embracement is required. It is through the encounter of individuals with the Church, that salvation made flesh is discovered. The Church unites humankind and God, continuing the unity effected in Christ.

In a real sense, the acts of the Church are the acts of Christ.

> All of this simply means that a sacrament, as a visible symbolic action of the Church, is not only the rendering present here on earth of Christ's mystery of saving worship, but also the Church's inward identification of itself, in faith, hope, and love with this mystery of worship. The ecclesial life of grace adds nothing to the fullness of Christ's grace, but is a sharing in that grace. The sacraments are therefore acts of the whole mystical body, of Christ and his Church. And indeed in this sense they are acts of Christ in and through his Church. Christ acts in the sacrament together with the people of God already realized and existing in the world.[17]

Ecclesial sacramental activity is Christological-historical activity. As Christ realized who he was as the word of the Father through his concrete actions in the world, so the Church realizes her nature as the historical extension of Christ through her actions. Christ was the medium of the Father. The Church is the medium of the word, Jesus. The Church is the word of God proclaimed in the words of men and women.

The Church exemplifies the same anthropological characteristics of language as did Jesus as the word. By proclaiming the word of God in history, the Church continues the disclosive work of Jesus. The Church applies his unique disclosure to every new historical, cultural, and geographical area of humankind's existence. Yet, the Church never totally matches the disclosive power of Jesus in all its word-events. The words of the Church remain the words of men and women expressing the word of God. Therefore, the proclamation of the Church can at times hide the word of God. On the other hand, there are times when the Church approaches close to the full disclosive power of the Lord and acts decisively vis-à-vis an individual's salvation. This proclamation is truly a sacrament of the word. In this case, the Church's proclamation is a continuation of Jesus' exegesis of history. It explains the present and keeps alive the Jesus story as a norm for humankind's future destiny.

Like Jesus, the Church is dualistically heuristic. The Church's proclamation of the word leads to a discovery of God and a discovery of what it means to be a man or women. This dual discovery is promissory and performative. In proclaiming the word, the Church implicitly proclaims prescriptions i.e., modes of being a Christian in the concrete historical situations of life. The Church's proclamation of the word is a testimony to its promissory and performative character. The words of the Church about the word always strive to awaken conforming-activity in those who hear.

Word and Sacraments

If sacraments are *symbols arising from the ministry of Jesus continued in and through the Church*, they are essentially bound to the word of God as proclaimed by the community of the word. The coincidence of the word and sacraments is three-fold. First, the reality realized in the proclamation of the word and in the symbolic activity of sacramental celebrations is identical i.e., the self-communication of God inviting humankind to participation in divine life. Second, the character of the realized reality is eschatological, definitive, and final in both instances. Third, the Church is the agent for both the proclamation of the word and the celebration of the sacraments.

The triple coincidence of proclaimed word and sacraments is not extrinsic. It germinates from the origin of the Church in the word and the existence of sacraments as ecclesial manifestations of this same word. "The power to preach the word of God by the authority of God and of his Christ, and the power to administer the sacraments to men are the basic powers of the Church which are constitutive of its essence."[18]

Care must be taken not to place the Church's proclamation of the word and the celebration of the sacraments on an equal theoretical plane. Primacy and priority must be given to the proclamation of the word.

> One cannot, strictly speaking, say that the saving activity of the Church includes the proclamation of the word and the use of signs. Rather, the proclamation of the Word is the activity of the Church that includes everything else. Even the use of the signs is fundamentally a saving preach-

ing of the Word for two reasons: First, because it is only the Word together with the thing that constitutes the sacramental sign, with the Word having the chief importance; secondly, however, because the significance of the sign itself is proclamation.[19]

"The use of signs is part of the Church's task of preaching the word, not *vice versa*."[20]

Once the sacraments are properly contextualized within the Church's proclamation of the word, it is necessary to underscore their unique place among all other proclamations. The Church legitimately proclaims many words in the fulfillment of its mission. But since this proclamation is in the words of men and women, it is marked by a variability. In sacraments, however, the ecclesial words fulfill the essence of the Church. In sacraments, the word of the Church is the proclamation of the word of God which signifies and effects salvation.

The primal place of the proclamation of the word over sacramental activity can also be seen in the classical discussion on the matter and form of the sacraments. The material element of the sacraments e.g., bread, water, etc., cannot be decisive in sacraments. Only the formal element can be decisive i.e., the words proclaimed over the matter. The basis for this affirmation lies in the impossibility and inability of finite limited objects to realize supernatural realities. As Rahner explains:

> . . . in the case of strictly supernatural realities . . . a purely natural thing in the nature of an *object* can never function as a sign in such a way that the supernatural reality could be attained through it alone. Whenever a reality of the world is to be a sign, indication and historical presence of a strictly supernatural reality, it can only be so when the spiritual, transcendental (subjective) openness, orientation of man, pointing beyond the finite to God himself, becomes an intrinsically constitutive element of this sign. But this implies that the supernatural reality can display itself only through the medium of the human *word* as long as it cannot present itself in its own proper reality, which is basically in the immediate vision of God.[21]

It is only the spoken human word, as an expression of human transcendence which allows the possibility of God's self-communication within sacramental celebrations. This does not imply a disregard for the material elements in the sacraments, any more than the primacy of the proclamation of the word would cause a neglect of sacraments in ecclesial life. Rather, it does imply that the material element of the sacraments can only be properly understood in terms of the formal element and that the sacraments can only be understood in terms of the Church's responsibility for proclaiming the word of God in the words of men and women.

Perhaps, one of the most significant theological advances of the Second Vatican Council was its recognition of the priority of proclaiming the word of God in the mission of the Church. This recognition had its impact on the *Decree on the Liturgy*. In this document, a vigorous effort was made to restore the primary place to Scripture in liturgical-sacramental celebrations. Sacraments were presented as expressions of the Church fulfilling its role as proclaimer of the word.

Conclusion

It might appear strange to begin investigating the theological dimensions of sacraments by turning to the word of God. This might appear more appropo to a theology of preaching or an examination of New Testament Christology. Yet, the word of God is the proper context for understanding the Church and its sacraments. Within the context of the word of God, the relationship between Jesus, Church, and sacraments becomes clear. The proclamation of Jesus, the word, is continued in the mission of the Church, a mission which is attained in the celebration of the sacraments.

It is impossible to theologically reflect on the sacraments without reference to ecclesiology and Christology. There are no sacraments that are not sacraments of the Church. There is no Church without Christ, the word of God. This chapter, therefore, establishes the specific context for theological reflection on sacraments.

Moreover, there is a clear line of convergence between the focal point of the word of God in Christian cultural behavior and the function of language within culture. The anthropological claims about the role and importance of language in general, find verification in the primary place and function of the word in Christian culture. Theological claims about the priority and primacy of the word do not contradict the behavioral sciences, but sustain their attestations. The word of God, the Church as proclaimer of the word, and the sacraments as concrete expressions of this proclamation bear the exegetical, heuristic, prescriptive, promissory, and performative characteristics of language in general and religious language in particular.

NOTES

1. K. Rahner, "What is a Sacrament," *Worship* 47 (1973), p. 275.

2. J. L. McKenzie, *Dictionary of the Bible*. (Milwaukee: Bruce Publ. Co., 1965), p. 939.

3. O'Grady, p. 90.

4. E. Schillebeeckx, *Christ the Sacrament of Encounter with God*. (New York: Sheed and Ward, 1963), p. 15.

5. *Ibid.*, p. 16.

6. K. Rahner, *The Church and the Sacraments*. (New York: Herder and Herder, 1962), p. 14.

7. *Ibid.*, pp. 14–15.

8. Schillebeeckx, p. 19.

9. O'Grady, p. 92.

10. K. Rahner, "The Word and the Eucharist," *Theological Investigations Vol. 4*. (Baltimore: Helicon Press, 1965), pp. 265ff.

11. *Ibid.*, p. 265.

12. Rahner, *The Church and the Sacraments* . . ., p. 18.

13. O. Semmelroth, "The Integral Idea of the Church," in *Theology Today Vol. 1*. (Milwaukee: Bruce Publ. Co., 1965), p. 137.

14. *Ibid.*, pp. 145–147.

15. Rahner, *The Church and the Sacraments* . . ., p, 20.

16. *Ibid.*, p. 22.

17. Schillebeeckx, *Christ the Sacrament* . . ., p. 79.

18. Rahner, "The Word and the Eucharist" . . ., p. 254.

19. M. Schmaus, *Dogma 5: The Church as Sacrament*. (London: Sheed and Ward, 1975), p. 17.

20. *Ibid.*

21. Rahner, "The Word and the Eucharist" . . ., p. 167.

9 SACRAMENTAL BEHAVIOR

Sacraments are realizations of the Church's task of being the living extension and presence of Christ in the world. They are proclamations of the word of God in the words and deeds of men and women. Each sacrament is radically linked to a facet of Jesus' ministry.

The sacraments of initiation continue Jesus' ministry of drawing disciples to himself and forming them into God's people. Baptism celebrates one's entry into the fellowship of faith. Confirmation seals in Jesus' gift of the Spirit which animates this communion. The Eucharist signifies and causes the unity of this communion by disclosing its key presupposition i.e., faith in Jesus' death and resurrection. Reconciliation continues Jesus' ministry of forgiveness. Anointing celebrates Jesus' ministry of healing. Marriage mirrors the relationship between Christ and his Church within the context of the deepest of human intimacies. Holy Orders continues the servant leadership of Jesus, drawing his followers closer and closer to the Father.

When the sacraments are celebrated the Church is celebrated, and Christ's saving ministry is continued. In fulfilling her missiological nature, the Church is being Christ's presence in history. As Christ realized his mission concretely and historically, the Church fulfills her mission in her concrete activities, especially in the sacraments. Christ, the Church, and the sacraments are not objects, ideas, or ideals. They are living, expressive, and dynamic organisms.

In our examination of "patterns of behavior," the goal of communal wholeness to social ritual activity stood out clearly. Ritual so structured behavior patterns that the quest for intimacy and communion was attained within the community. This chapter will focus on the Christian patterned behavior called sacraments. It will attempt to demonstrate that sacramental behavior has meaning in terms of establishing a real relationship to the ecclesial community, that sacramental behavior presupposes participation in the ecclesial community, and that sacramental behavior has as its first effect a specification of roles and relations within the Church communion. A reflection on the classical theorem of *sacramentum tantum, res et sacramentum, res tantum* in light of our anthropological data will guide this exploration.

The Theorem

Since the time of the great Scholastics, three elements have been identified within the composition of a sacrament: the *sacramentum tantum, res et sacramentum*, and the *res tantum*. Each term of the tripartate formula has a specific meaning and reference. The *sacramentum tantum* refers to the sign of the sacrament or the matter and form. In baptism, for example, the *sacramentum tantum* is the pouring of water and the recitation of the words "I baptize you. . . . " In the Eucharist, the *sacramentum tantum* is the bread and wine and the words of consecration. The *res tantum* refers to the final effect or the reality which becomes present in and through the sacramental celebration. This is nothing other than grace or participation in the life of the Trinity. The *res et sacramentum* is a reality produced prior to grace and distinct from it.[1] For baptism, confirmation, and holy orders, the *res et sacramentum* is called the sacramental character. For the other sacraments, it was called an embellishment or "ornation" of the soul.

A rather long and complex history preceded the final stabilization of this sacramental formula.[2] Its origins can be traced to the eucharistic controversy of the late eleventh century between Berengar, Lanfranc of Bec, Guitmund of La-Croix-St. Leofrey, and Alger of Liege. During this battle, the meaning and definition of the general term *sacramentum* began a process of refinement which later led to the explicit use of the tripartite formula by Anselm of Lyon in reference to the Eucharist. Peter Lombard later applied the formula to the other sacraments. It finally appears in an official ecclesiastical document, *Cum Marthae Circa*, by Pope Innocent III. In the theological schools of the thirteenth century, the formula's developed theological meaning appeared.

The medieval theologians did not aim at presenting a complete systematic sacramental theology by distinguishing three elements in a sacrament. They were simply carrying a theological position to its natural conclusion to avoid and correct potentially erroneous positions. It is startling to realize that any explicit Christology or ecclesiology is conspicuously absent from their sacramental teachings.

In fact, only several fragmentary truths have been indicated, for example, that Christ is the institutor of the sacraments and that the Church is their dispenser. In such a conception, therefore, the relationship between Christ, Church and the sacraments remains superficial and external, as though starting from Christ, one could arrive at the sacraments and their effects through the Church only *per accidens*, with no essential or intrinsic continuity among them.[3]

There was a profound truth, however, in the seminal insight of medieval theology. More contemporary theological reflection became its beneficiary.

Contemporary Interpretation

Nourished by Christological research and ecclesiological investigations, contemporary theology has corrected the lack of synthesis and correlation in the Scholastic sacramental treatises. One feature of the traditional tripartate formula has attracted special attention in the last decade, the *res et sacramentum* i.e., the reality produced prior to grace, distinct from it, yet entering into the attainment of grace.

Present theological reflection claims that the *res et sacramentum* is a "status in" or a "relationship to" the Church. Interestingly, this affirmation conforms not only to our presentation of sacraments as extensions of the Church's proclamation of the word of God, but also with the anthropological understanding of ritual's function within social groups. Two questions which flow from this contemporary theological claim circumscribe its elaboration. First, why does the *res et sacramentum* establish a status in the Church? Second, how do the behavioral studies on ritual evaluate this theological contention?

Sacramental activity contains a dual movement. God reaches down to humankind with his self-gift, inviting humankind to participation in his life. At the same time, the sacramental recipient ascends to God in his or her worship of the divine. Primacy and priority are attached to the descending movement of God, the initiator of the process. The worship character of the sacraments, even if secondary to the divine action, is intrinsic and constitutive to the sacramental process.

Jesus is the crossroad of the dual movements in sacramental activity. He is both God's self-gift and humankind's acceptance in worship. Offer and acceptance are unified in his person. This concurrence permeates his whole life, but is crystalized in his death and resurrection. In this event, the convergence of gift and worshiper becomes perfectly focused.

The real event of Jesus' embracing death in fulfillment of the Father's will is also the Father's vehicle for offering humankind a participation in his life and humankind's definitive acceptance of his offer in the pinnacle of worship. Christ's death, as the supreme act of worship, becomes clear when contextualized within the biblical understanding and meaning of worship. As previously noted, God issued three commands to those who were to be his people: to be a sign of his love, to offer true worship, and to care for the poor. By fulfilling the first and third of these responsibilities, Israel would fulfill the second. God did not require burnt offerings of slain animals as worship. His demand was more radical. Israel's worship was to be nothing less than an offering of their total selves. Their worship was to be a total dedication to the mission God assigned to them. The prophets condemned Israel for not worshiping God with this total commitment and dedication, especially in their neglect of social justice.

The New Testament writers depict Jesus as fulfilling God's demand for worship. He attained the perfection and fullness of divine worship in his death, in "laying down his life for his friends." Jesus' death was his total commitment to the service of the father. In a radical sense, there was nothing more to give. On Calvary, the irreversible, unsurpassable, and archetypical pattern of divine worship as obedience to God's will was definitively established.

If Christ's death is paradigmatic for worship of God, all human persons must travel the road to Calvary to fully worship the Father. Any form of divine worship is intrinsically and necessarily a participation in the Christological action of the "priest-victim" of Golgotha. This vision implies that there must be an access for men and women to be conjoined to the worshiping Christ. There must be a vehicle for humankind to participate in the death and resurrection of Christ, his great act of worship. The Church as Christ's presence in the world is this vehicle, especially when the Church celebrates the memorial of his death and resurrection, the Eucharist.

Participation in Christ's worship of the Father, which is also the acceptance of God's offer of salvation, has as an a priori participation or membership in the community called Church. As a member of the ecclesial community an individual is bound to Christ. Participation in divine life, or grace, is attained because the members of the Church have been conjoined to Christ's worship of the Father in the celebration of sacramental rituals.

> God does not simply give grace to the recipient of the sacrament, but first of all he makes him his cooperator in the salvation of the world, that is, co-offerer of the Mass. Precisely in, through and because of this

cooperation He makes him holy—this is the strict meaning of sacramental participation in divine worship in the present economy.[4]

A contemporary theology of the sacraments of Christian initiation verifies and further explains this scheme.

Baptism, confirmation, and the Eucharist all focus on incorporation into the death and resurrection of Christ and therefore, a deeper penetration and participation in the central faith-mystery which is the basis for the Church. Each of these sacraments effects a real change in one's relationship to or within the Church. At the core of this change lies one's status or role in the ecclesial community, especially in terms of its head, the Calvary Christ. What is this status or role? It is the *res et sacramentum*, the reality produced in sacramental behavior prior to grace, distinct from it, yet preparatory to grace.

> . . . the *res et sacramentum* is a habitual sacramental participation of the recipient in Christ the mediator, and an ontological incorporation into the Church of the Mass, so that through the reception of the sacrament the individual obtains a seven-fold *status* in the visible Church and becomes a habitual offerer of the Mass in participation in Christ the Priest-Victim.[5]

If the *res et sacramentum* is a participation in Christ's worship of the Father, and the Church is the extension of the worshiping Christ in the world, the *res et sacramentum*, by necessity, affects an individual's relationship to the Church.

A distinctive characteristic can be identified in the ecclesial status effected in the celebration of the different sacraments. In baptism i.e., infant baptism, a person becomes a passive offerer of the Eucharist. In confirmation, a person is designated as an active celebrator of the Eucharist. Holy Orders constitutes an individual as a public presider and minister of the eucharistic meal. Reconciliation makes one a contrite and therefore fruitful celebrator of the Eucharist. Anointing of the sick allows participation in the Eucharist as a fellow-sufferer with Christ. Marriage makes one a special offerer through conjugal love and family life. The Eucharist binds one physically and corporeally to the worshiping Christ as head of the Church who is sacramentally present.

If the schematic relation of Christ-Church sacraments is an accurate interpretation, the *res et sacramentum* cannot be a mere interpolation of data, but an essential insight for a sacramental synthesis. The cornerstone for this synthesis is the death and resurrection of Jesus. This event is concurrently his act of worship, God's offer of salvation, the reality continued in the Church, the event to which sacramental participants are related and conjoined in various modalities by the different sacraments, and the source and goal of all sacramental behavior.

It is one thing to assert that the *res et sacramentum* is a status or relation to the Church. It is quite a different issue to ask how the status or relation comes about or is established. For example, one can claim that the sacraments of Christian initiation make a person a full member of the Christian community. It is quite another task to describe how these sacramental behaviors effect membership.

An answer to the question of how sacramental behavior forms a status or effects membership in the Church can be found in the anthropological understanding of ritual. By applying our previous anthropological data on ritual to the rituals of the Christian community called sacraments, it is possible to uncover and isolate their power for effecting status and membership.

Prior to institutionalization, rituals act out or express attitudes, spirit, or feelings present within the social group. After institutionalization, rituals elicit from the members of the ritual community feelings, emotions, and behavior. In the present investigation of sacraments, they are to be understood as institutionalized in a strictly sociological sense. As formalized or institutionalized rituals, sacraments exhibit the characteristics of rituals, be they secular or religious.

A dynamic interplay between the individual, social group or "pseudo-species," and a lived experience-interpretation-expression of the meaning of human existence lies at the heart of formalized ritual. The vital exchange operative in the process of entrance into and continued existence within the world view of a particular community creates, integrates and reinforces an individual's relation to the social group and by necessity the various roles and status within the community. This fundamental affirmation describes in non-theological terms the proposed contemporary understanding of the ecclesial nature of the *res et sacramentum*.

The data uncovered in the investigation of the anthropological dimensions of ritual coalesces around relations and status between an individual and a community. Anthropological and sociological observation reveals the power of ritual to foster group communication, reduce and control intra-group conflict, and strengthen group identity and social bonding. Theoretical reflection penetrates the depths of the phenomenological data and notes that beneath any individual ritual situation, performance, or behavior, lies an attempted resolution of binary oppositions. It is ritual itself that fosters the resolution of these opposing forces by combining cognitive, motor, and volitional behavior to construct a more or less comprehensive vision of life among members of the ritual community. Ritual, at the same time, serves as the vehicle by which the communities' world view is mediated to new members and kept intact among the communities' previously indoctrinated constituency.

Whatever dimension of ritual might be selected for analysis, the mediation of a world view engendering and supporting integration amid the fracturing tendency of binary oppositions remains a constant constitutive element. A cursory reference to both psychological maturation and patterns of behavior bear this out.

A variety of rituals, spanning infancy to adulthood, support the realization of personality integration and maturation. The "negation of the ideal self," so intrinsically necessary for self-growth and interpersonal relations, finds its inception, continuance, and completion in and through rituals which open the path to communion with other members of the "pseudospecies." The various patterns of behavior operative in social groups testify to the efficacy of ritual's reinforcement of a community's world view expressed in their social drama. For example, the "way of intimacy" demonstrates the potency of the imagination's power in forming a community bond grounded in an original charter-event which is continually expressed and reenacted in ritual celebrations. The repetitive character of these ritual celebrations arises from the need for shared identity among the members of the social group and leads to legal prescriptions to ensure its achievement. The "way of social operationalism" records the invitation to deepen participation into the unitarian life of the community. The "way of interiorization" witnesses a community expectation that certain roles assumed within the group must transcend the purely functional and become personalized or biographical. A judge, for example, is expected to live as an upright law-abiding individual, or a priest is expected to emulate the values of a "holy" life.

Particular examples of the relational character of rituals could be multiplied indefinitely. More important than any individual example, however, is the perception of the interplay between the individual and the group and social roles effected by ritual behavior. Ritual essentially supplies the means for indoctrination, position, and correct relations within the ritual community. This is evident in a brief examination of the initiation process in any society or community. To remain as close as possible to our primary area of interest, initiation into the Church during the era of the great catechumenates of the second to sixth centuries is selected as an explanatory case.[6]

Three consistent structural elements emerge from a cross-cultural comparison of initiation processes: first, a separation from the old or former way of life; second, a period of indoctrination and testing whereby the community's world view and internal relations are introduced to the candidates for admission and a process of evaluation is applied to the candidates; and finally, the performance of rituals which celebrate the successful completion of the initiation process and terminate in the candidate's incorporation into the community with the accompanying rights of membership. This basic pattern was operative in the process of Christian initiation during the patristic age.

The basic scheme of separation, indoctrination, and incorporation was present in the great catechumenates. Those wishing to enroll as catechumens were to relinquish all ties with former employment or entertainment which was incommensurate with the Christian way of life, for example, service in the military or presence at the "Roman Games." After the fundamental sincerity of the candidates was ascertained, they were officially enrolled in the order of the catechumenate and began a process of indoctrination often referred to as illumination or enlightenment. During the period of indoctrination, which usually lasted three years, the candidates underwent both intellectual and spiritual formation in the world view and lifestyle of the Christian community. During Lent of the third year, those catechumens who applied and were judged worthy for full membership in the community entered an intensified process of spiritual formation which included the handing over of the Lord's Prayer and the Apostles Creed. At the Easter vigil, the high feast celebrating the central mystery of the Christian community's interpretation of human existence, the "elect," as they were called, completed the initiation process by celebrating the rituals of baptism, confirmation, and the Eucharist. Upon completion of these rituals, the candidates had become full members of the community as expressed by their participation in the rights of membership, i.e., the sacraments of initiation, especially the Eucharist.

Closer observation of elements in the initiation process of the catechumenate can clarify the power of ritual to establish relations and status within a ritual community. First, after enrollment in the catechumenate, the catechumen was in a passive, learning position, vis-à-vis those who were already members of the community. This was true not only in the formal sessions and gatherings of the catechumens, but also in the ritual celebrations of the community. The catechumens participated in the celebration of the Eucharist until the completion of the homily or instruction, at which time they left the celebration. The catechumens were not yet full members and were, therefore, prohibited from participation in the sign of full membership. They were considered members *in fieri*, in the making. The various prayers, blessings, and exorcisms recited over the catechumens in the name of the community by the various catechists, deacons, priests, and bishop bore similar witness to the status of the catechumens in relation to the community. With the candidates' gradual progression through the stages of the catechumenate, participation in the ritual of the community became intensified. The community entrusted more and more of its beliefs to the catecumens' care, e.g., the Lord's Prayer and the Creed. As ritual participation intensified, the catechumen was recognized more and more as one of the community's own.

What might appear as a hesitant attitude in the early Church by today's standards and practices was really the early Church's means of self-protection. Indoctrination of candidates for membership in the world view and lifestyle of the Christian community was an insurance of the continued health, integration and existence of the community. Without a process of indoctrination new members would pose a constant threat of internal conflict within the community.

The catechumenate placed the candidates in a relation among themselves as well as to full members of the community. The candidates were *liminal* persons and shared a bond with one another, characteristic of *communitas*. The catechumens as *liminal* persons fell between the normal positions assigned by law, custom or convention. They were neither pagans nor full members of the Christian community. In their liminal position, they participated in a bond of *communitas*, i.e., in an undifferentiated, equalitarian, direct, non-rational, existential, I-Thou relationship over and beyond any formal social bond. Vis-à-vis, the social bond of the initiated members of the Christian community, the catechumens stood as an anti-structure. The catechumenate as anti-structure in relation to Christian community as structure comprised the fertile Christian social drama. The catechumens' need for incorporation and indoctrination forced the community at large to reflect upon its own appreciation of the Christian world view and recognize the common bond which united them as a community (*gemeinschaft*) before the differentiating structures of Christian society (*gesellschaft*). The rituals of the Christian initiation process mediated the tension between structure and anti-structure. They required a return to the primordial experience or charter-event of the Christian community by both old and "new" members, and, at the same time introduced the "new" members into the existing social structure with its status and relations.

An investigation of the catechumenate also depicts the presence and operation of specific roles in the Christian community. Beyond the primordial unity of Christians, there were those in positions of leadership, education and administrative service. Catechists, deacons, priests, and bishop were specifically charged with the mediation of the community's world view to the catechumens and an evaluation of its acceptance by the catechumens. They were to exercise their functional role within the Christian community in the catechumenate, which in a real sense ensured its recognition once the catechumens had become full members. It is essential to bear in mind that the specialized role of these ministers was expressed not only in their cognitive status as teachers, but also, and more importantly, by their status in ritual celebrations. The correspondence between a particular status within the community and an expression, in fact a creation, of this status in ritual permeated the whole ecclesial milieu of the Patristic Church. "Confessors," those who were destined to be martyred for the faith but survived, were placed among the priests during the celebration of the Eucharist without any laying on of hands by the clergy. They were considered to have already been "ordained" by the Holy Spirit. Penitents were grouped together in the *Ordo Penitentis* where they prayed and fasted and underwent the rituals of reincorporation into the community.

From our example of Christian initiation, it should be clear that these sacramental behaviors created a status in and relation to the ecclesial community precisely because they were ritual behavior. Social status and social relations were expressed ritually, and ritual established and reinforced social relations and status. Herein lies the theological meaning of the *res et sacramentum* and the reason for its power or effectiveness.

Conclusion

The medieval Scholastic's division of a sacrament into three components was born from a need to avoid erroneous positions. In identifying the *res et sacramentum*, however, they forged a new ground which contemporary sacramental theologians have employed in their insistence on the essentially ecclesial and communal nature of the sacraments. This essential characteristic of the sacraments could be arrived at from a reflection on the word of God. To turn one's attettion to the *res et sacramentum*, however, adds further support to the contention.

Although contemporary sacramental theologians have capitalized on the medieval theorem, they have only pointed out that sacramental behavior establishes a "status in" or "relation to" the Church. They never explain how this is achieved. Once sacramental behavior is analyzed in terms of an anthropological understanding of ritual, the "how" can be properly understood.

Sacraments as religious rituals bear the power of all rituals within the context of their unique community. They effect "status in" or "relation to" the community precisely in their being ritual behavior. An anthropological understanding of ritual fills the theological gap on the issue of "how" the *res et sacramentum* comes about and functions.

Beyond the theological value of investigating sacramental behavior as an ecclesial and communal relationship, serious attention should be given to another *line of convergence* between the anthropological dimension of ritual and the theological claims about sacraments. The anthropological claims find collaborative evidence in a contemporary theological understanding of sacramental behavior. Moreover, the anthropological data permits a more complete and theologically sound exposition of sacramental behavior.

NOTES

1. Cf. Toshiyuki Miyakawa, "The Ecclesial Meaning of the 'Res et Sacramentum'," *The Thomist* 31 (1967), p. 386ff.

2. Cf. R. King, "The Origin and Evolution of a Sacramental Formula: Sacramentum Tantum, Res et Sacramentum, Res Tantum," *The Thomist* 31 (1967), pp. 21–82.

3. Miyakawa, pp. 381–382.

4. *Ibid.*, pp. 398–399.

5. *Ibid.*, p. 413.

6. For further examples within non-Christian cultures cf. Turner, *The Ritual Process*, pp. 5–43, and *Dreams, Fields and Metaphors*, pp. 166–271.

10 GRACE AND THE SACRAMENTS

There is, perhaps, no more elusive term in the whole spectrum of theological language than "grace." A survey of theological texts and manuals will find references to sanctifying, actual, infused, habitual, uncreated and created grace. If there is to be any understanding of the relation of sacraments and grace, a clarification of the meaning of the latter term is in order. The Belgian theologian, P. Fransen, knows the language problem well, and has cut through the verbal jungle. He writes:

> The theology of grace is in the main, the theology of God's love for us and of the love which God's first love has caused in us. *Grace* is the English word for the Latin *gratia*. Now *gratia* has acquired many secondary meanings, both in the technical language of the theologians and in the usage of the Church and the great Councils; but its prime Christian meaning comes from Scripture. The Latin Vulgate used *gratia* to translate the Greek word *charis*. All the sacred authors of the New Testament, Paul in particular, have borrowed from the Septuagint the term *charis* to render several Hebrew words conveying meanings reducible to three main ideas: condescending love, conciliatory compassion and fidelity. The basic sense of Christian grace, whatever its later and further technical or non-Scholastic connotations, should always remind us that God first loved us. Let that be its fundamental chord.[1]

Whatever title might be ascribed to the term grace, the reality expressed by the term is always the same: the life of God, Father, Son, and Holy Spirit offered to humankind as a free gift. Theological reflection on the reality of grace, however, has varied between the Eastern and the Western traditions throughout the centuries, between Catholics and Protestants since the Reformation. These different thrusts and interpretations have prevailed into our own age. Even in the Western tradition itself, minor and major shifts of emphasis dot the historical chart. Without becoming entangled in the complex history of the theology of grace, this chapter will examine three key issues: created-uncreated grace, grace as a communal phenomenon, and the sacramental causality of grace.

Created-Uncreated Grace

The distinction between created and uncreated grace is absent in the entire Eastern theological tradition and before the eleventh century in the West. Theologians were content to utilize the previous rich and fluid biblical-patristic understanding of *charis*. Grace was the relationship with a personal God historically revealed as Father, Son, and Spirit.

Disputes on infant baptism, the status of heretics, remaining in the state of grace without continual acts of faith and charity, etc., forced the Western theological tradition to analyze and clarify its understanding of *charis*. A tradition emerged which distinguished created and uncreated grace. Unfortunately, it often neglected the earlier vision of grace as an interpersonal relationship. Later, it vehemently reacted against the Protestant Reformer's teaching on grace and adopted a polemical, narrow, and stagnant interpretation of Trent's "Decree on Justification ." These two deficiencies impoverished the Western Catholic theological understanding of grace for five centuries. Created grace became little more than a quantitative reality individuals possessed. Overly sentimental and pietistic attitudes became embedded in the popular mentality on grace. Sacraments came dangerously close to being mere "grace machines" automatically dispensing "grace" to those not in sin. "The doctrine of grace, as set forth in classrooms and textbooks, was reduced to an uninviting short chapter on what had come to be called 'sanctifying grace,' and long chapters dealing with the endless disputes on the subject of 'actual grace.'"[2]

The "demise" of grace ended in the 1940's. Through the work of Maurice de la Taille, Karl Rahner, and Piet Fransen, the Western theological tradition slowly recovered the lost treasures of the biblical-patristic tradition. It is their rich understanding of grace which captures our imagination in exploring the theological dimension of sacraments. *Charis*, grace, is the final end, the *res tantum*, of sacramental behavior.

The distinction between created and uncreated grace arises from the assumption of differing vantage points i.e., whether one concentrates on the offer God makes to humankind or on the effect this offer realizes.

In theology, *uncreated grace* stands for God himself insofar as he communicates himself to man in love; in contradistinction to this, *created grace* signifies the effect God's self-communication produces on man. Evidently that result cannot be God himself; therefore it is something other than God, something created, a gift from God.[3]

Whether grace is viewed as God's offer or as the effect of the offer, a relational historical personal presence is implied. The offer is not made by an unknown, depersonalized, totally extra-historical power, but by the immanent Trinity expressed in history. Grace as a created relationship is neither notional nor abstract, but a real relationship with the Father, Son, and Spirit.

Uncreated grace is a totally gratuitous offer by God of his own life to humankind. It is the personal trinitarian love God brings to us. This love is thoroughly historical. It has been tied to the Incarnation of the Father's Son as the man Jesus who wins and offers salvation in his death and resurrection, and to the perduring presence of the Spirit in history until the end of time. Uncreated grace is the presence of the Trinity reaching down to us in the events of life, bidding us to accept their personal offer of mysterical and mysterious interpersonal love.

Created grace can be understood as distinct from the self-gift of Father, Son, and Spirit, but never in a fashion separate from reference to and origination in this prior and primary unity. "It is to be thought of only *within* and not *next to* or apart from the mystery of the trinitarian indwelling in us."[4] Created grace is the effect of the Trinity pitching their tent among us, transforming our sinful fractured existence into the full wholeness, harmony and integrity of our human destiny and potential.

Created grace is not the effect of the Godhead in its unity of nature, but in its historical manifestation. "It is the Father, the Son and the Holy Spirit, not as distinct but as it were interchangeable persons, but as they have revealed themselves to us, that is in the primordial originality of their reciprocal relations and properties."[5] Created grace is our relation to the Father as the origin and completion of all reality. It is our relation to the Son as the image of the Father i.e., the archetype of all creation, the loving and obedient servant. It is our relation to the Spirit who directs humankind outward to the world as witnesses to the Father's Son and inward to the depths of their hearts so that they will cling with total fidelity to the living God.

Many different terms have been marshalled in theological discourse to indentify the effect of God's presence on humankind. They all point, however, to one reality: that through grace we share in the gift of divine life. Participation in divine life is by necessity relational, corresponding to the relational existence of the Trinity. There is a relation to Christ who imprints his image on us and in whom we become servants and sons and daughters of the Father, through the power of the Spirit. This relationship to Christ effects a real healing and elevation in us.

From our estranged human condition, God takes us up into his glory. The wounds inflicted by sin are healed. This healing is not imaginary, but real. Grace does not merely rearrange the surface of our lives, nor is it an "overlooking" of sins, nor a decision "not to imput" our sins. The effect of grace reaches to the depths of our very being to radically attack the source of all alienation and sin i.e., egocentrism. By becoming servants in and with Christ, egocentrism is destroyed by relationship. Our inner selves are adapted by the Father's gratuitous forgiveness and our proper relation to God and one another is restored.

Grace affects more than healing. It also elevates us by making us sons and daughters of the Father. This is the *supernatural* effect of God's gift of self. As sons in the Son, we participate in divine life. As the Greek Fathers noted, we are divinized. This would be impossible under our own power. But the healing of the Father's forgiveness makes us his children by uniting us to his Son. In grace, God becomes *Abba*, Father. In grace, we live his life.

Our immediate union with Christ is also an immediate union with the Father and the Holy Spirit. It would be difficult to improve on Fransen's lucid description:

> The immediate union with the Son brings with it a union with the Father and with the Holy Spirit; both these unions are likewise immediate, and both bear the mark of the characteristic property of the respective divine persons.

> The origin of all grace can be traced to the election by the Father. To him belongs the initiative in granting grace. And as the prime cause he is also the ultimate end; we are called to the Father as the final goal of all grace. He calls us to himself through grace by adopting us as his children, by uniting us with his Son, by extending the inner trinitarian relationship of Fatherhood to us, wherever we are—or better, by assuming us as adopted children into his relations of love with his Son. His divine "I," which from all eternity utters to his a loving "Thou," is addressed to us as well; He raises us and unites us with his Son, saying, "You are my well-beloved sons." And this precisely is the life of grace. . . .

> The Holy Spirit reveals his own personality in us. It is through the power of the Holy Spirit that the Father impresses the image of the Son on us. In his role as Spirit of the father and the Son, he existentially actual-

izes this image and carries it to the perfection and fulfillment of a personal acceptance. This he does in a twofold manner. First, inwardly he moves us, joined with the Son, to union with the Father in an upward filial surrender, directing us to the Father and "driving" us on in faith, hope and charity. Second he simultaneously animates us to display outwardly a complete "obedience to the faith" by our Christian witnessing.[6]

Clearly, the relational character of the effect of grace (created grace) reflects the relational character of the original gift (uncreated grace), the life of the Blessed Trinity. God coming to us as Father, Son, and Spirit simultaneously changes us from within so that we hunger for his love of which he makes us partakers. Created grace originates, continues, and is completed in the indwelling of the Trinity.

Grace as a Communal Phenomenon

To stress the interpersonal character of grace as a relationship between the Father, Son, and Spirit and an individual should not lead to a categorization of grace as an individualistic affair. Grace is an active love of God for an individual in the wholeness of his or her personhood. At the same time, this active love of God binds individuals together in an inseparable union of participated love expressed in the *koinonia*, Church fellowship. Individual participation in divine life and ecclesial fellowship are two inseparable aspects of the one reality of grace, especially in the context of sacraments.

The insistence of a solidarity or fellowship in grace finds support on many levels of reflection. The data accruing from an investigation of ritual in psychology, sociology, and anthropology converged on the *existential fact* of human interrelatedness and solidarity. An individual stands alone in the world. Every man and woman participates in the greater family of humankind. Therefore, if a man or woman stands before God, this presence must always be in some fashion a corporate presence of all who form the human family.

From a theological perspective, the interpersonal character of human existence participates in and reflects the interpersonal character of God. The individual persons of God are so for and in each other that they are intensely themselves. The Father so loves the Son that nothing of the Son is negated or lost. This mutual non-destructive love spirates the Spirit who likewise remains a distinct person. The human person, formed in the image and likeness of God, parallels the characteristics of love present in God. In reaching out to the other, an individual discovers and realizes his or her true self. No one can omit *interpersonal coexistential love* without truncating his or her very self. The paradox of God is the paradox of man and woman. What appears to imply self-abrogation is the only real path to self-discovery and integrity. God is God in the absolute quality of his interpersonal love. Man becomes man in his interpersonal love. If grace is the indwelling of God, and the characteristic of God is interpersonal love, one should expect that an individual's participation in divine life will draw him or her more deeply into communion and solidarity with those who likewise share the divine gift. This vision is woven throughout the Hebrew and Christian Scriptures.

In the Hebrew Scriptures, God offers mercy and faithful love to Israel, if she will enter into a covenant with him. God will be *gracious* to his people. It is essential to notice that the covenantal promise and response is made primarily to the whole people. The Hebrew Bible presents the great divine saving act as the actual formation of Israel into God's people. In bringing Israel into existence and forming them as a people, God calls them his own and saves them. This is evident in the titles ascribed to Israel: *laos tou theou*, the people of God, and *ekklesia tou theou*, the assembled of God.

The solidarity of Israel, vis-à-vis the covenant and grace, finds lucid expression in both the criticism and the vision of its prophetic tradition. Israel's sin is not merely the failure of individuals to remain faithful to the covenant, but their turning from God as a whole people. As a nation, Israel transgressed the covenant stipulations. The positive vision of the prophets is likewise corporate. The hoped for destiny portrayed by the prophets is a positive attestation that Israel as a nation would return to the covenant. Moreover, all nations on earth would be joined with them at the banquet of the great king.

The Christian Scriptures continue the notions of solidarity and community underpinning the Old Testament. In the New Testament, Jesus is presented as proclaiming and ushering in the Age of the Kingdom. In this age all nations are invited to participate in the reign of his Father. Christ is this kingdom enfleshed in human history. He is the living expression of the Father's kingship. He fulfills the prophetic hopes. By drawing and acquiring a people to himself for the father through the power of the Spirit, he wins and effects redemption for both Jew and Greek.

The historical gift of Jesus to humankind is the gift of trinitarian love and the effect of this gift is participation in trinitarian love. The kingdom, as already begun yet not fully realized, is life under the rule and reign of trinitarian love. This is the radical basis for Christian existence. Love is the law of the kingdom. The acceptance of the Father's kingship is manifested and expressed in the love of persons one for the other. Love of the neighbor is the measure of loving God. Of this, Christ is the prototype. As the first Epistle of John beautifully explains:

> Beloved, let us love one another because love is of God; everyone who loves is begotten of God and has knowledge of God. The man without love has known nothing of God, for God is love. God's love was revealed in our midst in this way: He sent his only Son to the world that we might have life through him. Love then consists in this: not that we have loved God, but that he has loved us and sent his Son as as offering for our sins. Beloved, if God has loved us so, we must have the same love for one another. . . . God is love and he who abides in love abides in God, and God in him. Our love is brought to perfection in this, that we should have confidence on the day of judgment, for our relation to the world is just like his. Love has no room for fear; rather, perfect love casts out all fear. And since fear has to do with punishment, love is not yet perfect in one who is afraid. We, for our part, love because he first loved us. If anyone says, "My love is fixed on God," yet hates his brother, he is a liar. One who has no love for the brother he has seen, cannot love the God he has not seen. The commandment we have from him is this: whoever loves God must also love his brother. (1John 4:7-21).

Participation in the kingdom of God effects a common brotherhood and living fellowship among persons. God as Father, Son, and Spirit has come to humankind with open arms to embrace and draw all people into the unity of his heart. The loving God is the radical basis for the ecclesial *koinonia*.

The first visible manifestation and realization of the kingdom of God proclaimed by Christ was the faith and presence of those who believed in him as the revelation of the Father. He formed these believers into a community. God's love was for each of these individuals, but never apart from his love for the whole community. The indwelling of the Trinity fashioned a bond of grace that was the source of unity among them.

There is an essential link between an individual's participation in the life of the Trinity and a relation to the community formed by Christ's redemptive actions. Grace and Church are not indifferent realities. They share a common origin and goal. By definition, grace is the free offer of God's love made in Christ, especially in his death–resurrection. This charter-event is the basis and center of the Christian world view. For Christians, therefore, it is inconceivable that grace should ever stand apart from Christ. He is the mediator of immediate grace. He is the visibility of "invisible grace."

An "invisible" and a "visible" aspect can be detected in grace. "Invisible" grace is the Father, Son, and Spirit coming to us in an immediate fashion, and, in our acceptance, an immediate participation in their life of love is realized. "Visible" grace is the mode or form through which the offer is made. To the extent that grace is "visible," it is mediated.

The visible mediated character of grace is not an appendage to a doctrine of grace, but arises from the structure of human existence. God's self-gift was made in the historical Jesus. The Incarnation represents the definitive mode of God's participation in the human world. If all shades of Docetism are to be avoided, the humanity of Christ as the structural norm of the relation between God and humankind must be taken seriously. "Visibility," bodiliness, and corporeality are intrinsic to the revelation and self-communication of God. If humankind is to "hear," "see," "feel," "know," etc., God, there are a priori structures to the human person which necessitate that the relevation and self-communication of God exist within space and time, place and history. This requires mediation or "visibility."

In the time of the historical Jesus, grace was mediated through his person. After his death, the need remained for "invisible" grace to be visibly mediated and constitutively tied to him as the definitive and final revelation and way to the Father through the power of the Spirit. It is our contention that the continuing mediation of grace is bound to humankind in general and the fellowship of the Church in particular.

Our previous presentation of the relationship of Christ and the Church offers evidence for the Church's role in continuing the mediation of grace. First, the ecclesial community is the manifestation of the kingdom's arrival. The *koinonia* characteristic and constitutive of its members is the effect of their participation in the life of the Trinity. Second, Christ wins redemption by gathering this people together and continually offering them to the Father as his own. Their being together as a *koinonia* is the manifestation of continuing redemption and grace in the world. Third, the Church is the continuing mode of Christ's ministry of redemption by being a sign to the nations of the Father's love, visibly and historically demonstrated in love for one another and all who cross their path. In short, the Church is the continuing mediation of "invisible" grace by being the visible manifestation and presence of the now "invisible" Christ.

No attempt is being made here to usurp or replace Christ as the sole mediator of immediate grace. There is no substitute for Christ and there can never be. We are demanding, however, that the necessity of the visible manifestation of grace demands a visible presence of Christ. The Church has this mission and responsibility from its author and head, Christ.

The visibility of the Church implies that it is a structured society, a *gesellschaft*. As the visible presence of Christ, the mediator of grace, the Church is also a communion, a *gemeinschaft*. It is on the level of ecclesial communion, ecclesial *koinonia*, that the witness to and effect of grace shine within the ecclesial body.

The "summary" statements in the Acts of the Apostles (2:42–47; 4:32–35; 5:12–16) describe three predominant characteristics of the Jerusalem Christian communion. They break bread in memory of the Lord, share all things in common, and care for the poor. In non-theological terms, this community is characterized by the sociological notes of *communitas* and primary groups. Communitas is the bond uniting individuals over and above any formal bond established by social structure. Before any differentiation of roles or ministries within the ecclesial organism, there is first the unity and equality of all who have come to believe that Jesus is Lord. On this level, the main characteristics or primary groups are exhibited. The members coexist in face to face association. The associations are unspecialized. There is an intimacy and permanence among the members.

The basis for communitas in the Christian fellowship is the indwelling of the Trinity which binds its members together under the power of the Spirit. This unity is expressed in the great Christian symbol of the Eucharist, the body and blood of Christ. This is marvelously expressed by St. Paul in 1 Corinthians 10:17, "We, though many, are one body, because we partake of the one bread," and the ancient eucharistic prayer of the Didache:

> Just as this bread which we break, once scattered over the hills, has been gathered and made one, so may the Church too be assembled from the ends of the earth into thy kingdom. For glory and power are thine forever.[7]

The Christian *koinonia* as *communitas* and primary group is the visible mediating mode of God's offer of grace through the one mediator, Christ. As communion, fellowship, or *gemeinschaft*, the Church enters into and participates in the dynamic self-communication of God and its realization in the indwelling of the Trinity.

Grace is not restricted to the ecclesial sacramental system. Grace exists outside the sacraments, the same grace that exists within them. Since our specific concern is the relationship between grace and the sacraments, however, we will concentrate on *how* the Christian fellowship enters into the mystery of the indwelling of the Trinity vis-à-vis its members. To accomplish this, a return to the sacramental formula *sacramentum tantum, res et sacramentum, res tantum* is necessary.

The *res et sacramentum* is a relation to or status within the Church. It is prior to, yet involved in, the efficacy of grace. Consequently, the ecclesial community participates in the "effecting" of grace in its sacramental celebrations i.e., the *sacramentum tantum*. Incorporation into or deepening participation within the ecclesial fellowship is the vehicle by which God's self-communication is accomplished within sacramental celebrations. This conclusion is necessary since the very communion into which one is incorporated or more intensely bound has the Trinity as its foundation and the indwelling of the Trinity is grace, the *res tantum* of the sacraments.

The Christian fellowship of love is the effect of God's love present within the members of the Church. The love expressed by these members is not merely a human love, but a love perfected by God in the sacramental celebrations. The *koinonia* constitutive of membership in the Church is simultaneously the effect of participation in the life of the Trinity.

The *sacramentum tantum* is the symbolic ritualization by the ecclesial *koinonia* of God's presence among his people. In this expression, the Church realizes what it is charged to be i.e., a fellowship with Christ as its head and center. Ritualization also realizes the *koinonia* by being the gathered community of Christ drawing its members deeper into the mystery of Trinitarian love. This is the *res et sacramentum* of the Christian sacraments. By being related to the Church, one is placed within the locus and opened to the love of God or grace, the *res tantum*.

There is nothing less here than the living organism of the mystery of redemption continually unfolding in the historical pattern established in the paradigmatic Christ-event. In being bound to the fellowship, which has its origin in the Trinity, Christians participate more deeply in this divine mystery. Increased participation leads them to renewed and recurring expression in symbolic rituals.

The sacraments of Christian initiation exemplify the relationship between the *res et sacramentum* and *res tantum* we have attempted to describe and refine. The Christian tradition is cognizant of a fundamental opposition between sin and grace. Before entrance into the Christian community, an individual is viewed as harnessed by sin, whether "original" or personal. The designation "original" refers to a condition present in every person before free decision or choice which radically affects their existence. "Original sin" is a real condition of being estranged from God. It is the absence of the indwelling of the Trinity which is the ultimate destiny of every person. Personal sin refers to this same void, but arises from free choice and decision on the part of the individual. In either or both cases, the reality inoperative in an individual is the active-accepted loving presence of the indwelling God.

Both "original sin" and grace are mediated realities. "Original sin" is mediated by the world, society, or social structures that present the meaning of life and a value system judged alien by the Christian tradition. Grace is mediated by Christ through his visibility, the Christian community.

How does one move from "original sin" to grace? In the first place, the movement is already the free activity of the invisible God calling an individual to himself, and at the same time, the visibility of Christ's Church introducing an individual to the Christian paradigm of existence and making him or her a member of this community through the process of Christian initiation.

The process of Christian initiation demands a separation from the former way of life and the world view which underpinned it. It establishes a period of indoctrination, examination, and testing designed to remake an individual as a member of the Christian "pseudospecies." It celebrates rituals which express the new reality the individual has become in the Church through the activity of God and Christ's Church.

During the period of indoctrination, the individual is truly being bound more and more deeply to the fellowship of the Christian community, since his or her acceptance of the self-communication of God is through the acceptance of the world view of the Christian community. The growing intensification of membership reaches a climax—when the individual and the Christian community concurrently discover "I am," he/she is a Christian. This is effected by the indwelling of the Trinity, recognized by the community, and expressed in the ritual of Christian baptism. In a real sense, grace (*res tantum*) is being made a member of the Christian community (*sacramentum et res*), celebrated (*sacramentum tantum*) in the sacraments of Christian initiation.

Sacramental Efficacy

Grace is God himself, Father, Son, and Spirit dwelling within and individual. Grace is both individual and communal, immediate and mediated. One question remains on the relationship between grace and the sacraments. How do they affect grace? This issue has been the great stumbling block of sacramentology. A correct understanding of grace as a relational reality coupled with an understanding of sacraments enriched by an anthropological understanding of ritual, allows a possible explanation which avoids the danger of mechanical causality.

The distinguishing feature between "sacramentalists" and "non-sacramentalists" usually emerges on the issue of sacramental causality or efficacy.[8] Sacramentalists are committed to the fundamental law of sacramentology: *significando efficiunt and efficiendo significant* i.e., the sacraments signify what they affect and affect what they signify. Non-sacramentalists usually reject this theorem.

Unfortunately, the discussion over sacramental efficacy has been marred by polemics, misunderstandings and over-simplified explanations. It is well advised to attempt a clarification of terms involved in an analysis of sacramental causality, especially the term *opus operatum*, or *ex opere operato* as it is more commonly known.

The term *opus operatum* pre-dated the Council of Trent. It exerted a strong influence on the medieval concept of sacraments. From the time of Trent, however, it became a hallmark of religious polemics between Catholics and Protestants. Every Catholics from this time onward learned that the sacraments "produce" or effect grace *ex opere operato*. In opposition to this Catholic slogan, the Protestants raised their own cry of *Sola Fidei. The Protestants, above and beyond the polity of polemics, were concerned that the Catholic position removed God's freedom and the gratuity of his gift by binding him to an external rite. Catholics wanted to stress that the efficacy of the sacraments rested on God and not the holiness of the minister or the recipient.*

The two "ecclesial ships" still seem to be passing in the night on this issue. Many Catholics do interpret ex opere operato in an uncritical, unrefined, and overly simplified theological fashion which comes dangerously close to magic. Many Protestants have failed to reexamine the rich pre-polemical traditions which do offer a basis for it to correct understanding and interpretation. It is important, therefore, to examine what happens to the term at and after the Council of Trent and what its proper theological meaning intended to affirm.

Canons 6, 7, 8 on the sacraments in general record Trent's position on *opus operatum* and allied issues. Canon 6 states:

> If anyone shall say that the sacraments of the New Law do not contain the grace which they signify, or that they do not confer that grace on those who place no obstacle in their way, as though they are only out-

ward signs of grace or justice received through faith and are but certain marks of Christian profession whereby among men believers are distinguished from unbelievers, *anathema sit.*

Canon 7 notes:

If anyone shall say that grace, so far as God's part is concerned, is not imparted through the sacraments always and to all men even if they receive them rightly, but only sometimes and to some persons, *anathema sit.*

Canon 8 remarks:

If anyone shall say that by the sacraments of the New Law, grace is not confered *ex opere operato*, but that faith alone in the divine promise is sufficient to obtain grace, *anathema sit.*

A fast reading of these canons does give the impression that Trent did in fact present a magical understanding of *opus operatum.* A more historically informed reading of the Council's position adjusts and corrects this initial impression.

Both in the preceding Scholastic tradition and at the Council of Trent itself, there was a consciousness of the primordial role of faith. This was explicitly affirmed in Chapter 7 *On the Nature and Causes of Justification of the Sinner.* It teaches,

. . . instrumentalis item sacramentum baptismi, quod est 'sacramentum fidei', sine qua nulli unquam contigit justificatio.

. . . the instrumental cause is the sacrament of baptism, which is the sacrament of faith, without which no man was ever saved.

In the Latin text, the *sine qua* can only refer to faith which is feminine, and not baptism which is masculine. Consequently, the decree is teaching that no person has been justified without faith.

There was, however, a determined effort at Trent to avoid a strong emphasis on faith since the Lutherans had waved the banner of *sola fidei.* Moreover, Trent did not attempt a complete theological exposition. The bishops only wished to correct what they considered as heretical doctrines. In this sense, Trent's treatment of sacramentology is incomplete. The situation was further complicated after the Council by the unavailability of its *acta* i.e., the daily record of the floor debates and interventions. The growing Catholic-Protestant polemics only hardened spirits and rigidified positions. A general "nominalistic" flavor to theology permeated the Catholic tradition. All the groundwork and foundation was laid for a mechanical understanding of *opus operatum* in theological circles from the sixteenth century into our own day. As Rahner has noted: "The idea of the *opus operatum* in fact current, contains an element of what might be called physical certainty of functioning, which does not belong to it in a more accurate theology."[9] This conception is but one step removed from magic.

Laying aside polemics and mechanical conceptions, it is possible to perceive a valid theological meaning to the term *opus operatum* in the sacraments. Negatively, the term implies that the causal conferral of grace is not continugent on the holiness of the minister or the sacramental recipient, but on the positing of the sacramental sign.[10] This negative statement is a secondary note. Positively, and primarily, the term *opus operatum* refers to the abiding, irrevocable, and eschatological promise by God of grace for an individual. To claim that the sacraments effect grace *ex opere operato* is to affirm that sacramental actions are really actions of Christ. *Ex opere operato* and "in the power of the mystery of Christ" mean the same thing.[11]

Opus operatum is a Christological affirmation about the central mystery of Christian faith i.e., the Trinity has offered humankind a participation in their divine life through the Christ-event. The sacramental actions of the Church as the presence of Christ's offer of the Father's love through the power of the Spirit are efficacious.

The term *opus operatum* does not remove all uncertainty or doubt concerning an individual's salvation or participation in grace. Even Trent taught,

> . . . the necessity, if the sacrament is to be received fruitfully by an adult, of a right disposition: active cooperation in the reception of the sacrament with faith and love. Consequently, the sacrament in its concrete reality involves, like the *opus operantis* (the disposition of the recipient) an element of uncertainty about grace, of doubt about its factual efficacy. With the sacrament a person knows just as little as he does with his "subjective" actions performed in faith, whether it has really given him God's grace, just as little, and just as much. There is after all an undeniable fact which is hidden in the popular view of the sacraments by what the average person thinks *opus operatum* implies.[12]

Although God's offer of grace is guaranteed in the sacramental actions of the Church, the factual efficacy of the sacramental actions can never be an absolute certitude that an individual lives in grace. St. Thomas and the great Scholastics knew this well. "For them *opus operantis* was essentially related to the *opus operatum*, as the *personal aspect* in the justifying process of any sacrament, that aspect by which a free and responsible person accepted God's grace conferred by the sanctifying efficacy of the sacramental rite, that is by virtue of the *opus operatum*."[13] *Opus operatum* does not negate human responsibility and freedom. It demands it. Sacraments are *factually* efficacious in their faith-acceptance.

Clarification of confused terms does not fully answer the key issue of sacramental causality or efficacy i.e., the question and explanatory theories of how the sacraments affect what they signify and signify what they effect. The history of sacramental theology records many proposed solutions to this problem. Other authors have sufficiently recorded and explained the various classical positions. Our concentration will focus on more recent attempts to find a satisfactory explanation, attempts which conform to the anthropological understanding of the power of ritual. As a background, however, the main thrust, assets, and deficits of the classical positions will be presented. These positions cluster into four areas: physical, moral, occasional, and intentional causality.

Physical Causality

In Scholastic theology, physical causality can be divided into two types: dispositive and perfective. In dispositive physical causality, the term *physical* refers to reality as such, independent from anyone actually thinking about it. The word *causality* refers to the bringing about of grace. The word *dispositive* or disposition is more difficult to define. Medieval theologians were well aware that nothing was able to produce grace. God alone was the source of grace. The sacraments did, however, produce, cause or bring about a disposition to grace. They offered two examples to explain their notion of this disposition. First, in human generation the parents so caused or disposed the arrangement of matter through intercourse-conception that, given God's ordinary providence, the soul of a child must be infused. "The parents are not the immediate efficient causes of the soul's being, but, granted God's normal providence, they cause the soul to be in these elements (material), and thus they are the dispositive physical causes of the soul."[14] Second, when a seal is imposed on wax, the wax conforms to the form or image of the seal. The wax, in the very act of the seal being imposed, assumed or possessed a disposition to the form of the seal.

In the sacraments, the adherents to dispositive physical causality claimed a similar disposition arises. The sign of the sacraments was such, through the power of God, that when it was placed in the recipient of the sacrament a disposition for grace was present. The recipient of the sacrament was being adapted to grace and the disposition to grace created through the sacramental sign was fulfilled.

Unfortunately, the two examples utilized in explaining dispositive physical causality have serious flaws when applied to sacraments. In the case of the body-soul, there was some attempt made to include some active participation of free responsible persons in the disposition. A poor biological understanding of human conception, however, minimized active participation. In the example of the seal-wax, there was a twofold deficiency. First, the agent of the action was different. With a seal, man is the agent. In the sacraments, God is the agent. Second, the wax only conforms to the image of the seal in a totally passive modality. Passivity is not the core of sacramental relations between humankind and God. In sacraments, men and women are free active subjects.

The dual intentions of dispositive physical causality were well directed, in spite of their inadequate examples. They were correct in recognizing the impossibility of humankind causing grace in any fashion. Yet, whoever cooperated with God's gift of grace in the sacraments, to the extent that they were able, would receive his self-gift. Man could not produce grace, but he could bring about a disposition to grace. In the sacraments, the sacramental sign effected a real disposition to grace, and in view of this disposition, God really and freely offered himself.[15]

Perfective physical causality originated in the sixteenth century when grace became more and more envisioned as a physical quantitative reality, and sacramental causality was explained with mechanistic overtones. In this position, the sacramental sign was envisioned as a direct and immediate cause of grace itself, and not as an operational sign.

> The rite of a sacrament is an immediate physical cause of grace. The term perfective means that the outward rite is a cause which goes directly to grace, without the intermediation of the symbolic reality; the term physical affirms the objectivity and reality of the causality. God, by using the sacrament as an instrument, adds to its natural powers a created transitory impulse comparable to the movement and direction given by a man's hand to an instrument such as a pen. The sacraments are both causes and signs, but they are not causes inasmuch as they are sgns, but inasmuch as God adds this ontological passing enhancement of their physical entity.[16]

God alone is the primary cause of grace. The sacraments are instruments he employs in the Church to effect grace during the ritual celebrations.

The danger of perfective physical causality lies in the sacraments necessarily being instruments of causality. Some claimed that this was defined by the Council of Trent. This is not the case. Trent taught that the sacraments *contained* grace. It allowed the various theological "schools" to work out exactly how this happened.

In reducing sacraments to instruments, perfective physical causality came dangerously close to magic. They saw no necessary connection between the sacramental sign and grace. The true and necessary symbolic character of the sacraments was pushed to the background. Yet, insofar as the sacraments are signs, they are not primarily physical realities but signifiers.

Moreover, it is all but impossible to identify any free responsibility in the sacraments' recipient in the perfective physical causality's scheme. When taken to an extreme, this position leads to a totally passive interpretation of the role of people in the acceptance of grace. Unfortunately, this possibility often became reality in the popular comprehension of the sacraments among Roman Catholics, and still exerts pressure today.

Moral Causality

In the theory of moral causality, the sacraments are less causes and more propitiatory acts or prayers. The term *moral* in this context means "trying to convince." The sacraments, as prayers, have a moral value or worth which moved God to bestow his grace. Consequently, "the connection between the sacraments and grace is not merely God's antecedent determination to give grace whenever the sacrament is administered, but is something in the sacrament itself."[17]

In presenting sacraments as prayers or acts or worship, moral causality has pinpointed a dimension of sacraments which should never be omitted from theological analysis. A phenomenological description of what goes on in sacramental celebrations would surely insist that the people gathered together are praying to their God. "The symbolic actions of the sacraments, to all unprejudiced observers, to those not blinded by the 'smooth, solid, mechanical concepts' of the manuals, are very evidently prayers of the Church. To receive a sacrament, the faithful come together . . . and they pray to God. These are acts of worship."[18]

The deficiency of moral causality is one of omission rather than commission. It simply does not go far enough. The theory correctly identifies the sacraments as prayers, but it fails to demonstrate the link between the sign of the sacrament and the effect realized in and through the sacramental sign. "The theory of 'moral' causality, whether it admits it or not, must acknowledge a causality in regard to God which is then retracted by explaining that the real nexus is that between God and grace: God wills the grace as dependent on the sign, but does not will this grace because of that sign."[19] Ultimately, moral causality dissolves any real efficacy in the sacramental sign.

Occasional Causality

Occasional causality is the legacy of the "Franciscan" school and Nominalism. For the Occasionalists, there is no intrinsic necessary connection between the sacraments and grace. God has simply promised that on the occasion of sacramental celebration he would confer grace. "There is no power in the sacrament itself which causes grace, but God makes the sacrament an infallible condition for his own immediate action on the soul."[20]

The position of the Occasionalists is comprehensible once their fundamental distinction between *de potentia absoluta* and *de potentia ordinata* is understood. *De potentia absoluta* refers to God's absolute power. *De potentia ordinata* refers to how God has actually chosen to use his power. No created reality can ever bind God vis-à-vis his absolute power. He is absolutely free. If God willed, he could bestow grace even on someone in "mortal sin." In his ordinary power, however, God has *actually* decided and revealed a certain course of action or way to salvation. An element in this path is sacramental life.

For the Occasionalists, it is unprofitable to search for interconnections and explanations in sacramental activity. It is more valuable to know exactly what God has decreed and to follow it. Grace is present in the sacraments simply because God has desired to save us. Sacraments are celebrated because God has promised to bestow his grace.

Intentional Causality

In the last decade of the 19th century, Louis Billot became very sensitive to the dangerous tendencies toward mechanism in the theories of sacramental causality prevalent at the time. He could not accept the sacraments being reduced to a material or physical level. He insisted that they were first and foremost signs. Therefore, he returned to the old sacramental axiom: *causando significant et significando causant*, and developed the theory known as "Intentional Causality".

Billot and his followers employed a juridical model to explain sacramental causality. The sacraments were envisioned as causing a *right* to re-

ceive grace. The recipient had a "legal title" to grace.[21] Sacraments established a "contract" between the recipient of the sacrament and God,
similar to the binding contract between the seller and buyer of property. In
both cases, the contract is binding on both parties and there is a real trans-
action or transfer.

Intentional causality's goal of salvaging the unity between sacramental activity and efficacy was a positive advance in theological reflection. It
failed, however, in its concrete application. The juridical model employed
to illustrate sacramental causality fell far short of the relationship between
God and humankind in sacramental activity. No juridical model can sufficiently maintain the relationship of freedom, responsibility, and mutual
personal activity which defines sacramental life.

In all four theories of sacramental causality, the common deficiency is
the inability to take seriously the sign character of the sacraments. Only by
exploring the symbolic character of sacraments can an escape be found
from inadequate explanations of sacramental causality. It is this emphasis
on the symbolic nature of sacraments which characterizes contemporary
reflection on sacramentology, and at the same time, shines through an anthropological study of ritual.

Symbolic Causality

Three European theologians, K. Rahner, P. Fransen, and E. Schillebeeckx, have been responsible for the renewed focus on symbolism and
symbolic activity as a theoretical key to understanding sacramental efficacy. Each author journeyed back to Thomas Aquinas as a launching pad
and added more contemporary philosophical and theological insights to
construct a "symbolic causality". They recognized that Thomas' position
had certain deficiencies.[22] He had not developed the relationship between
ecclesiology and sacramentology, which reduced his understanding of sacramental character as a deputation to worship to a narrowly individualistic
interpretation. Moreover, although he had a germinal recognition of the
key role of the word of God in sacraments, even referring to it as a *signum*
(sign) and form of the sacraments, his understanding of the relationship
between the word of God and the sacraments remained purely formal and
in the background.[23] Yet, there were two key insights in the *Summa* which
could stimulate the reconstruction of sacramental causality. First, Thomas
"makes it clear that according to his convictions the primary and most
radical point of departure for our understanding of the sacraments is the
concept 'sign' and so of 'symbol'".[24] Second, the person of Christ is the
center of sacramental efficacy.

A clear development can be detected from Thomas' commentary on Lombard's *Sentences* to his own theological perspective on sacraments in the third part of the *Summa*. In the former, he merely repeats the various positions of the earlier masters of theology, using the term *ex opere operato* for sacramental efficacy.[25] In the latter, he totally avoids this term and substitutes *virtus passionis Christi, mysteria carnis Christi*, etc. In the *Summa*, Thomas returned to "the true source of sacramental sanctification, the glorified Lord who works in us through his Spirit".[26]

Thomas rejected both the moral and occasional models of sacramental causality. Convinced of the "sign" or symbolic character of the sacraments, he developed *instrumental causality*. In the *Summa* III, 62,5 he wrote:

> I answer that, as stated above (a,1) a sacrament in causing grace works after the manner of an instrument. Now an instrument is twofold; the one separate, as a stick for instance; the other united, as a hand. Moreover, the separate instrument is moved by means of the united instrument, as a stick by a hand. Now the principal efficient cause of grace is God himself, in comparison with whom Christ's humanity is a united instrument, whereas the sacrament is a separate instrument. Consequently, the saving power must needs be derived by the sacraments from Christ's Godhead through his humanity . . .

Thomas knew well that ultimately only God could be the cause of grace and that Christ is the center and vehicle for the bestowal of grace in the sacramental actions. What exactly, however, did Thomas mean when he called the sacraments "separated instruments"?

Medieval theology faced a perplexing problem in ascribing a real causal role to sacraments in the efficacy of grace. How could something material and corporeal effect a spiritual reality? Thomas grasped this problem clearly.[27] Yet, he insisted that the sacraments are involved in "producing" grace as instruments of the principle cause, God. This is clear in *Summa* III, 62,1:

> I answer that, we must needs say that in some way the sacraments of the New Law cause grace. For it is evident that through the sacraments of the New Law man is incorporated with Christ: thus the apostle says of baptism (Gal. 3:27): *As many of you who have been baptized in Christ have put on Christ*. And man is a member of Christ through grace alone.
>
> Some, however, say that they are the causes of grace not by their own operation, but insofar as God causes grace in the soul when the sacraments are employed. And they give as an example a man who on pre-

senting a leaden coin, receives, by the kings command, a hundred pounds: not as though the leaden coin by an operation of its own, causes him to give that sum of money; this being the effect of the mere will of the king. Hence, Bernard says in a sermon on the Lord's Supper: *Just as a canon is invested by means of a book, an abbot by means of a crozier, a bishop by means of a ring, so by the various sacraments various kinds of grace are conferred.* But if we examine the question properly, we shall see that according to the above mode the sacraments are mere signs. For the leaden coin is nothing but a sign of the king's command that this man should receive money. In like manner the book is the sign of the conferring of a canonry. Hence, according to this opinion, the sacraments of the New Law would be mere signs of grace; whereas we have it on the authority of many saints that the sacraments of the New Law not only signify, they also cause grace.

We must therefore say otherwise, that an efficient cause is twofold, principle and instrumental. The principle cause works by the power of its form, to which form the effect is likened; just as fire by its own heat makes something hot. In this way none but God can cause grace: since grace is nothing else than participated likeness of the Divine nature, according to 2 Peter 1:4, *He hath given us most great and precious promises; that we may be (Vulg.,—You may be made) partakers of the Divine nature.*—But the instrumental cause works not by the power of its form, but only by the motion whereby it is moved by the principle agent: so that the effect is not likened to the instrument but to the principle agent: for instance the couch is not like the ax, but like the art which is in the craftsman's mind. And it is thus that the sacraments of the New Law cause grace: for they are instituted by God to be employed for the purpose of conferring grace. . . .

Thomas' key insight is that the proper nature of an instrument enters into the accomplishment of causality. He applied this insight in responding to the objection that sacraments cannot cause grace insofar as they are material and grace is spiritual.

Every instrument has a twofold action i.e., its instrumental action moved by the power of the principle agent and its proper action which belongs to it by nature of its form. Consequently, the craftsman makes the couch and his ax is moved by his power. Yet, the ax accomplishes its instrumental action only because it is its own proper action i.e., for an ax to cut. The sacraments operate similarly.

> . . . the corporeal sacraments by their operation, which they exercise on the body that they touch, accomplish through the Divine institution as instrumental operation on the soul; for example, the water of baptism, in

respect to its proper power, cleanses the body, and thereby inasmuch as it is the instrument of the Divine power cleanses the soul: since from the soul and body one thing is made. . . . [28]

In Thomas' framework, the sacraments have an instrumental power for attaining the effect of grace, which is dependent on and only operative in view of God as principle cause. In this sense, he affirmed that the sacraments contained the grace they signified and effected. He identified the presence of grace in the sacraments in two ways: first, as in a sign; second, as in its cause. These two elements are inseparable. The signifying and causal power of the sacraments are essentially conjoined.

Rahner, Fransen, and Schillebeeckx capitalized on Thomas' affirmation of the sacramental axiom: *significando efficiunt et efficiens significant*. They fleshed outt the implications of this axiom for sacramental causality with an additional consciousness of its relation to a theology of the word, Christology and ecclesiology. Rahner employed a doctrine of "intrinsic symbolism" to expose the full power of symbols to make present the reality they signify. Fransen explored the dynamic power of symbolic activity in human behavior to understand sacramental efficacy. Schillebeeckx pursued a similar orientation, although in his early writings he was unable to accept a "causality of symbols" as an adequate exposition of sacramental causality.

Rahner

In *Church and Sacraments*, Rahner explicitly identified his position as the "causality of symbols."

> With the approach we have been using, it can become clear that the sacraments precisely as signs are causes of grace, that it is a case here of causation by symbols, of the kind that belongs to what by its very nature is a symbol. "By such natural symbols" or intrinsically real symbols, we mean for our purpose here, the spaciotemporal, historical phenomena, the visible and tangible form in which something that appears, notifies its presence, bodying forth this manifestation really distinct from itself.[29]

Sacramental efficacy is not a notion or reality added as an appendage to the sign character of the sacraments. Sacraments are efficacious precisely because they are signs, or more specifically, symbols.[30]

Symbols point to another reality, make it present, but are not identical to the reality symbolized. In symbolization, two elements must be distinguished i.e., the dependence of the actual manifestation on what is being made present, and the difference between what is manifesting and what is made present. The example of the human body as a symbol of the self will clarify this dependence and distinctiveness.

The body as a symbol of the real person *me* is both a symbol of the self and a manifestation of the self. The manifestation of self through the body is dependent upon and presupposes the real existence of the total self. Yet, in a real self, the self is distinct from the manifesting body i.e., it is not identical to the body. In this example, "What is manifesting itself points to its own identity and existence by manifesting itself in this manifestation which is independent from itself."[31] The body as a symbol is the cause of the total self which it signifies, by being the way in which what is signified (the total self) affects itself.

Rahner applied this theory of "intrinsic symbolism" to both the Church and the sacraments. For him, the Church is the symbol of the eschatologically victorious mercy of God expressed in Christ for all humankind,

> ... through her faith, believed and proclaimed, in God's eschatologically victorious grace in Christ, the Church is the sacrament of the world's salvation, because she portrays and presents that grace in the world as eschatologically victorious, as a grace that will never depart from the world and which, despite all pitfalls along the way, drives the world invincibly towards the perfection of God's kingdom. The sacramental sign of this grace is an efficacious sign, not in the sense that it produces otherwise non-existent God-willed grace, but because, through the sign, grace willed by God brings itself into historical manifestation and thus renders itself historically visible.[32]

The Church is the symbol of Christ. As symbol, the Church by being itself manifests Christ, makes him present, but is not absolutely identical to him. As in the case of the total self being the possibility for the body as symbol, Christ is the possibility for the symbolic power of the Church. The Church is a symbolic cause for the presence of Christ whom it signifies by being the way in which Christ effects his presence in the world. This relational scheme is especially true for the sacraments.

> Christ acts through the Church in regard to an individual human being, by giving his actions spacio-temporal embodiment by having his gift of grace manifested in the sacrament. This visible form is itself an effect of the coming of grace; it is there because God is gracious to men; and in

this self embodiment grace itself occurs. The sacramental sign is the cause of grace inasmuch as grace is conferred by being signified. And this presence (by signifying) of grace in the sacraments is simply the actuality of the Church herself as the visible manifestation of grace.[33]

Sacramental efficacy is bound to the sacramental symbolic function of making Christ present in its visibility, which visibility has as its a priori God's self-communication to humankind in Christ through the Spirit.

It is doubtful as to whether Rahner's doctrine of "intrinsic symbolism" can be proven. Its foundation lies in the area of metaphysics and it functions paradigmatically. One can only examine existential life and evaluate whether or not it conforms to experience. "Intrinsic symbolism" either works or it doesn't. This interpretation of sacramental causality, however, takes seriously the sacramental axiom of the sacraments effecting what they symbolize and symbolizing what they effect.

Fransen

Fransen's exploration of *symbolic activity* has further refined and extended Rahner's notion of symbolism. He has pointed out a contention which permeated the first half of this text i.e., that human existence is through and through a symbolic existence. The symbolic nature of reality pervades human life.

Unfortunately, the scientific-technological flavor and character of contemporary culture has often clouded and confused the true symbolic character and dimension of human existence. In this milieu, signs and symbols have often become weakened and impoverished. This "poverty of symbols" has in many respects intensified the contemporary cultural crisis.

In spite of the predominating technological reductionalism, Fransen powerfully maintained that symbolic activity is the root of all human activity, and that the genesis of symbolic activity is rooted in the body-spirit polarity of the human person.[34]

> Man cannot act or even exist except in symbolic activity, because he is inextricably a spirit in matter. He cannot realize himself except in gestures; he cannot think except in words and language. Since his symbolic action is also a true activity, the only activity of which he is capable, "his actions effect what they signify." This great sacramental principle is also the principle of our whole existence.[35]

The principle of human life and the principle of religious symbolic activity are the same.

The symbolic character of human activity is not restricted by grandure or import of the performance. In all our actions, even in what are considered private personal thoughts, there is always a visibility no matter how miniscule, which is a manifestation of a deeper invisibility i.e., the acting person realizing who he or she is in the activity.[36]

Every human activity is contextualized. It is in reference to its context that human symbolic activity discovers its full meaning. For example, a kiss between long separated friends who meet after several years presents one meaning and realization of potentials. A kiss between a man and woman celebrating their fiftieth wedding anniversary realizes a quite different potential. A kiss between lovers who have endured a trying period of argumentation and pain is still another realization of potentials. In each instance, however, human activity is symbolic. The context of the symbolization reveals the significance and meaning of the activity.

Religious symbolic activity follows the trademark of all human symbolic activity. Consequently, sacraments attain their full meaning in terms of their context. The meaning of sacramental activity is enshrined in the context of the religious community in which they are celebrated, or better, which enacts them as expressions of the reality and potentials which are the "spirit" embodied within the community.

> Sacraments are never things, they are not "something." They are, as everybody can see who leaves his books and enters a Church, an action, a *liturgical action*, in which different persons exercise their own activity. They are symbolic activities of a special kind, that is ritual and ecclesiastic. Their symbolization finds its final and full meaning in the religious community in which they are performed, that is in the Church, simply because they are essentially "corporate" symbols of a religious community.[37]

Fransen's insight echoes the results drawn from an anthropological analysis of ritual. Every community expresses its world view or interpretation of the random experiences of life in ritual activity. It is in and through ritual symbolic activities that the very heart of the community or "pseudospecies" finds its realization, fulfillment, and verification.

Fransen located the efficacy of sacraments in the efficacy of all symbols i.e., the activity of realizing what is being symbolized.

> *Every symbolic activity possesses its own efficacy*, precisely because it is an activity. If there is any difference in efficacy, this cannot be caused by the nature of the person who is at the origin of the activity. Christ, real

man and real God in the unity of one divine person, acted as we do according to the laws of symbolic activity, expressing in words and gestures his invisible divine intentions and actions. But because his humanity was united with his divinity in the mystery of the hypostatic union, his human symbolic activities possessed a divine efficacy. We are only human, and yet our symbolic activities possess a very limited though real efficacy.[38]

Sacramental efficacy arises from religious symbolic activity.

In Fransen's view, there is no need to search for a secondary notion, such as instrumental causality, to defend sacramental efficacy. Only a myopic understanding of the concept "sign" in a static rationalistic thought system will require further supplementation. This is not to infer that instrumentality is wrong, but that in a rich understanding of symbolic activity it is unnecessary. Since, "in the unity of his person, every person, and this includes Christ too, each according to his or her own dignity and power possesses in and through his or her symbolic activity both the symbolic manifestation of what he or she intends to do, and at the same time and *in the same moment*, the realization of his or her symbolic activity."[39]

Fransen's theory of symbolic activity included two "laws of symbolization." First, there is the law of appropriation. When the content and meaning of a reality is supercharged and bursting with richness, so that a particular symbol is incapable of expressing this richness, "we see how human nature looks spontaneously for more symbols, integrating them into the initial symbolic activities in the desperate effort to equal what must ever surpass any full expression."[40] In more anthropological terminology, symbolic activity is heuristic. In an attempt to capture the fullness of meaning, which is the a priori for a symbol and what the symbol makes present through signification, the human person and the human community advert from one symbol to the next in an unending process of transcendence which always evades final resolution and full completion.

Second, there is the law of extension. "Every symbol, which from its fundamental meaning and context possesses a central importance for life, tends to extend itself in similar, although only analogical, symbolic action."[41] Fundamental, supercharged symbols permeate the life of an individual and a community in allied but not identical arenas. For example, the Eucharist has permeated all areas of Christian life e.g., morning and evening prayers, benediction, and eucharistic processions. Under the law of extension, all "extended" symbols will be interpreted in relation to the fundamental and foundational symbol from which they are extended.

Schillebeeckx

Schillebeeckx followed a path similar to Rahner and Fransen, although in his early writings he was only willing to accept a causality of symbols in relation to Christ. He adhered to the sacramental axiom: *significando efficiunt et efficiend significant*. In the sacraments, however, he insisted that the human sign-activity was the personal act of Christ the High Priest.[42] "Consequently, we must say that because it realizes the symbolic activity of Christ in his Church, the sacrament causes salvation as a sign in the full human sense of the word and thus not as a mere indication of something 'beyond.' "[43]

Schillebeeckx distinguished between a "causality of symbol" for the immediate acts of the historical Jesus and an "instrumental causality of symbol" for the symbolic acts of Christ through his ecclesial visibility. He argued that there was a different instrumentality in the two instances. The historical body of Christ was an *instrument conjunctum*, whereas the ecclesial acts of Christ are *instrumentum separata*.

Schillebeeckx exercised a caution in his use of "instrumentality" for the human nature of Christ, "for human nature is certainly not an instrument of the person, but rather the mode of his existence. Thus the (bodily-spiritual) humanity of Christ is a mode of existence of God the Son himself."[44] Christ's human interiority belongs *hypostatically* to the person of the Son of God. It was for this same reason that Aquinas added the nuance "conjoined instrument" to the body of Christ. Unlike his bodily acts, his "ecclesial" acts do not participate in the hypostatic union, even though they are identified with the glorified body of Christ in heaven. Consequently, it is more proper to speak of an "instrumental causality of symbol" in reference to sacramental efficacy.[45]

Certain questions can be raised against Schillebeeckx's interpretation. First, did the position he espoused at the time of *Christ the Sacrament* . . . rely too heavily on a scholastic model of thought, especially in its Christology? Second, even though the relation between Christ and the Church is not hypostatic, could not the unique bond between Christ and his Church specified by his permeating presence through the Spirit, sufficiently ground a "causality of symbol" without the addition of instrumentality?

Schillebeeckx wrote his doctoral dissertation on Thomas' sacramentology. Beyond a doubt, *Christ the Sacrament* . . . relied heavily on a Thomistic orientation and content. This text did not develop a "new" sacramentology grounded in a phenomenology of encounter. Rather, it employed this new philosophical insight to clarify and expand the more important elements of sacramentology contained in the classical treatises.

Consequently, Schillebeeckx's work suffered from some of the limitations of the Thomistic model, "instrumental causality" being a case in point. If one remains within the Thomistic system and Aristotelian categories, "instrumental causality" can be conceded. There are, however, "other ways of thought which might enable us to come nearer to the *personal* mystery contained in every sacrament,"[46] for example, a symbolic causality grounded in symbolic activity as co-natural to the human person.

Schillebeeckx was correct in denying that the Church was hypostatically joined to the risen-glorified Christ. Yet, there is a real and unique relationship between Christ and the Church which is more intimate and powerful than the term "separated instrument" suggests, a unity which could sustain a "divine" efficacy for sacraments.

In our previous chapter on "Word and Sacrament" the bond between Christ and the Church was clarified. It was maintained that the Church is the people of God and body of Christ to the extent that it is united to Christ through the power of the Spirit. The ecclesial community only exists in its members being conjoined by their shared participation in Trinitarian life, formed in the image of the Son and animated by the Spirit. At the core of all the Church's activity lies the radical foundation of the indwelling Trinity. There is no comparable unity in human existence. This unity, although not hypostatic, is so essential to the nature and existence of the Church, that the actions of the Church are intrinsically bound to the actions of Christ and participate in his divine efficacy insofar as they are symbolic actions. Schillebeeckx's more recent writings suggest his agreement with this position.[47]

Understanding sacramental efficacy in terms of symbolism and symbolic activity is harmonious with the data gleaned from an anthropological exploration of ritual. Ritual activity as symbolic behavior brings about an integral vision of life. It makes meaning out of random experiences. Ritual or symbolic activity, within the context of a particular community, is a constituative center where both individuals and the whole social group realize their deepest possibilities through the utilization of their cognitive, imaginative, motor, and emotional faculties.

The Christian rituals, called sacraments, are efficacious precisely because they are the symbolic activities of the Christian community. In sacramental activities the meaning of life is made present i.e., communion with the Father, Son, and Spirit or grace. The sacraments "work," "give grace," are "encounters with the risen Lord" because they are symbolic actions of the community of God's people which is the visibility of Christ in history, Christ who is the symbolic activity of the Father through the Spirit.

Conclusion

The issue of grace is a concern for every Christian tradition. It is the ultimate question for every Christian Church insofar as it offers an answer to humankind's quest for ultimate meaning in this life and after death. The meaning of grace has been disputed both within and between different Christian communions. This chapter has outlined key facets to this elusive reality within the specific context of Christian sacraments.

Grace is not a quantitative reality. It is a qualitative relationship between an individual and God in his historical manifestation as Father, Son, and Spirit. Above and beyond all proposed distinctions and types of grace stands the radical biblical revelation. God wishes to communicate and share his interpersonal love and life with every man and woman. The factual attainment of this mutual love is grace.

God's offer of love is his totally free gift. It is totally gratuitous. There is nothing any human person can do to demand it. This is uncreated grace. Created grace is our relation to the Father, Son, and Spirit. It is the effect uncreated grace has on us. This effect can never be considered as separated from God's initiative in uncreated grace. It is even inaccurate to portray created grace as our response to God's gracious offer of self. God and humankind are never equal partners. Even our active "yes" to the divine invitation is not an independent human response, but a personal free act in cooperation with God who works in us. Without God's inner movement which accompanies the divine invitation, a human person would be incapable of responding positively to the offer of participated Trinitarian life.

Grace is simultaneously individual and communal. The biblical testimony to this *fact* desperately needs to be recovered and disseminated today. Neither element should be dwarfed by the other. The love of God is offered to real people in the concreteness of their individual life. Grace is my relationship with a God who is interested in my individuality and uniqueness. But this divine love is factually manifested and affected by my being with the community of people God calls his own. I am uniquely loved by God within the corporate solidarity of humankind in general and the Christian communion in particular. Grace and Church are not merely related theological phenomena. They are co-existential expressions of the one reality of God's self-gift as offered invitation and realized participation in Trinitarian life.

The intimacy of grace and Church is lucidly expressed in sacramental life. As expressions of the Church's nature, the sacraments effect the grace they signify. As ecclesial symbolic activities, the sacraments make present the risen Christ who calls the participants to enter more deeply into his love of the Father through the Spirit by intensifying their mutual love for each other which expresses the *koinonia*, the fellowship, the essence of the Church and grace. Sacramental efficacy is symbolic causality.

If these key dimensions of grace can be embraced and maintained by the different Christian communions, the theological and pastoral comprehension of the meaning of grace will be embellished, remnants of polemicisms will be neutralized, and perhaps the distance which separates Christian communities from union with one another will be shortened.

NOTES

1. P. Fransen, *The New Life of Grace*. (New York: Seabury Press, 1973), p. 15.

2. *Ibid.*, p. 96.

3. *Ibid.*, p. 87.

4. *Ibid.*, p. 98; also, K. Rahner, *The Trinity*. (New York: Herder and Herder, 1970); and, C. Ernst, *The Theology of Grace*. (Notre Dame: Fides Press, 1976).

5. Fransen, *Intelligent Theology*, p. 94.

6. Fransen, *The New Life . . .*, p. 56. For a comparison of the Eastern and Western approaches cf. R.D. Zimany, "Grace, Deification, and Sanctification: East and West," *Diakonia* 12 (1977), pp. 121–144.

7. Cf. L. Deiss, *Early Sources of the Liturgy*. (Collegeville: The Liturgical Press, (1967), p. 14.

8. Cf. D. Tappeiner, "Sacramental Causality in Aquinas and Raher: Some Critical Thoughts," *Scotish Journal of Theology* 28 (1975), p. 243: "The sacramental principle involves the crucial assertion that the sacraments are means in a causal sense, for the transformation of spiritual power through material elements. This assertion of genuine causal efficacy for sacraments, however it is explained, is that which ultimately divides all who are actually sacramentalists from all non-sacramentalists."

9. Rahner, *The Church and the Sacraments*, p. 26.

10. *Ibid.*

11. Schillebeeckx, *Christ the Sacrament . . .*, p. 83.

12. Rahner, *The Church and the Sacraments*, pp. 25–26.

13. Fransen, *Intelligent Theology*, p. 131.

14. B. Leeming, *Principles of Sacramental Theology*. 2nd edition. (London: Longmans, 1960), p. 289.

15. Cf. J.P. Kenny, *The Supernatural*. (New York: Alba House, 1972), p. 86, wherein the concept of *dispositio ultima* is explained in relation to created and uncreated grace.

16. Leeming, p. 288.

17. *Ibid.*, p. 287.

18. Fransen, *Intelligent Theology*, p. 104.
19. Rahner, *The Church and the Sacraments*, p. 37.
20. Leeming, p. 287.
21. Rahner, *The Church and the Sacraments*, p. 35.
22. Cf. K. Rahner, "Introductory Observations on Thomas Acquinas' Theology of the Sacraments in General," *Theological Investigations Vol. 14.* (New York: Seabury Press, 1976), p. 151.
23. *Ibid.*, p. 152, "But so far as Thomas Aquinas is concerned this connection between a theology of the word and a theology of sacraments still remains totally in the background." Also, Tappeiner, p. 245, "This recognition of the 'word' was itself only formal because the relational aspect of the sacrament was overshadowed by the ontological aspect. The 'word' was reduced virtually to a formal validation directed more to the material element than to the persons involved."
24. *Ibid.*, p. 153.
25. Cf. Schillebeeckx, *Christ the Sacrament . . .*, pp. 100–109.
26. Fransen, *Intelligent Theology*, p. 103.
27. Cf. *Summa* III, 62 1 obj.1; 62,3 obj. 3; 62,4 obj.1.
28. *Ibid.*, III, 62,1 ad. 1.
29. Rahner, *The Church and the Sacraments*, p. 37. On the various positions cf. L. Renwart, "Efficacité des Rites Sacramentels," *Nouvelle Revue Theologique* 92 (1970), pp. 383–397.
30. K. Rahner, "Considerations on the Active Role of the Person in the Sacramental Event," *Theological Investigations Vol. 14.* (New York: Seabury Press, 1976), p. 177.
31. Rahner, *The Church and the Sacraments*, p. 38.
32. Rahner, "What is a Sacrament?," p. 281.
33. Rahner, *The Church and the Sacraments*, p. 39.
34. Cf. P. Fransen, "Symboliek en Bijbelse Taal," *Bijdragen* 28 (1967), pp. 152–175; also, the whole tradition stemming from M. Merleau-Ponty.
35. Fransen, *Intelligent Theology*, p. 117.
36. *Ibid.*
37. *Ibid.*, pp. 136–137.
38. *Ibid.*, p. 138.
39. *Ibid.*, pp. 138–139.
40. *Ibid.*, p. 141.
41. *Ibid.*, p. 142.
42. Schillebeeckx, *Christ the Sacrament . . .*, p. 90.
43. *Ibid.*, pp. 90–91.
44. Cf. Fransen, *Intelligent Theology*, pp. 114–115.
45. *Ibid.*, p. 140.
46. *Ibid.*,
47. Cf. E. Schillebeeckx, *Revelation and Theology.* (New York: Sheed and Ward, 1968); *The Mission of the Church.* (New York: Seabury Press, 1973).

11 SACRAMENTS AND ECCLESIAL ROOT METAPHORS

Throughout Part Three of this investigation, the lines of convergence between the behavioral sciences' analysis of ritual and theological affirmations on the key elements of Christian sacraments has been stressed. Up until this point, the convergence has focused on specific dimensions i.e., the word of God, sacramental behavior, and grace. In order to complete a theological reconstruction of sacraments in relation to a behavioral analysis of ritual, an additional area must be examined i.e., sacraments and root metaphors.

It was previously claimed that rituals express the world view of a particular culture. Is this true of Christian ritual, Christian sacraments? Do the Christian sacraments express the fundamental Christian root metaphor? This chapter will attempt to answer this question. First, however, it is necessary to retrace our steps and present a brief summary of ritual's relation to root metaphors. This backtracking will bring our question into proper focus.

Ritual and Root Metaphors

Cultural communities necessarily discover and express meaning within the cluster of binary-oppositions which shape human experience. Root metaphors issue forth as products of this constitutive enterprise. Within them, one finds the culture's attempted resolution of experienced data and expressed world hypothesis.

Root metaphors are analogical, primordial, and operational. As analogical, they attempt to comprehend, relate, and resolve the multiple facets of experienced reality in terms of one element which is selected as the "clue," model, or paradigm for the total network or system. As primordial, they fall within the category of "first principles" or *creencias*. They are the foundations for the whole system of thought and action within a culture, without necessarily being available in conscious reflection or common sense. They are similar to cultural archetypes buried deep within the cultural unconscious. As operational, root metaphors are the focal points or nodal images of the social drama. They are expressed in the social structure and await new birth in the anti-structure. Their operational character is correlational rather than juxtapositional.

The genesis of root metaphors lies in the anti-structure with its dimensions of liminality and communitas. In this fertile zone of creativity and dynamism, symbols "given" and "present" in reality are arranged to shape an interpretive scheme of experience which is expressed through a culture's rituals. Before institutionalization, these rituals express feelings and emotions. They form the structure of the primordial root metaphor. They also express the meaning of the metaphor which forms the deepest content of the bond of communitas within the social group, even though the content of the bond usually remains prereflective or unconscious. After institutionalization, ritual elicits feelings and emotions. It functions to guarantee the socialization of new members by indoctrinating them into the basic world vision or root metaphor expressed in the community's ritual; and, it reenforces the metaphor in old members. Ritual is the instrument for the social transmission of root metaphors.

Insofar as the bond of communitas is experienced and operative in institutionalized ritual, these rituals are "strong," "have meaning," and reaffirm a culture's root metaphor. The social structure will be preserved. Insofar as the bond of communitas is weak or absent, the power of ritual as community-building will be hollow and the root metaphor increasingly impotent. The existing social structure will be challenged. The "social drama" will ensue with its potential for new metaphors and new rituals to express them.

Root metaphors are at the nerve center of cultural life. They are the life-force of a culture. Ritual is also indispensable to culture since it *is the* vehicle for the transmission of metaphors. Ritual and root metaphors exist in sympathetic vibration. Health in one strengthens the other. Weakness in one threatens the other.

Christian Sacraments and Ecclesial Root Metaphors

Christian communities are cultures within humankind. One should expect that Christian communities will be comprised of and operate within the structural elements and social dynamics controlling cultural units.

Consequently, the Christian communities should be characterized by rituals which are grounded in and expressive of their distinctive root metaphor, their distinctive vision of life's meaning. Christian sacraments should express the fundamental Christian root metaphor.

There can be no doubt that the Christian sacraments exhibit the key dimensions of ritual. Do they, however, fulfill the most radical function of ritual i.e., disclose Christianity's distinctive metaphor? This question is not extrinsic. If it can be positively demonstrated that they do, the main orientation of this theological investigation will find validation. Moreover, the significant theological place and function of sacraments within Christian culture will be established.

Our initial thrust into sacramentology focused on the word of God, Jesus. He is the foundational metaphor of Christian culture. His life is the analogical clue to Christian culture. This is the Christian "mystery of faith": Christ has died, Christ is risen, Christ will come again. It is in terms of this mystery that the constituency of the Christian community "resolves" the experienced binary-oppositions of life into positive meaning.

The opposing forces of life-death structure Jesus' meaning as the Christian root metaphor. The resolution of these forces is an affirmation of positive meaning i.e., from life through death to life. The birthplace of the Christian faith, of the Christian world view, is the conviction that the "Lord is risen," death is overcome. This "Easter faith" is so fundamental to the Christian vision that its oral and written traditions contain "proofs" of its factuality i.e., the empty tomb, the Emmaus account, the appearance stories.

The fundamental root metaphor of Jesus' resurrection engages a dynamic application and extension process in the Christian community. The community revisits Jesus' life-events and unfolds their deeper meaning in light of his resurrection. In this adventure, a continuity is recognized between the whole life of Jesus and the final events of his death and resurrection. The Christian community also applies this foundational paradigm to the future. All new events, tensions, and binary oppositions are "resolved" in reference to the metaphor of Jesus' death-resurrection. Past, present, and future are placed beneath Jesus' culminating actions.

Slowly, but with insightful adeptness, the whole cosmos is placed under the Christian paradigm. The death-resurrection of Jesus becomes an all encompassing charter-event for Christianity. In this capacity, the death-resurrection event is the source of the specifically Christian world view and identity, as well as the "first principle" which governs all other Christian metaphors, in both their construction and operation.

A cursory glance at the various metaphors operative within Christian culture testifies to the above contentions, especially the insight that when binary-oppositions are subsumed under the death-resurrection of Jesus, positive meaning is attained. For example, one can interpret the universe as meaningful or absurd. Under Christ it is meaningful for there is a God who is known as Father and who loves humankind. In human existence, there is good-bad, or in Christian terminology, grace-sin. Good/grace is life in Christ. Bad/sin is life apart from Christ. Life in Christ promises eternal happiness. Life outside of Christ promises eternal darkness and damnation. Sickness-health is resolved into life for those who "believe in" Christ. Master-servant (leader-follower) is resolved in becoming like Christ i.e., the servant of everyone.

It appears that whatever potentially oppositional elements which could be clustered under death find their "resolution" in the contrary elements which could be clustered under life. In the Christian world view, all potentially harmful and "negative" experiences within the binary-oppositions of human existence are minimally neutralized and maximally positivized within the fundamental Christian root metaphor of Christ's death and resurrection. Employing the conceptual framework of Levi-Strauss, one could say that the death and resurrection of Christ is *the* cognitive myth of Christian culture.

Anthropology has demonstrated the intrinsic relation of root metaphors and ritual. One would expect that Christian root metaphors would find their expression in Christian rituals called sacraments. These Christian ritual celebrations, employing symbols, language, gesture, sight, and sound, should point to and make present the metaphor of Christ's death and resurrection. Two sacraments in particular, baptism and the Eucharist, succeed in this venture. In these ritual celebrations, the celebrators move from one pole of binary-oppositions to another by being linked, bound, or identified with the charter-event constituting the Christian community and expressing its foundational root metaphor.

Interestingly, the Christian theological tradition has always underlined baptism and the Eucharist as the premier sacraments. Their heightened position arose from their intimate grounding in and expressiveness of Christ's death and resurrection. The Eucharist re-enacts the charter-event which sustains the whole Christian world view. Baptism celebrates and effects membership within the community which lives this world view and thereby establishes a right and responsibility to participate in the ritual of the Eucharist, the unique re-enactment of the fundamental Christian metaphor. Baptism is imaged as a plunging into the death of Christ so that life in Christ might be secured. In a real sense, baptism is the Eucharist begun (*in fieri*) and the Eucharist is baptism completed.

　　In the eucharistic ritual, a complex heuristic structure forms a unity between Israel's Passover, the Last Supper, Calvary, and the community celebrations of past and present Eucharists. In this ritual, various experienced events, realities, or ideas are clustered under the poles of death or life. This can be expressed in the following chart.

	DEATH ⟶ LIFE	
Israel	Egypt	Promised Land
	Slavery	Freedom
	Death	Life
JESUS	Earth	Heaven
	Slavery, Suffering	Freedom, Happiness
	Physically, emotionally broken	Resurrected Life
	Death (broken bread-wine)	Nourishment, Service
Christian	Earth	Heaven
Eucharist	Slavery, Suffering	Service
	Death	Eternal Life

In each instance, the negative pole is transformed into the positive pole in and through the ritual which expresses the fundamental metaphor i.e., from death to life. This pattern holds true for baptism. An individual is immersed into water to die, so that they might rise to new life in Christ as a member of his body, the Church. This perspective can also be graphically represented.

	DEATH ⟶ LIFE	
Christ	Cross	New Life
	Tomb	Appearance, Presence
Individual	Immersion	New Life in Christ
Candidate	Buried with Christ	Son/Daughter of God
Christian	Alien	Member
Community	Exclusion	Participation

We find here verification of what was previously expressed in the preceding chapter i.e., ritual providing access to a charter-event and its previous re-enactments. In the case of the Christian sacraments as rituals, especially baptism and the Eucharist, this operational principle is found at work. Moreover, this process of contact and identification secures the communication and transmission of the fundamental metaphor which sustains the whole cultural system, even if it be on an unconscious level. In the case of Christian culture this metaphor is the death and resurrection of Christ. Through the repetition of Christian rituals, the Christian world view is further reinforced and the "unfinished business" of concretely fulfilling its exigencies can be taken up again and again.

Similar schemes can be constructed for the sacraments of reconciliation, anointing of the sick, holy orders, and marriage. In each instance, a potential negative interpretation and experience are transformed and positivized by being placed under the metaphor of Christ's death and resurrection in the context of ritual performance. Our main purpose, however, is not to explore each of these sacraments, but to gain a perspective on the whole of sacramentology. One further step is required in this enterprise. A claim was issued that ritual and root metaphors arise from the antistructure with its characteristics of liminality and communitas. This claim must be tested. Do Christian root metaphors and the rituals which express them actually originate in the social drama of structure—anti-structure? Once Christian culture became "structure," did its metaphors and rituals participate in the unending processual dynamism of the social drama? The Last Supper—the Calvary event and its celebration in the sacrament of the Eucharist provide a test case.

It can be shown that the total constellation of Jesus' ritual supper-death bears the anti-structural marks of liminality and communitas which eventually emerge as the structure of a new "pseudospecies." Furthermore, the level of communitas present in the structure of Christian culture, through the ritual celebration of this charter-event, was, is, and will be decisive for the continued existence and concrete form of the existing Christian social unit. The biblical accounts of the Last Supper provide an entrance to this data.

Any analysis of the biblical reports of the Last Supper is wrought with complex and, at times, unresolvable issues. The date, type of Jewish meal, context, liturgical influences on the development and final redaction of the texts, and the fundamental meaning of the Last Supper are only a few of the elements requiring investigation. Without overlooking the importance of the debates surrounding these areas and cognizant of their ongoing nature, certain affirmations about the Last Supper are possible. First, the Jewish feast of Passover was the context for the celebration of the Last Supper, even if the actual event was not a Passover meal. Second, the biblical redactors portray Jesus as presenting the meaning of his ensuing death in terms of this ritual meal. Third, the meaning of the Jewish Passover undergoes a transformation and reinterpretation by Christ in the "report" of the biblical writers. Finally, this ritual meal was to be continued by the followers of Jesus "in his memory." In short, it is within the context of a Jewish ritual meal of liberation that Jesus is reported to have expressed the meaning of his life which is completed and fulfilled (*telos*) on Calvary.

If the present scheme of ritual in general and religious ritual in particular are valid, it should be demonstrable that Jesus' Last Supper-Calvary event is anti-structural and initiatory of the social drama. Moreover, this ritual which expresses the fundamental Christian root metaphor should be characterized by the liminality and communitas of the participants. Such seems to be the case in the development of the Christian Eucharist.

Jesus and his disciples never purported to be anything but Jews. The Passovers they celebrated prior to the Last Supper could be characterized as structural within the context of the Jewish "pseudospecies" of which they were a part. At the celebration of the Last Supper, however, an anti-structure found its birth. The language, interpretive meaning, and actions of the Last Supper-Calvary event constituted a breach with the accepted meaning of the Jewish Passover ritual. This breach did not require or imply a total segmentation or separation from Judaism. Neither Jesus nor his disciples gave any indication to this effect. Even after the death of the Master, his band of followers remained closely bound and linked with Judaism.

In time, the breach spawned in the Last Supper-Calvary event developed into a crisis. The distinctive character of Jesus' and his followers' Judaism was recognized as radically different from other Judaic sects. Christians made bold attempts to demonstrate homogeneity with the Jewish tradition and its world view, but this redressive action fell short. Judaism could no longer accept the "Christian" interpretation and convictions about Jesus as being consistent with its vision of life and history. Consequently, Christianity slowly emerged as a "culture" or "pseudospecies" in its own right. What was antistructural vis-à-vis Judaism became structural.

Jesus and his followers shared the characteristics of liminality and communitas indigenous to the anti-structure. At the Last Supper the liminality ascribed to Jesus by the biblical authors did not lie in his particular ritual actions, but in the meaning or interpretation given to these actions.

> To break bread and give thanks, in just the way Jesus did, was an obligation for every devout Jew. Jesus was neither instituting a new ritual nor telling his friends to continue an existing ritual: it would be pointless to command something that would go on in any case. The real meaning therefore falls on the last half of the command. Do this *in memory of me*. That is, whenever you do this in the future, whenever you gather for a meal and do what we have done so often together, you will be remembering *me* in what you do. What Jesus did, then, was to attach a new meaning to the most ordinary ritual in Jewish life—indeed, to the only ritual or corporate act he could be sure his disciples would do together regularly in any case.[1]

Jesus' liminal condition was further intensified after the supper in his crucifixion-resurrection event, which in turn further specified the meaning of "remembering him." V. Turner has provided a list of liminal properties compared to properties of a status system. A comparison of this list with the biblical record of the Last Supper-Calvary constellation is astonishing. Turner recorded twenty-six potential liminal properties:

Liminal Properties	Status Properties
Transition	State
Totality	Partiality
Homogeneity	Heterogeneity
Communitas	Structure
Equality	Inequality
Anonymity	Systems of nomenclature
Absence of property	Property
Nakedness/or uniform clothing	Distinctions of clothing
Sexual continence	Sexuality
Minimalization of sex distinctions	Maximalization of sex distinction
Absence of rank	Distinctions of rank
Humility	Just pride of position
Disregard for personal appearance	Care for personal appearance
No distinctions of wealth	Distinctions of wealth

Unselfishness	Selfishness
Total obedience	Obedience only to superior rank
Sacredness	Secularity
Silence	Speech
Suspension of kinship rights and obligations	Kinship rights and obligations
Continuous reference to mystical powers	Intermittent reference to mystical powers
Foolishness	Sagacity
Simplicity	Complexity
Acceptance of pain and suffering	Avoidance of pain and suffering
Heteronomy	Degrees of autonomy[2]

In the biblical texts of the Passion narrative, to one degree or another, all twenty-six possible properties of liminality are associated with Jesus. Other biblical texts, extending to the "Infancy Narratives" recorded different liminal characteristics. Liminality does not apply exclusively to Jesus, it is also extended to his followers, although not to the same intensified degree. His disciples are to live as pilgrims, accepting each other as brothers and sisters, live without care for riches, be servants to all, be humble and unselfish, remain faithful to the "way" etc. . . .

Beyond liminality, Jesus and his followers shared the bond of communitas. During his ministry, his relationship with the disciples was direct, face to face, and existential. In the liminal situation of his immanent death, he ate a shared common meal of liberation. After his death, his followers assumed a life of *koinonia*, a fellowship grounded in his death and resurrection as the meaning of human life. This *koinonia* partially reflected a realization of Jesus' "High Priestly Prayer for Unity" found in the 17th chapter of John, the completion of the "Last discourse." The communitas grounding the Christian *koinonia* was to be the hallmark, the rule, and the charter of the Christian "pseudospecies."

The liminality of Jesus and the spontaneous communitas of the "believers" survived insofar as Jesus and his disciples were anti-structural to Judaism. When Christianity became a structure in its own right, its liminal characteristics were, to a certain extent, neutralized and the bond of communitas became both normative and ideological rather than spontaneous.

The level of communitas in Christian culture viewed as structure will be the evaluative principle and criterion of the strength of its particular historical expression. If communitas is high, the particular Christian social structure will survive. Should communitas be low, the particular Christian social structure faces the possibility of disintegration. The intensity of communitas will be determined both by the acceptance or rejection of the fundamental root metaphor of Christ's death-resurrection, and the power of the cultural rituals or Christian sacraments to express and reinforce this metaphor by joining its members to this original charter-event and its past re-enactments. If Christian rituals, and especially the Eucharist, render present the charter-event of Christ's death and resurrection, the communitas of the *koinonia*, the unity and fellowship of all believers, will pervade and permeate the Christian social structure and verify its meaning. If Christian rituals cloak the foundational Christian metaphor, the social drama will vividly materialize within the Christian social structure itself and cry out for revision.

Communitas as an essential element for the preservation of cultural life assumes heightened importance in the Christian "pseudospecies" when placed within the present theological understanding of grace. In a real sense, the fundamental metaphor of Christ's death-resurrection and grace are one and the same reality. Christian sacramentality claims that the presence of God's offer of love and salvation is mediated through the community of his people. The gathered people of God are the Church, are the Christian culture, to the extent that they live the *koinonia*, the fellowship of those who share the communitas of Christ. The absence of communitas within the Christian community is a distortion of its root metaphor and a corruption of its culture.

It is interesting to realize that these fundamental insights have so often been attested to in Christian theological tradition. Theologians have pointed out that the Eucharist is both the sign and cause of unity in the Church. They have located the Church where the Eucharist is truly celebrated. They have noted that the Church is most herself and what she should be in the celebration of the Eucharist. Almost all movements of reform and renewal in the Christian structure have been prophetic demands to return the Church to a more real, concrete, and commensurate expression of the communitas which should sustain all its dimensions, operations, hopes, designs, and activities. This was the great proclamation of the *Decree on the Liturgy* at the Second Vatican Council. In this decree, ". . . the priority is given to the entire people of God as actively and responsively constituting the Church, before consideration of diverse ministries, inclusive of the *diaconia* based on holy orders."[3] "Secondly, and correlative to this basic concept of the Church, is the Constitution's underscoring of the dignity and role of the laity, based on their sacramental deputation to cult through baptism (confirmation)."[4] Only when the performance of Christian rituals, especially the celebration of the Eucharist, expresses and elicits communitas will the fundamental metaphor of Christ's death-resurrection be capable of sustaining a meaningful life amid the diverse tensions of binary-oppositions.

Christian sacraments should function as expressions of the fundamental ecclesial metaphor of the Christian faith. All of them, and the Eucharist in particular, aim at sustaining the Christian world view as a system of meaning for the random experiences of life, experiences containing both curses and blessings, pleasure and pain, fulfillment and frustration, life and death. In their ritual actions, Christians are joined to their Christ-centered charter-event made present through the power of their imagination and their clustered symbols. Christ, the meaning and mystery of human life, is the focal point of Christian ritual behavior.

The vision of sacraments as expressions of ecclesial root metaphors bears striking resemblance to our previous affirmations on the relation between the *res et sacramentum*, grace, and symbolic causality. Sacramental rituals, first and foremost, create a relationship between an individual and the community. In being drawn deeper into the community, the *koinonia*, God's self-gift of grace is mediated to the participants. Within the Christian world view, the attachment, interiorization, and conformity to the root metaphor of Christ's death-resurrection, in and through the re-enactment of this charter-event, is the attainment of salvation or grace. In their ritual symbolic activities, the Christian "ritualizers" are unified with the Father, through the Son, in the power of the Spirit, all within the visibility of the community of believers who are expressing themselves in symbolic activity.

Conclusion

This chapter commenced with a question. Do the Christian rituals, called sacraments, express the Christian root metaphor of Christ's death-resurrection? Our response has been affirmative. Christian sacraments exhibit the dimensions of ritual within the context of Christianity's distinctive world view. They function to take the random "stuff" of life with its tensions and, by placing them within the Christian paradigm, resolve them into positive meaning. In this regard, Christian sacraments express and reinforce the social structure of the Christian community, a social structure which was born in the "social drama" with Israel.

There are distinctive values in examining Christian sacraments in relation to root metaphors. First, the specificity and uniqueness of the Christian world view becomes obvious. Believers can become so caught up in the multiple issues of sacramentology that a vision of the whole is omitted. In relating Christian sacraments to root metaphors, one is brought face to face with the heart of Christian faith and the heart of sacramentology i.e., the death and resurrection of Jesus. Second, the relation of sacraments and root metaphors clarifies the real purpose of sacraments. Since the expression of root metaphors is ritual's primary function, the main purpose of sacraments is to proclaim, make present, and realize the effects of Christ's death and resurrection. There are, no doubt, many reasons why people participate in sacraments. The main reason, however, should be contact with the charter-event which encompasses all the experiences of life, interprets them, and gives them meaning beneath the Christian paradigm of the Paschal mystery. Sacraments offer this contact in and through the ritualizing Christian community. Third, in relating sacraments to root metaphors, a theological framework emerges which does justice to both the anthropological and theological dimensions of ritual in general and Christian ritual in particular. This framework permits a real interrelatedness and essential bond between human symbolic activity, the Christological and ecclesiological foundation of sacramentology, and the interpersonal-communal character of grace.

When sacraments are envisioned as expressions of the Christian root metaphor, sacramental theology reaches a higher vantage point of reflection. Such a sacramentology is nourished by the richness of the behavioral sciences and the best of its own theological tradition.

NOTES

1. T. Guzie, *Jesus and the Eucharist*. (New York: Paulist Press, 1974), p. 46.
2. Turner, *The Ritual Process*, pp. 106–107.
3. G. Diekmann, "The Constitution on the Sacred Liturgy," in *Vatican II: An Interfaith Appraisal*. John H. Millas, (ed.), (Notre Dame: University of Notre Dame Press, 1966), p. 20.
4. *Ibid.*

SUMMARY: PART THREE

In reconstructing a theology of sacraments for our contemporary age, two general observations stand out. First, sacraments are a melting pot for a blending of various theological disciplines. Second, by applying the behavioral sciences' insights into ritual to the key theological dimensions of sacraments a path is opened for a deeper penetration into the meaning and operation of sacraments *per se*.

A contemporary sacramental theology commences with a theology of the word of God. Jesus as the Father's word is the primordial sacrament. He is paradigmatic for all further sacramental affirmations. This implies that the elements constitutive of him as the word should be present and operative in all sacraments. Paramount among these elements was his bodiliness which gave him visibility and historicity. His body was the vehicle for his self-actualization. It was also the locus for God's self-gift of love and humankind's acceptance.

Our Christological starting point led to ecclesiological affirmations. The Church is the continuation of the Christological paradigm in history. It is the medium for the risen Christ's visibility and tangibility. It is his presence in the world. The Church is the sacrament of the risen Lord.

In proclaiming the word, the Church fulfills its mission and purpose. This proclamation requires visibility or enfleshment. The testimony to this enfleshment is the very corporate body of the Christian community in the union of its members. In being a *koinonia*, a Christian fellowship is what it was meant to be.

Sacraments are ecclesial in nature. They are first and foremost the Church proclaiming the word. The sacramental proclamation of the word, however, is unique among the many words the Church proclaims. In this proclamation, the very nature or essence of the Church is realized. In the sacraments, the saving love of God manifested in Christ for an individual is actually made present and realized. In sacraments, the Church not only speaks the word, but "performs" the word, it makes the word visible in action.

There is a direct bond between sacraments, *koinonia* and grace. When the proclamation of the word is made flesh in the Church, the Christian fellowship, the *koinonia*, is intensified. This ecclesial community, made one in Christ through the Spirit, mediates the offer and invitation to divine life which is the very basis for its existence and identity. This *is* sacramental action! It should also be noted that there is an essential communal dimension to all three realities i.e., *koinonia*, grace, and sacraments. They can never be isolated, individualistic affairs.

One and the same efficacy pervades Christ, Church, and sacraments. These realities make present what they signify without being identical to the signified. This presupposition underpins our whole endeavor. If symbols and symbolic activity do not exist, the efficacious power of rituals in general and Christian sacraments in particular can only make sense by a commitment to some "magical" principle, even though references to a "divine power" or "divine will" are conjured up to avoid this criticism. If the Incarnation is to be taken seriously, God has chosen to act within the dimensions of space and time and to respect the structural elements of humankind. A theology of sacraments need not attempt to escape from this condition. Comprehension of God's self-communication· manifested in Christian sacraments can be attained by exploring the full richness present in reality as a given. The action of the divine appears in the environment of humankind or not at all.

The value and importance of sacraments attains increased stature when contextualized by an anthropological understanding of ritual. The behavioral sciences depict ritual as the most natural, normal, and even necessary human activity. It is the key to personal growth, integration, and continued personality equilibrium. It fosters social communication and social relationships. It expresses the root metaphor which distinguishes a culture from all others. Without ritual, individuals and whole cultures face the threat of dissolution.

Our application of the anthropological data on ritual to Christian sacraments was not primarily intended for the construction of a sacramental apologetics, although the evidence is more than entertaining. Rather, the insights accruing from the behavioral sciences afford indispensable data for a theological comprehension of sacraments. Too often in the past, sacramentology concerned itself with little more than statements of the *what* and not the *why* and *how* of sacramental activity. Hopefully, our theological perspective demonstrates that an application of the anthropological insights into ritual to sacraments takes theological discourse beyond declarative statements to an understanding of sacramental operations which in turn deepens one's original theological comprehension. There is no need for reductionism in this method. Our claim that Christian sacraments follow the operation and functions of all ritual does not negate the distinctiveness of the Christian sacramental claims. On the contrary, it discloses the real unique center of Christianity i.e., its root metaphor of Christ's death and resurrection. Sacraments continually express and reinforce this Christian world view, and in doing so, bring all reality under the paradigmatic Christ.

PART FOUR
SACRAMENTAL MODELS

Every theological system utilizes a particular model to explain its unique vision or orientation. The sacramental theology proposed in the previous pages presumes its own particular model, i.e., *celebration*.

This section will outline the main elements of the celebration model and contrast it will alternative models which have been influential during the last decade of reflection on the meaning and operation of sacraments.

In explicitly identifying the model at work in our sacramental theology, it is hoped that certain presuppositions or unconscious conviction which have influenced our theological effort might be thematized and thereby clarified.

12 CELEBRATION: TOWARD A REVISED SACRAMENTAL MODEL

Contemporary scholarship is fascinated with models. These instruments for comprehension have assisted both theoreticians and practitioners in all fields of research to delve more deeply into the foundations and structures of their respective intellectual arenas. Theology itself has born much fruit through the analysis and application of models to its systems and discourse. Models have brought to consciousness and highlighted the basic presuppositions and limitations which underpin all theological endeavors.

Models can be described as exploratory devices of scholarship which organize data in a working hypothesis; and, preconceptions coloring cognition and comprehension of reality.[1] On the one hand, models structure experience and realities in such a way that a discovery of previously overlooked insights is evoked. Models are heuristic. On the other hand, models exert a determining force on how reality is perceived and understood. Usually this determining force remains hidden or unconscious. One's theological understanding of the Church is a good example of these two dimensions. There are a variety of models for the Church e.g., institution, herald, communion, sacrament, servant, etc. Depending on which model is selected, every other dimension of the Church will be interpreted and evaluated in correspondence to it. Therefore, an institutional ecclesial model will present ministry in the Church in terms of hierarchical function. When questioned why ministry is restricted to the hierarchy, a person will frequently respond: that is the way it is, and rarely acknowledge that they have opted for an institutional model. Models are always there, but are usually presupposed and unconscious.

There are three types of exploratory models: physical, logical, and theoretical (conceptual). Physical models usually attempt a scale reproduction of the object they are trying to represent.[2] For example, a model of a house is constructed in miniature size to a gain an idea of its design and structural relations i.e., the proportionate sizes of the rooms. Logical models attempt to reveal a particular reality through the axioms, rules, or definitions of logic.[3] For example, the sun emits energy without appearing to significantly shrink over a long period of time. Einstein used a logical model to penetrate the mystery of this phenomenon i.e., $E = M C^2$. The various disciples of mathematics exemplify logical models. The theoretical or conceptual models work on a principle of *selectivity*. It is a "closed system which provides a meaningful selective representation of reality."[4] In the theoretical model the key aspects which are thought to more or less correspond to the core or essence of the reality under investigation are selected as the hinges for understanding the whole reality. For example, an inventory of ecclesial elements will note institutions, sacraments, preaching, service, politics, communion, piety, etc. In the theoretical model, one of these elements will be selected as expressing the depth of the Church and function as the umbrella under which all other elements will be interrelated and explained. It is important to note that the selected element(s) functions symbolically i.e., making present the reality of the Church without being identical to it or exhausting its meaning.[5]

Beyond evoking discovery, models prejudice and color our comprehension of reality. Models are reminiscent of the "first principles" or *creencias* which were claimed to be at the heart of the present cultural crisis. Models lie submerged in individuals, "schools of thought," and whole cultures. In a real sense, they are the ground of thinking and understanding.[6] It is the unconscious or submerged character of models that fuels their vital power. A change in these basic unconscious models involves nothing less than the creation of a new culture, a new historical period, or a new scientific theory. This is obvious when one compares the understanding of man and the universe in American and European cultures, the Middle Ages and the Enlightenment, or the Ptolemaic and Copernican universe.

Any attempted reconstruction of a theological discipline implies a shift in models. This is true of the present revision of sacramental theology which has turned to the anthropological sciences as a source for its theological reflection. Consequently, a new sacramental model has been implied. This chapter will try and outline the presupposed model of *celebration*. Celebration is a theoretical model. It has been preferred to the physical and logical models for two reasons. First, there is a flexibility in a theoretical model absent from the other types. Second, and more importantly, the symbolic character of the selected element which makes the theoretical model work corresponds to the symbolic character of the Christian sacraments. The rich symbolic arena of sacramental life often resists exact definition or reduction to logical statements.[7]

Before focusing on *celebration*, it is valuable to examine three alternate models which have been operative in sacramental theology during the last century. "Late-Scholasticism," "Mystery-Presence," and "Interpersonal-Encounter" offer a background against which the distinctiveness of the *Celebration* model can be traced and historically contextualized.

Scholasticism after the Fifteenth Century

The origin, formation, and mutation of Scholasticism's sacramental vision is extremely complex.[8] Consequently, generalizations should be issued hesitantly. Nevertheless, it is possible to point out two questions reverted to by the Scholastic tradition which hint at its sacramental model. The first question centered on the composition of the sacraments. The second question studied sacramental causality.

The genesis of Scholasticism's understanding of sacramental composition can be traced to Scripture and the Fathers of the Church.[9] In Scripture, a ritual action is always coupled with a word or prayer. The Church Fathers, Augustine in particular, applied this scheme to their interpretation of sacraments. These ecclesial rituals were considered to consist of matter and spirit i.e., the phenomena observed (*elementum*) and the words (*verbum*) pronounced in using the *elementum*. Augustine wrote: *accedit verbum ad elementum et fit sacramentum.*[10]

In the early Middle Ages, Augustine's terminology underwent a linguistic evolution. *Materia* replaced *elementum*. *Forma sacramenti* or *forma verborum* replaced *verbum*.[11] Linguistic changes rather than philosophical reorientation were the causes for this substitution. The early Scholastics, and even Aquinas, were not yet employing *materia* and *forma* in terms of Aristotelian hylomorphism, but attempting to express the earlier tradition in their contemporary Latin.[12] After Thomas, however, hylomorphism dominated Scholasticism and *materia* and *forma* assumed their new technical meanings.[13]

The separation of *materia* and *forma* from the biblical-patristic tradition in the sixteenth century led to a "thing-like" conception of grace. *Materia* and *forma* = *res*. In the situation of sacramental behavior, this *res* was grace.

By the sixteenth century, and continuing to some extent into our own age, sacraments are some*thing* which causes grace, which is itself some*thing*. The journey into a physical-quantitative model had commenced.

Causality was the second issue dominating the Scholastics' discussion of sacramentology. A positive intention pervaded their investigation into this subject i.e., to insure the gratuity of God's self-gift and to avoid a too thing-like understanding of grace. Unfortunately, the notions of efficacy and causality, emerging from their efforts, proved not only unsuccessful but deleterious.

The complexities surrounding the Scholastics' doctrines of causality are no less involved than those surrounding sacramental composition. First, the sacraments "work" *ex opere operato*. Second, the sacraments signify what they effect and effect what they signify. Whether dispositive, physical, moral, occasional, or intentional, causality is examined, the absolute freedom and gratuity of God's self-gift is vigorously defended. These Scholastic theories, however, all fell short in explaining how the sacraments cause grace. This deficiency arose from the limitations inherent in their models. They tended to view the sacraments mechanistically i.e., the sacraments produce grace as a machine produces good, or magically i.e., God has simply deigned that when these words were spoken grace would be offered. Even the more personalistic position of Aquinas grounded in the passion, death and resurrection of Christ went undeveloped.

Once the physical-quantitative notion of grace was coupled with a mechanical understanding of causality, the model prevalent among so many Christians of the past and present, solidified in its mechanical-physical form. The great Scholastics would never have accepted this interpretation. Thomas, Scotus and Bonaventure would have found it abhorent. Yet, later authors, who claimed these "greats" as the initiators of this vision, secured the mechanistic-physical model as the unconscious model for Christian sacramentology for over three centuries.

One is not surprised to note the Protestant tradition of the sixteenth century warning of a manipulative tendency operative in the late Scholastic orientation. Man's ritual performance could so easily be envisioned as shackling the divine. The Protestant tradition correctly saw that late Scholasticism had fallen into the very trap they hoped to avoid.

The victory of the mechanistic-physical model in Roman Catholicism was costly. The sign/symbol character of sacraments was forced to lie dormant in forgotten theological traditions. Every attempt to awaken this lost perspective raised cries of heresy. A mechanistic-physical model of sacramentology simply had no room for symbolism or symbolic activity. The questions of "validity of performance" and "accumulation of graces" slowly became the exclusive thrust of sacramental investigations and writings.

The mechanical-physical model of late Scholasticism proves inadequate for penetrating into the meaning of sacraments on three fundamental levels. First, grace and the sacraments are not things. Grace is the living God freely coming and offering himself to man. Sacraments are first and foremost symbolic activities. It is impossible to reduce or understand the relation between God and humankind as the relation between physical objects. Second, the late Scholastic model fails to include any reference to the relationship between sacraments, grace, the word of God, and the Church. One has the impression that it is quite possible to locate sacraments and grace in an extrinsic position to Christ and the community of believers. Sacraments and sacramental grace, however, can never be understood except as bound to Christ, the sacrament of the Father, and the Church, the sacrament of Christ. Sacramentology is necessarily Christological and ecclesiological. Third, the mechanical-physical model ascribed a passive attitude to the recipients of sacraments. Sacraments are some*thing* individuals "attend," "watch," or "receive" rather than community rituals in which they actively participate and share. Sacraments are never individual private affairs. They are communal symbolic activities.

Among the various Scholastic positions certain positive values can be identified. For example, moral causality stressed the sacraments as prayers. This is a perennially valid fact. Occasional causality recognized the need to maintain the total gratuity and freedom of God in his self-gift. Physical causality emphasized the real nature of God's activity. Sacraments and grace are not imaginary. Yet, taken as a whole, the physical-mechanical model which emerged in late Scholasticism and perdured to the twentieth century fails to express adequately the present data on sacramentology.

Mystery—Presence (*Mysteriengegenwart*)

A variety of forces coalesced between 1920 and 1950 to create a general dissatisfaction with the individualistic, mechanistic, and quantitative models prevalent in sacramentology. Husserl's phenomenological method initiated a new philosophical direction on the continent. Two world wars had jarred and dissipated the utopian climate instilled by Hegelian optimism. One positive effect amid the tragedy of the wars surfaced. Many theological scholars gained a freedom for research. They returned to the libraries and read the Scriptures, Fathers of the Church, and the great Scholastics with "new eyes." From the settling dust of warfare emerged a new and well-informed theological vision.

Liturgical renewal was one of the first concentrations in twentieth-century Europe. New hope for vibrant worship in the Christian Churches emerged from the liturgical investigations undertaken in the Benedictine abbeys of Solesmes in France, Maredsous and Mont-Ceasar in Belgium, and Maria Laach in Germany. The climate was ripe for the formulation of a new sacramental model. This potential became fact in the work of Dom Odo Casel (1886–1948) a monk of Maria Laach and the distinguished proponent of the *Mysteriengegenwart* or "Mystery-Presence" model.

> Casel (and the lively controversy around his work) gave perhaps the greatest single impetus to the general movement in theology and spirituality away from the individualistic, sometimes excessively objectivised approach characteristic of the post-Renaissance period up till the last decade of the nineteenth century.[14]

Casel elaborated many of his ideas in the liturgical review under his direction from 1921–1941, the *Jarhbuch für Liturgiewissenschaft*. One main idea almost exclusively predominated his life's work: ". . . to expound the theological aspects of the liturgy" and see "in the Eucharist a re-enactment of the mysteries of Christ by his Church (Mysterienlehre)."[15]

Two goals specified Casel's theological enterprise. First, he wanted to avoid the individualism of decadent Scholasticism and return to the rich theological tradition of the Father's. Second, he aimed, with the assistance of Husserl's phenomenological method, at unearthing the Christian *Kulteidos* i.e., the core of Christian worship and the Christian sacraments. He began his reflection with an examination of the Greek Mystery religions.

In the ancient Greek world there was a keen sense of *moira* (fate). The "gods" controlled the destiny of man. The one escape from the fates was the Greek Mystery religions. In these religions the members could obtain the *secret* and gain *soteria* (salvation). The mysteries consisted of secret rites and symbols reserved for the initiated. It was thought that knowledge of the mysteries assured personal advantage either in this life or after death. Salvation (*soteria*) consisted in this advantage or good fortune.[16] Casel believed

> that the concept of Christian mystery in worship, in the exact sense in which he understood it, had been historically speaking the Christian response, true and transcendental, to those general religious aspirations of mankind which were manifested in ancient times in the abberations of the pagan mystery cults.

In these pagan ritual mysteries, thought Casel, under the symbol of the rite of worship, representing the historical vicissitudes of a divine supposed to be a savior, above all his death and resurrection (e.g., Mithros, Isis, and Osiris), the initiate was persuaded to relive himself, by way of worship and through a mysterious assimiliation, of those same vicissitudes of the god, above all his death and resurrection, and thus obtain soteria, salvation.[17]

The main difference between the mystery religions and the state cults was their emphasis on the intimate and personal relationship between the initiated and the gods. The gods honored in the mysteries were considered to have visibly appeared on earth, undergone human sufferings, and rediscovered good fortune, salvation or eternal life. The actions and experiences of the gods were not buried in the past, but actually made present in the cultic actions of the Mystery religions. The presence of the gods was realized in sacred actions, words, and symbols. It was considered a real and objective presence, not just intentional. It was in and through the rituals of the Mystery religions that access was gained to the gods, the participants were unified to them, and salvation was gained.[18]

Casel attempted to identify the *Kult-eidos* (essence of cult) of the Mystery religions. He tried to explain how and in what manner divinization or salvation was attained. He concluded that in the system of the Mystery religions, salvation was not a purely spiritual reality, but something tangible, audible, and perceptible in the context of their worship or cult. Casel envisioned these various elements coagulating to form the essence of worship i.e., "Mystery-Presence." The *Mystery* is a cultic action, a sacred action, in which a saving event is made *present*. In performing the specific rite, the worshiping community takes part in the saving event and procures salvation.[19] In a visible rite, a divine reality is made present to the participants. Mystery, for Casel, is always equal to "Mystery-Presence" i.e., the idea of mystery necessarily and unavoidably implies that the divine reality is brought into the presence of the worshiping community.

Casel proceeded to apply his insights and discoveries to Christian worship and the Christian sacraments. In this case, the saving action or event was Christ's historical redemptive actions. Christian sacraments made these actions present to the worshiping community who were united to them and, thereby, attained salvation.

According to Casel, there is rendered objectively present in the sacramental act of worship not only the *effect* of Christ's historical redemptive actions and especially the Passion; in other words, there is made objectively present not only grace; but also the past redemptive action itself, in particular the Passion on Golgotha, not indeed in all the least circumstances of persons and environment, but, as he says, in what was essential in that action, in its substance.

Thus according to Casel, in the rite which in the liturgy is performed in space and time. Christ's historical redemptive actions on earth and especially the Passion are "commemorated" in the sense of being rendered objectively present, re-presented, and be it noted, numerically the same, although—and this must also be carefully noted in Casel's position—in a way of their own completely unique.[20]

Christ's presence in the sacraments is a "Mystery-Presence."

For Casel, "Mystery-Presence" was isolated as the point of selection for his sacramental model. There are both real advantages and disadvantages to this selection. Positively "Mystery-Presence" breaks out of the individualistic and mechanistic post-Renaissance Scholasticism and returns to the rich tradition of the Fathers of the Church with their emphasis on the relation between sacraments, Christ, Community, and grace. Casel's vision correctly identifies the sacraments as communal acts of worship, as liturgy.

Moreover, Casel's "Mystery-Presence" secures the freedom and gratuity of God's self-gift, and links this self-gift to the historical offer of salvation made in Christ as the revelation and presence of God in humankind's world. Grace is also properly understood as a participation in the redemptive acts disclosed in the person of Jesus the Christ who is really and objectively present in the worshiping community of the believers.

Casel's "Mystery-Presence" model also leans in the direction of personalism. In a real sense, his model paves the way for the "Interpersonal-Encounter" model developed in the late 1950's and early 1960's. "Mystery-Presence" is concerned with personal causality and symbolic activity. Sacraments, for Casel, are activities which focus on the person of Christ, the revelation of the Father.

The final advantage of Casel's model is more difficult to articulate. "Mystery-Presence" contains the needs for affirming a sacramental model grounded in the "giveness" of God's presence i.e., God as the ultimate cause for the sacramental celebration. Too often, sacraments are envisioned as creating something new. Joined to this attitude is an ill-founded optimism that God can be totally understood and his operations digested and explained. Casel's "Mystery-Presence" is a healthy reminder that the sacraments celebrate realities that have already become present, even though they may not have attained their full significance and meaning.

Humankind can never be exempt from reflection and reason, but humankind will never exhaust the activities of a God who transcends the limits of human analysis and dissection, while at the same time respecting the structures and processes of human existence. Sacraments do not conjure up God. They vividly make present, express, and deepen within the sacramental participants the love of God which is already and always present for his people.

Casel's "Mystery-Presence" model is not without is limitations and deficits. In the first place, the data available for verification and substantiation of Casel's interpretation of the Greek Mystery religions is meager. This should not be surprising. Secret cults rarely leave behind documentation of their operation and doctrines. It is therefore difficult, if not impossible, to ascertain exactly what their *Kult-eidos* actually was and how this was related to their overall religious synthesis.

Casel was too optimistic in his portrayal of the "Mystery-Presence's" influence on the Fathers of the Church. He contended that the Greek Fathers were initially opposed to the Greek Mysteries, but with the increase of Greeks entering the Christian community, their past religious practices, thought patterns, and language were evaluated more favorably. Eventually, in Casel's opinion, the Greek Fathers employed the dynamisms of the Greek Mystery religions to interpret and explain the Christian meaning of the sacraments. He singled out the rites and teachings surrounding the catechumenate and the sacraments of initiation to defend this position. Unfortunately, as in the case of the Greek Mystery religions themselves, very little is known about the interpretation of the Greek Mystery religions from the texts of the Fathers.

A philosophical objection, however, is the most significant one posed to the "Mystery-Presence" model. Casel merely posits the presence of God in the saving acts of Christ in the sacramental celebration. He fails to explain how this "Mystery-Presence" comes about. One has the impression that Casel hints toward the typical *theandric* nature of Christ's activity i.e., Christ as a human being belongs to the order of human existence and his actions are therefore temporal and passing; as God, however, Christ's actions are supra-temporal and eternal. Undoubtedly, this position faithfully represents the tradition of the Church Fathers, but Casel posits it without defending the logic of its possibility.

On the whole Casel's intuition and goals were good. He was able to break through an impoverished Scholasticism and open up new vistas in sacramental theology. The inspiration emerging from his model of "Mystery-Presence" is, however, more valuable than its content.

"Interpersonal-Encounter"

From disillusionment and the pain of the world wars a second philosophical movement was born in Europe. French "Existentialism, the varied survivors of the holocaust and Christian thinkers rediscovered and expounded the importance and value of the human person. Two words predominated the discourse among psychologists, philosophers, and theologians: *Personalism* and *Encounter*. False utopianism had succumbed to the admission of humankind's potential for choosing destruction and oblivion. Nostalgia for the past had yielded to the need for rebuilding a dismembered social order in the present. Yesterday's hopes had faded and life could never again be exactly the same. Some believed that "tomorrow" might never arrive. Meaning, if it ever could be found, it could only come today, in the now, in the present. Only face to face relationships could offer an answer.

Theologians capitalized on the European intellectual climate. The feelings, hopes and language of the times were more amenable to Christian thought than in many ages. *Personalism* and *Encounter* were themes which reached the core of Christian faith and doctrine, even though post-Reformation Scholasticism had failed to underline their constitutive character. From the 1940's onward, a theological reconstruction was undertaken which attempted to interpret and express Christian revelation and doctrine within these prevailing categories. The model of "Interpersonal-Encounter" was to predominate not only sacramentology, but the whole theological enterprise.

Proponents of the "Interpersonal-Encounter" model focus on the relationship which exists between persons as their point of selection. This relationship is generally characterized as a mutual acceptance, acknowledgement and enrichment of one another in gratuity and freedom. Three elements stand out in this model. First, an encounter is a meeting between two or more persons who are in an "I-Thou" rather than an "I-It" relationship. Second, the encounter transpires in the present, the now. Third, the encounter is a mutual self-giving performed in equality and freedom. Two theologians in particular exemplified the application of this model to sacramentology: Otto Semmelroth and Eduard Schillebeeckx.

In his book, *Kirche als Ursakrament*, Semmelroth pointed out a double or dialogical movement in every sacrament. He called these the sacramental movement and the sacrificial movement. He employed the image of a marriage relationship to elucidate the difference between these two movements.

Semmelroth considered the encounter between God and man in sacraments to be the "male movement." God takes the initiative and reaches down to humankind. He initiates his gesture of salvation, offering man the opportunity to participate in his Trinitarian life. Semmelroth considered the activity of God to be both gratuitous and authoritative (effective).

The sacramental encounter between God and man also had a sacrificial dimension. Semmelroth called this the "bridal movement." The sacramental participants respond to God's self-gift by offering him their prayers, faith, and commitment.

The important perspective in Semmelroth's thesis is not his particular explanations of the sacramental character, but his insistence on the *dialogical character* of the sacramental relationship between God and humankind. The encounter itself is God coming to man. Man's response to this offer is accepted grace, or the actualization of his potential relationship with God. Semmelroth's choice of terminology to describe the dialogical movements will find strong contemporary objection and reservation. The attachment of masculine overtones to God's offer and feminine overtones to humankind's response will be vigorously challenged by scholars sensitive to the women's liberation movement. His choice of the word sacrifice will also come under scrutiny. In its deepest sense the word *sacrifice* means a public act of worship or faith, which accepts God as God. Unfortunately, common parlance has understood the term to imply either pain, suffering, immolation or destruction.

Schillebeeckx entitled his treatment of sacraments in general *Christ the Sacrament of Encounter with God*. Originally, he was to have published a two volume work: *De Sacramentele Heilseconomie*. Volume One of this tome appeared in 1952 with the final page presenting the outline for Volume Two. This second part, however, has never appeared. *Christ the Sacrament . . .* was published in 1963 as its replacement.

Although Schillebeeckx's title indicated *Encounter* as his sacramental model, he did not really build a sacramentology on the basis of a phenomenology of encounter. Rather, he used the model of encounter to collect and organize the "classical" elements of sacramentology. His model did allow, however, for a new and deeper meaning to emerge from these classical treatises and theses.

Schillebeeckx created a new perspective or framework for sacramentology by employing his "Encounter" model. He was able to view Christ as the sacrament of God, the person/place where the unsurpassable meeting between God and humankind unfolds. In his vision, the Church was the sacrament of the risen Christ, his presence in the world, the community within which the love of Christ for humankind is historically concretized and made present. Schillebeeckx located both sacramental efficacy and causality in the encounter with the risen Lord in and through the Church.

The "Interpersonal-Encounter" model manifested in the works of Semmelroth, Schillebeeckx, Rahner, Fransen and others had profound advantages. Their sacramental theology, and understanding of sacramental grace in particular, reflected more accurately the biblical record of God's revelation to humankind. More importantly, the necessity of personal involvement, commitment and faith returned to sacramental discourse as a critical corrective of the passive mechanical-physical attitude dominating the three earlier centuries of reflection on sacramentology.

"Interpersonal-Encounters" demand mutual activity, self-giving, freedom and acceptance. Grace as a participated relation in the life of God, who has manifested himself in the life of Jesus, present in the Church through the power of the Spirit, demands no less. A clear example is given here of how the point of selection in a theoretical model controls and limits theological discourse. The choice of "Interpersonal Encounter necessitates a structure founded on interpersonal relationships. Within this perspective, it is impossible to conceive of grace as some*thing* that can be quantitatively accumulated. It is likewise impossible to have totally passive interpersonal relations wherein the free and loving exchange of selves could be realized mechanically. The "Interpersonal-Encounter" model demands that grace be described if at all, in qualitative relational terms which require personal activity.

The "Interpersonal-Encounter" model is not without its limitations. At times, the impression is given that the present time mode is exclusively important. It seems that the now is over-emphasized to the detriment of the past and the future. No person or community, however, can exist without a meaningful past which is made present in the ritual celebration. Similarly, any sacramental activity which does not look forward to the future with expectation and actually exert an influence in the development and construction of the future will be forgotten and buried in an unknown historical past.

The "Interpersonal-Encounter" model also faces the danger of deteriorating into a privatized individualism, a "me and God" attitude. The magnified contemporary fixation on the self and, "What does it mean for me?" can distort the true dialogical character of any encounter. While the love God offers is always personal and immediate to an individual, it is also a mediated love. The sacramental encounter with God is always in and through the community of the Church as the presence of Christ in the world.

Finally, the "Interpersonal-Encounter" model can overlook an important and necessary element of the sacramental theological tradition originating in St. Augustine and surviving in the writings of the mystics. This element is the *givenness* of God's presence in the core and depths of humankind. Only the gratuitous giveness of God's presence can be a sturdy ground for sacramental celebrations.

Celebration: A New Sacramental Model

The anthropological data on ritual guiding and informing our theological reconstruction of sacramentology and the exigency of the limitations of the previous sacramental models offers an impetus to search for a new model. The point of selection in this model is *celebration*. It is believed that in viewing the sacraments as celebrations, the positive elements of Scholasticism, "Mystery-Presence", and "Interpersonal-Encounter" can be salvaged and their limitations rectified. Furthermore, it is believed that the celebration model opens sacramental theological reflection to the vast nourishment available from the anthropological investigation into ritual in general.

The term *celebration* has a specific meaning as it is employed in our sacramental model. *A celebration is a communal activity by which a community manifests, symbolizes, and makes present to their individual selves and the members of the community the reality of a joyful, consoling, enriching reality-event.* In this definition, a celebration is both a symbol and a model. A celebration points to a reality and makes it present, without being identical to the reality. It also structures reality into a particular form or order so that a particular reality-event can be understood.

Two further elements of a celebration require notation and explanation if the term's meaning is to be stated more accurately. First, any celebration presupposes that the reality-event being celebrated is already there, already present. This presence is a given The givenness of the reality-event is presupposed to the extent that celebrations function symbolically, for all symbols have as their *a priori condition of possibility* the reality they are symbolizing, the reality they are making present. For example, my body can only be a symbol of myself because there is a self to be symbolized. Likewise, there can only be a celebration because there has been or is a reality-event to be celebrated or made present.

It is the richness of the reality-event itself that grounds the celebration. In and through the celebration, however, the reality-event becomes more real, more intensely present. The actual celebrating (and therefore symbolizing) of the reality-event enables its depth of meaning and givenness to unfold and become more real and meaningful to both the individual "celebrants" and the celebrating community as a whole. This framework is exemplified in a twenty-fifth wedding anniversary. The reality-event being celebrated is twenty-five years of shared life and love. The celebration, with its manifold elements of party, song, dances, family, friends and stories allows the givenness of the shared life-love to become more real to the individuals, the gathered community, and even others beyond the community who hear of the celebration.

Second, celebrations are repetitive. They usually appear in a definite time pattern or cycle. On a regular basis the community celebrates the reality-event. Through the repetition of the celebration, a bond is maintained with the reality-event and the community is capable of sustaining a shared identity among its members. This shared identity will reflect not only the consciousness of participating in the particular historical celebration, but more significantly a shared world view and history grounded in the reality-event itself. For example, nations regularly celebrate their founding date, religious communities celebrate the feast and significant events of their originator, and families celebrate birthdays. All of these various celebrations hearken the participants back to their origins wherein their common identity is disclosed and discovered anew.

The above definition/description of celebrations is in concert with the anthropological dimensions of ritual. In fact, all celebrations are rituals. They involve two or more persons, are repetitive and have adaptive value. Celebrations as rituals link the participants to a charter-event (reality-event) and previous re-enactments of this event, in which process *unfinished business* is uncovered and taken up as a task to be completed. Celebrations as rituals evoke feelings, attitudes and patterns of behavior in order to create a unity and bond among the celebrators, a bond which is based on the meaning of the charter-event (reality-event).

Temporality and Personalization

Among the multiple dimensions emerging from a phenomenology of celebration, two facets in particular are germane to the function of celebration as a model for sacraments. First, celebrations possess a temporal dimension i.e., a memory of the past, a location in the present, and a hopeful expectation of the future. Second, celebrations include a process of personalization grounded in a dual/dialogical movement of internalization-externalization.

Celebrations are human events. They participate in human historicity exhibited in its triple modality i.e., past (*anamnesis*), present (*kairos*), and future (*eschaton*). A reduction of any temporal mode weakens the full richness of celebration and can result in a warped comprehension of its meaning. Each temporal mode or dimension contributes to the richness, fullness and depth of its meaning.

Very frequently the word "commemoration" is employed as a synonym for celebration. Both "sacred" and "secular" communities commemorate past events. Revealed religions, especially those which recount the entrance of a diety into human history, secure a special place for the commemoration of past events. Caution should be observed in the use of the word "commemoration" or memory, since it can have a variety of meanings. A clarification of its meaning in the context of celebration is essential.

Memory can be a purely intellectual affair e.g., remember the "good old days." Memory can be understood as an incentive to motivation or behavior e.g., remember the reward/punishment. The richest meaning of memory is, however, the making present here and now of the effects of a past reality-event (charter-event). This particular understanding of memory (*anamnesis*) dominates the Judeo-Christian comprehension of their religious ritual celebrations, especially the celebration of the Passover-Exodus and the Eucharist-Last Supper/Calvary. In these ritual celebrations of past reality-events, their effects are again made present in the ritual community. In this scheme, it is important to underscore the interdependence of the reality-event and the ritual celebration. The givenness of the reality-event, charged with significance and meaning, grounds and causes the celebration. Concurrently, it is the givenness of the reality-event itself which is disclosed and made present in the ritual celebration. This rich meaning of memory as *anamnesis* in the Judeo-Christian sense is the one presently employed in the context of celebration.

The actual celebration of a reality-event transpires in the present temporal mode. The present is not to be taken as a mere cyclic repetition of the past (Greek understanding), but a linear development from the past (Hebrew understanding). It is significant that the shift from a cyclic to a linear understanding of time arose within the context of Israel's religious ritual celebrations. Van Rad has astutely demonstrated that while actually celebrating her religious festivals, Israel began to look back into her past. Israel came to the comprehension that what Yahweh had effected in the past, Yahweh was effecting today in the present. From the distance of the present, the depth of meaning, the fuller effects, and the various implications of Israel's past reality-event (charter-event) were more completely revealed and comprehended in their being made present in and through the religious ritual celebration. Furthermore, in the actual performance of the ritual celebration the participants were made one with the past events now present in their celebration. A continuity of past and present was forged which grounded a continued identity. As previously noted, the basis for this identity and historical bond was the givenness of the reality-event. An example of this identification through participation in ritual celebrations is apparent in the Old Testament varients on the number of Israelites who participated in the original Exodus event. This number varies from two tribes, to twelve tribes, to 10,000 people. These numerical differences can be understood in terms of the increasing population of Israel who participated in the Passover meal and were, therefore, considered to have actually made the journey from Egypt to the Promised Lane.

The celebration of a reality-event in the present is a *kairos*, a critical opportunity, a blessed time. During the time of the celebration the community, as a whole and as individuals, exist in a supercharged occasion. The opportunity is available for abandonment to the meaning of the reality-event. The potential is made present for participation in their origin, identity and reason for being together as a community.

Celebrations are more than a memory (*anamnesis*) and a present re-enactment (*kairos*). Celebrations are marked with an expectation, a hope to celebrate again. The actual repetition of certain celebrations attest to this important perspective. A particular reality-event (charter-event) will only be celebrated to the extent that it is envisioned as valuable and meaningful for the future.

The richness, depth and meaning-significance of the reality-event itself determine its accessibility for future celebrations. If the reality-event survives the test of time, it will exert a determining power on the future by shaping its possible limits and offering a reference point for interpreting the future's meaning. If the meaning of a reality-event is weak or insignificant, it will slip into the unknown past and be void of a future.

The future dimension of celebration correlates with the dynamism of the social drama. Reality-events are celebrated and determinant of the future because they resolve binary-oppositions and ground a comprehensive world view emerging from a root metaphor. Ritual celebrations express and sustain this global vision forming a social structure. Insofar as the social structure is high in *communitas*, it will be strong and stable. In this case, the ritual celebrations which express it will be continued in the future. A dmiminished *communitas* will threaten the social structure and make it vulnerable to challenge and potential dissolution. Ritual celebrations sustaining a collapsing social structure and root metaphor will be transformed or totally discarded. New root metaphors with accompanying ritual celebrations will emerge from the anti-structure and inherit re-enactment in the future.

Along with temporality, celebrations include a process of personalization grounded in a dynamism of internalization-externalization. The first movement in any celebration is internal. The ritual participants, as individuals and community, are turned inward to the source and foundation of the celebration i.e., the givenness of the reality-event. The process of "turning in," "contemplating," or "listening" allows the significance and meaning of the reality-event to arise within the consciousness of the participants and become fixed as the meaning and purpose of their coming together. Internalization aims at union, intimacy, and the neutralization of separation and distance. Language, gesture, and symbolic activity are activated for its attainment.

In the celebration, internalization gives way to externalization. As individuals and community, the participants reach out to one another to express the meaning and effect of the experienced reality-event. In the process of externalization, the participants become living acting symbols. In and through the participants, the reality-event discloses its depth of meaning. The celebrating community becomes the living vessel of its meaningful treasure.

The process of personalization unfolding in celebrations affirms a fundamental truth and condition of human existence. The full meaning of any reality is disclosed and discovered in-relation-with-others. The human person and the human community reach their fullest comprehension and participation in a reality to the extent that they are a being-together. The psychological, anthropological, sociological, and philosophical data on ritualization are radically affirmed in this declaration. The great variety of "psychological schools" all highlight the importance of others in the development of personality. Sociology has as its scientific presupposition the relational character of human existence. Contemporary philosophy underlines co-existence as a radical principle of human life. In our relation-with-others the richness of life and love are unfolded, a richness in which we participate. Celebrations, as human events, mirror the dialogical character of human life. All true celebrations will exemplify the dual move ments of internalization-externalization.

Sacraments as Celebrations

The *celebration model* has three perimeters. First, the basis of any celebration is the reality-event itself. In the ritual celebration of the reality-event, its meaning is unfolded. Second, celebrations are fully temporal. They originate in the past, transpire in the present, and yearn for the future. Third, celebrations are both a "turning in" and a "turning out," individual and communal. Does the celebration model, however, adequately serve the reality of sacraments? Is it evocative of their meaning and reflective of their relational elements?

In our definition/description of *celebration*, three main features can be isolated: first, a way of being together (community); second, a manifestation and symbolic activity; third, a reality-event as a *given*. Each of these elements corresponds to an indispensable dimension of sacraments. Sacraments are symbols arising from the ministry of Jesus continued in and through the Church, which when received in faith are encounters with God, Father, Son, and Holy Spirit.

Sacraments are thoroughly ecclesial. They are always sacraments of and through the Church. The Church is not to be considered first and foremost as a hierarchy or clergy, but a community, a *koinonia*, a way of being together in Christ. More specifically, sacraments are symbolic activities of the ecclesial Christian community. They are community patterns of behavior in which the nature of the community is expressed and realized. In its sacramental activity the Church becomes what it was meant to be i.e., the historical presence of Christ in the world offering the Father's love to humankind. Sacramental economy is always an ecclesial economy.

This vision of sacraments conforms to both the Hebrew and Christian Scriptures' vision of the saving activity of God. In both records, God saves his people in the action of bringing them together and forming them into a people. For both the Jew and the Christian, the charter-event of their respective salvation is at the same time the origin of their being a community i.e., the Exodus and the Last Supper-Calvary.

The communion of people is the basis for God's self-communication, his self-gift. The Church as the gathered people of God living the fellowship of *koinonia* grounds sacramental life. God is the agent of this community. He is the one who gathers them into a community.

It is in their being together as a community that the consciousne-s, experience, and actuality of their being saved is realized, a salvation in which they participate as individuals. This is the theological significance and meaning of the *res et sacramentum* as a relationship to or status within the Church. The ecclesial *koinonia*, the Church fellowship, is also the mediation and concurrently, the effect of grace (*charis*) within a theological perspective. It is evident that *celebration* and sacramentology are both grounded in community as a way of being together.

Sacraments are symbolic activities. They express and realize in ritual form the presence of the living God offering himself to the community; and, at the same time, they are the acceptance of God's love by the community in their act of worship. Sacraments are more than symbols. They are fundamentally activities or modes of expression involving the totality of the participants i.e., their cognitive, volitional, emotional, and physical dimensions.

Sacraments are performative. People "do" sacraments. Precisely as ritual activities, sacraments make present the offer of God's love. Through these community ritual activities, the participants are joined to the death and resurrection of Christ and conformed to the meaning of this event. The participants are united with Christ through the power of the Spirit in his worship of and obedience to the Father. Union with the Trinity is exactly what grace and salvation are all about.

Sacraments begin and terminate in the reality-event of God's loving kindness and faithful presence for his people. Sacraments trace their origin to the entrance of God in human history, his gathering of a people to himself, and his abiding with them in the power of his spirit enfleshing his love in their midst. Sacraments are celebrations of this joyful, consoling, fulfilling reality-event. God's love for humanity manifested in the charter-event of Christ's death-resurrection is the fundamental metaphor which resolves the binary-oppositions of life into a positive meaning system. God himself is the cause of the sacramental celebration which has as vehicle, goal, and effect, a deeper union of the participants with the approaching God and one another.

Within the model of *celebration*, faith and worship stand out as dominant principles. The ground of any celebration is the givenness of a reality-event. Sacraments will be celebrated when the participants are in communion with the reality-event of God and his love. Faith is the a priori condition for communion with God. Faith alone gives humankind access to the meaning and depth of God. Only in faith will the sacraments be encounters with the living God, and faith is already a gift.

Sacraments are expressions of faith and by necessity expressions of worship. Faith's discovery of God can only issue in sincere worship. The essence of worship is giving thanks and praise to God by placing one's whole self in obedience to his will. This was Jesus' worship of the Father. In worship, sacraments are tied to day to day living. This is the true prescriptive characteristic of all ritual: the acceptance of its meaning as constitutive for concrete life. Role must become personal and communal biography. The crux of sacramental faith and worship lies in the acceptance or rejection of the Christian root metaphor as paradigmatic for the interpretation of reality and concrete life in society.

Absence of faith will dull sacramental celebrations and hinder the revelatory power of their symbols and symbolic activity. The impoverished condition of worship in many ecclesial communities is often linked to outdated and culturally foreign patterns of behavior. This observation is often valid. Yet, the present sacramental crisis may lie at a much deeper level. The more serious obstacle resides in the impoverished state of experiential faith. The real personal knowledge of God operating decisively in human history is so often absent. Yet only from this vantage point, only when experiential faith identifies God as the purpose, cause, and goal of sacramental life will the sacraments as ecclesial celebrations attain their full significance and final meaning.

The advantages of the *celebration model* can be articulated in relation to the models previously summarized. First, without negating the positive thrust of the "Interpersonal-Encounter" model, it corrects its telescoping of time and individualistic tendencies. The full dimensions of temporality are restored to sacramentology by the celebration model. Sacraments commemorate the past. They link the participants to Jesus' ministry and meaning by making the offer of salvation incarnate in his person, present again to his people. Sacraments are celebrated in the present. Now is the time, the *kairos*, of grace when God embraces his people. Sacraments point the Christian community to the future, when salvation will be fully attained. The three temporal modes of sacramental celebrations tie the Christian community to human history. The past dimension links the community to its origins and identity. The present dimension sustains the community in the now. The future dimension establishes the reality-event of God's love as the hoped for future and the evaluative principle of ecclesial planning and performance. Sacraments are communal ritual activities. They are ecclesial in nature while including the active role of the individuals who comprise the community.

Second, the *celebration model* avoids any indication that sacraments operate mechanically or physically. Celebrations are human behavior. Celebrations operate in human symbolic activity. Agreeing with the "Interpersonal-Encounter" model in opposition to the late-Scholastic model, *celebration* employs the idiom of persons rather than things to understand the interaction of God and humankind in ritual activity.

Finally, the celebration model overcomes the philosophical deficiency of Casel's "Mystery-Presence" model. Casel had failed to explain the presence of God in the sacramental activity of the community. In the *celebration model*, the presence of God operates in a fashion consistent with the presence of the reality-event in any true celebration. The *celebration model* relies on and appeals to the data on ritual in general to substantiate its claims. The real battle is not fought on whether Christianity "works" in its sacramental activities. This is only a skirmish. The real war focuses on whether there is symbolic activity, root metaphors, and rituals which express them. Once these realities are accepted and one enters the Christian world view, sacraments are the most normal activities in the world.

The danger implicit in the *celebration model* is the danger implicit in sacramentology *per se*. In this vision, celebration presupposes belief, faith in the reality-event. This is not to suggest that faith is dangerous or noxious. Rather, it is to claim that the judgment of faith's actual presence should be proclaimed with a certain precariousness. Who can say with absolute surety, "I believe," "we believe"? Doubt always seems to be a structural element of faith. Yet, the celebration model rises or falls on a faithful commitment to the reality-event of the Christian God as ground and givenness of sacraments. If commitment to the meaning of this reality-event is absent from sacramental celebrations, they will be empty expressions. Without faith, sacraments rapidly degenerate into magic and eventual oblivion.

Among the four models proposed for sacraments, the *celebration model* seems to reflect best the dynamism of a reconstructed sacramentology. Sacraments are not things, but ritual activities which follow the constitutive structures of ritual in general. The *celebration model* corresponds to the data supporting our theological claims about sacraments in general. Celebrations begin with common human experience. This was the starting point for our sacramental reconstruction. Celebration involved both the individual and the community. Our sacramental analysis demonstrated the correlation of these two poles in relation to ritual. Celebration is concerned with the transmission and evaluation of meaning. This was the consistent theme as our new sacramental ediface was being forged.

One further element commends celebration as a model for sacraments. Celebrations are symbolic activities. They are performative and penetrating. Only a model open to expressing the full depth of reality can evoke discovery of God's mysterious love and self-gift to humankind. Celebration is open to this task and in many ways attains this goal.

NOTES

1. Teodor Shanin, "Models and Thought," in *Rules of the Game*. (London: Tavistock Publ., 1972), pp. 1–22; also, F. Ferré, "Mapping the Logic of Models in Science and Theology," in *New Essays on Religious Language*. (New York: Oxford

University Press, 1966), pp. 54–93; and R.P. Scharlemann, "Theological Models and Their Construction," *The Journal of Theology* 53 (1973), pp. 65–82.

2. *Ibid.*, p. 8.

3. *Ibid.*

4. *Ibid.*

5. Although the selection functions symbolically, symbol and model should not be absolutely identified. Cf. Scharlemann, pp. 69–70.

6. Cf. Ortega Gasset, pp. 381–382; J. H. Newman, *Lectures on the Present Position of Catholics in England.* (Dublin, 1857), p. 26; Shanin, p. 16; Black, p. 239; and S. Toulmin, *Foresight and Understanding: An Inquiry into the Aims of Science.* (Bloomington: Indiana University Press, 1961), pp. 42–43. J. Walgrave has analyzed the relation of cultural change and theological understanding in *Geloof en theologie in de crisis.* (Kasterlee: De Vroente, 1966).

7. Cf. Shanin, p. 8.

8. Cf. D. Van den Eynde, "The Composition of the Sacraments in Early Scholasticism," *Franciscan Studies* XL (1951), pp. 1–20, 117–144, XLI (1952), pp. 1–26; also, E. Schillebeeckx, *De Sacramentele Heilseconomie I.* (Antwerp: Bilthoven, 1952).

9. Cf. Schillebeeckx, *Christ the Sacrament . . .*, pp. 92–95.

10. *Joannis Evangelium* 80,3 (Pl., 35, 1840); cf. Van den Eynde, p.4.

11. Cf. Van den Eynde XL, pp. 14– 20; and Schillebeeckx, *De Sacramenele . . .*, pp. 368–369.

12. *Ibid.*, p. 20. Hugh of St. Cher appears to have been the first to employ *materia* and *forma* in a hylomorphic sense.

13. For a definition of hylomorphism cf. Schillebeeckx, *Christ the Sacrament . . .*, p. 93 n.5.

14. *Ibid.*, p. 55 n8.

15. "Casel, Odo," *The Oxford Dictionary of the Christian Church 2nd Edition.* (London: Oxford University Press, 1974), p. 245.

16. J. de Baciocchi, *L'Eucharistie.* (Tournai: Descless & Co., 1964) p. 23: "Ces *mystères* consistaient dans des rites secrets et symboliques strictement réservés aux initiés; ils étaient censés assurer à leurs adeptes des advantages dans vie presénte ou apres la mort, un bonheur plus ou moins participé de celui des 'immortels' dont ils évoquaient les adventures (mythe) en les faisent, plus ou moins revivre (rite) par les initiés. Le bonheur ainsi procuré s'appelait souvent comme dans les christianisme, le salut, *soteria*."

17. Vaggaginni, p. 105.

18. Cf. Thédore Filthaut, *La Théologie Des Mysteres: Exposé De La Controverse.* (Tournai: Descless & Co., 1954), pp. 88–89.

19. *Ibid.*

20. Vagaginni, pp. 104–105.

21. G. Von Rad, *The Message of the Prophets.* (London: SCM Press, 1968), pp. 77–99.

13 THE CHALLENGE
OF THE CRISIS

In this concluding chapter we will return to the starting point of this theological enterprise, the idea of crisis. This "revisiting" will not be a mere repetition. Our penetration into the significant dimensions of ritual and Christian sacraments equips us for a fresh look. From this widened horizon, what may well be the key theological question for the next decade and beyond is cast before our minds and beckons our serious reflection and eventual action.

Anyone who theologizes on Christian sacraments will be required to respond to three attitudes which either minimize or dismiss Christian ritual. First, there is the frame of mind which reduces the meaning of Christian ritual by equating it to rubrics. In this case, attention is lured away from the real significance of Christian sacraments as expression of the Christian root metaphor and focused on the style, directions, or "smoothness" of the ceremony. Second, there is the attitude which identifies Christian ritual as magical rites. In this instance, Christian sacraments are reduced to "dated," "primitive," and "archaic" behaviors belonging to a previous era of humankind's history which has been surpassed by an empirical-scientific consciousness. This evaluation portrays Christian ritual as an attempt to escape from "real" post-industrial life. Third, there is the judgment which dichotomizes community and individual. In this situation, Christian ritual is indentified so strongly with one of these elements that the other is excluded. Usually, the tendency will be to reduce sacraments to private affairs. Taken to its ultimate conclusion, the necessity of any ritual will vanish as extrinsic to "*my* relationship with God."

These three critical attitudes must be judged ill-founded and incorrect from the theological vantage point of this text. Christian sacraments are not rubrics, they are not magic, and they do not bifurcate individual and community. A rebutal could always be issued that our defense of sacraments against these attitudes is self-serving and based on deniable theological presuppositions. It was for this very reason that our theological vision turned first to an anthropological analysis of ritual by non-theological sciences. Any rebutal to our theological contentions must also critique the findings of psychology, sociology, and anthropology which support our theological convictions. The lines of convergence between a behavioral and a theological understanding of ritual's operation and meaning are too strong to dismiss one without the other.

A serious investigation of ritual discloses its importance, function, and meaning not only for religion, but also for the vitality of individual and corporate secular existence. Psychology, sociology, and anthropology uncover various functions and dimensions to ritual which locate it at the nerve center of human life. One walks through this investigation being slowly convinced that men and women are ritual beings through and through. Ritual appears to be the most natural and normal event, happening, or performance in the world. It is endemic to and constitutive of human existence. It cannot be simply cast aside or overlooked without detrimental consequences.

Ritual is a medium or vehicle for communicating and sustaining a particular culture's root metaphor, which is the focal point and permeating undercurrent for its world view. Through ritual's operation, life's binary-oppositions are contextualized within a culture's metaphor and "resolved" into positive meaning for a culture's individual members and the social unit as a whole. Ritual fulfills this function by placing the ritual participants in contact with the original charter-event, its past re-enactments, and its present celebration. Having again seen and "tasted" the center and goal of their lives, the members of the ritual community can take up the "unfinished business" of aligning themselves and all reality to the central metaphor. A people's ritual is a code for understanding their interpretation of life.

Christian sacraments exhibit all the characteristics of ritual in general. They are normal and necessary for Christian culture. They are the medium or vehicle through which the Christian root metaphor of Christ's death-resurrection is expressed and mobilized to "positively" resolve the binary-oppositions of life. Through sacramental rituals, Christians are bound to the Paschal mystery and participate in its gift of divine life which is mediated through the gathered community as the presence of the risen Christ in the world.

Our anthropological understanding of how ritual in general "works" has permitted a deeper penetration into the true significance of two classical sacramental theorems i.e., *sacramentum tantum, res et sacramentum, res tantum* and *causando significant et significando causant.* Moreover, it has provided a framework in which a real relationship between the word of God, Church, *koinonia*, causality, grace, and symbolic activity can be radically affirmed and explained.

Our efforts in constructing a sacramental theology could be compared to piecing together a picture-puzzle. Various sciences, both theological and nontheological, have contributed the pieces which form our data. Each piece is unique and irreducible to any other. Yet, side by side, the pieces fit together to form an image or mosaic. As more and more of the image emerges, the more clear the whole arrangement becomes and the more facilely the remaining pieces correlate. Finally, the puzzle is completed and all the pieces are grasped as a whole.

From the beginning to the end of our sacramental "puzzle" is a long journey. Its completion, however, does not finish our theological task. Rather, it urges us to return once again to our beginning, the idea of crisis and readjust our understanding of what it is all about. There is a sacramental crisis in the Church, but in view of the whole sacramental mosaic it appears to be symptomatic of more serious problems i.e., the crisis of faith and the crisis of membership spawned in the crisis of culture.

It might seem surprising that an investigation of sacramental theology would lead to an identification of faith and membership as the real crisis confronting the Church. It would seem more natural for fundamental theology or ecclesiology to note their instability or threatened existence. Without diminishing the theological voices from these theological specialties who have warned against a mediocrity of faith and limpyness of membership, it might well be that sacramental theology is *the* theological arena where the true crisis of the Church is best illumined.

Since a contemporary sacramental theology draws its data from the behavioral sciences, biblical studies, Christology, ecclesiology, and its own specific tradition, it has a unique advantage of being receptive to and influenced by multiple insights, tendencies, and needs. What might go undetected in another discipline, could be recognized in sacramental theology by its repetition in different areas of data. This appears to be the case in the discernment and identification of the contemporary ecclesial crisis.

Clues to the Crisis

Although the crisis of faith and the crisis of membership spawned in the crisis of culture have been suggested as the key contemporary ecclesial question after the completion of our sacramental "puzzle," hindsight can detect many clues to its presence throughout the construction of our sacramental mosaic. Each of these clues, in one way or another, directs our attention to either commitment, faith, or membership.

First, the change in unconscious presuppositions which underpins all cultural life was portrayed as the predominant cause of the present sacramental crisis. The Church itself stimulated this cultural shift by progressively guaranteeing the autonomy of the human sciences and the world. A cultural change, however, implies the possibility of new unconscious presuppositions or first principles. There is a real danger that the emerging contemporary culture will have no room for Christianity within its paradigmatic model of life. Secularization could lead to a *secularism* which would structure society and its institutions in such a manner that religious faith and affiliation are no longer judged as values.

Second, ritual was seen as endemic to personality development. It was the vehicle for the transmission and appropriation of values which fostered personality maturation and membership in a particular "pseudospecies." Through ritual, the "pseudospecies" also presented individuals with a "negative identity" i.e., what they were not to become if they were to be and remain members of that unique community. Adolescence was the culmination of this personal and social growth process with its self-appropriation of the "pseudospecies" world view which began a life-long embracement of its ideology.

Can the Christian "pseudospecies" presume that its present ritual activity will allow its neophites to attain a solidarity of convictions in a mass communications network which reinforces shifting cultural values in a pluralistic world? Will ideological alternatives prohibit life-long commitment to the unique Christian vision? Have the alternative lifestyles and value options born in cultural change fostered the accomodation of Christianity's. "negative identity" to such a degree that its members could embrace almost any ideology or value system without surrendering their unique Christian indentity? What will be the criteria which identify Christian distinctiveness? What will be the norms for membership in the Christian "pseudospecies"?

Third, our sociological analysis of ritual uncovered a prescriptive dimension. The world view expressed in and through a community's rituals makes demands on the participants. They are to personalize and adhere to the meaning expressed in the ritual's enactment. Role and status are to become personal biography. Ritual is a constant challenge to work at completing "unfinished business."

Christian ritual is as prescriptive as any other. It requires personal adherence to Jesus and a continual conversion of one's whole life to the message of the Gospel. Christian ritual demands a living active faith and demands its continual intensification. Theoretically, there can be no opposition to these affirmations. Are they true factually? What quality of faith is demanded in today's Church? Does Christian ritual actually demand that its participants prioritize the task of transforming "unfinished business"? Has the radical message of repentance and Christian love been locked up in Church or brought to the marketplace of ordinary daily life? Is not this problem a continual ecclesial tension? Does not Christianity prescribe a world-transforming faith? Why hasn't the world been transformed? In the midst of cultural transformation, can any other question be more fundamental?

Fourth, anthropological studies revealed a continual tension of the "social drama" operating in a culture. There is a processual flow of structure-antistructure. Should a culture's root metaphor cease being adequate for resolving experienced binary-oppositions due to its own impotence or that of its rituals, a crisis will appear and eventually find resolution in the arena of ritual. Ritual is the medium for root metaphors.

If a crisis is recognized in Christian sacraments, our attention should be properly directed to the root metaphor of Christianity, the paschal mystery, as the real arena of the crisis. Does this metaphor factually resolve life's experienced binary-oppositions? Are Christian rituals actually making the metaphor clear or are they cloaking it? Have these rituals lost their power of engendering and expressing the bond of *communitas* which should flow from the metaphor? What redressive action can be taken to answer the critique of the anti-structure?

Each of the above clues arises from a non-theological science. Yet, they raise the question of either commitment or membership in relationship to cultural change. Moreover, they find strong resonance in our theological affirmations concerning the Christian sacraments.

In our theological vision, sacraments are ecclesial celebrations of faith. They are proclamations of the word, Jesus. The factual proclamation in the celebration of sacraments presupposes that people have believed in this word. This Christian faith is not first and foremost an intellectual assent to an idea. Rather, it is an active adherence and total commitment to the person of Jesus as the ultimate revelation of God and, therefore, the ultimate meaning of life.

As ecclesial celebrations of faith, communal dimensions permeate the sacraments. Their performance (*sacramentum tantum*) establishes or intensifies an individual's relationship to or status within (*res et sacramentum*) the people called Church. Sacraments affect membership and specify an individual's community role. Sacraments are a medium or vehicle through which God offers his love and life (*res tantum*) to humankind. God's self-communication of grace is not made without reference to or location within the community of his people. His saving grace is historically manifested in and through an individual becoming a member fo the Christian *koinonia* or intensifying this membership. Faith, membership, and grace are intrinsically related to form the central dimensions of the Christian sacraments.

An Overview of the Crisis

Hindsight can detect clues throughout our development of a sacramental theology which hint beyond the symptomatic sacramental crisis to a deeper ecclesial turbulence. Further speculation of what the crisis is about and what appropriate response can be marshalled by the Church to answer its challenge can be sketched from the framework of our sacramental mosaic.

Sacraments fulfill in Christian culture the same significant function ritual performs in any culture. Rituals express and sustain root metaphors. Christian sacraments proclaim Christ's paschal mystery and incorporate the multiple experiences of life within this paradigm. Through a ritual process, Christians are presented with an answer to life's questions. The Christian answer is the mystery of Christ.

Meaningful participation through ritual in any culture's root metaphor or world hypothesis presumes belief, be it pre-conscious or thematized. Adherence to the Christian root metaphor is called faith. The Christian tradition has constantly affirmed two prerequisites for faith: the hearing of the Gospel, the Jesus story, and the inner working of God who illumines our minds and hearts to comprehend the meaning of the Gospel and embrace it as true. Our initial grasp and commitment to Jesus is the act of conversion, the birth of faith. This is to be followed by a life-long perduring of faith, a constant and consistent conformity of our lives to the life of Jesus.

Christian faith is both personal and communal. It is a response emerging from the depths of an individual's personhood and involving the totality of who they are. This response, however, is contextualized by a community. It is the community which originally proclaims the Gospel heard by an individual, a community which keeps the Jesus story alive. It is the community which sustains the life-long continuance of faith. It is a community formed by a shared common faith which its individual members profess. This is beautifully expressed in the *Rite of Baptism for Children*. After the renunciation of sin and the profession of faith, the priest and the congregation give their assent to the profession: "This is our faith. This is the faith of the Church. We are proud to profess it, in Christ Jesus our Lord." Faith attaches an individual to the Christian *koinonia*. Shared faith is a criteria for membership in the Christian community.

Christian sacraments are ritual proclamations of the word, Jesus, by the Church. They place their participants in contact with the original Christian charter-event and root metaphor. They make the center of Christian faith *really present* through symbolic activity and the creative use of the human imagination. They express faith, membership and grace, and they intensify faith, membership and grace. Christian sacraments are both signs and causes.

If ritual is indigenous to every culture and community, if it is the medium for the expression and reinforcement of a culture's belief, Christian sacraments cannot be extrinsic to Christian faith. Rather, they are central to the continuing life of faith which follows upon the act of conversion. They are an evaluative gauge of faith's, membership's, and the Christian root metaphor's strength at any juncture of the Church's history. If there is a crisis in any of these elements, it should manifest itself in the arena of Christian sacramental life.

There is no immediate need for a factual demonstration of the sacramental crisis. The initial chapter of this text verified its presence and identified its causes. There is an urgency, however, in raising a general consciousness that the crisis goes deeper than many have portrayed or expected it. It reaches down to the very heart of Christianity. The sacramental crisis indicates that the basis for the Christian world view is being called into question. It suggests that people are increasingly abandoning the Christian root metaphor as the key reality which brings meaning to their experience of life. It suggests a decline in membership which implies fragile faith.

Explanations of the decline in membership and active faith can pursue two general lines of analysis. First, individuals are not adhering to the Christian root metaphor because it is not being adequately expressed. Either the present structure of the sacramental system lacks the necessary wholeness which interrelates each of the sacraments with the others and their origin in and expression of the paschal mystery; or the way, style, or form of the actual ritual performances do not adeuqately symbolize the Christian root metaphor. The language and symbolic gestures in the actual celebration of the sacraments is so mutated that it cloaks the paschal mystery and focuses attention on other realities. In this first explanation, the crisis is located in the rituals which are hindering the metaphor.

Second, the Christian root metaphor itself is being challenged by alternate world views, be they other religions, philosophies, or political-economic systems. The power of the paschal mystery to resolve the binary-oppositions of life is being radically questioned. In short, the decline of membership and active faith is a witness to the "social drama." Christianity as structure is being challenged by alternatives which are anti-structural to it. Depending on one's optimism or pessimism, the social drama has entered the crisis phases and redressive actions are being marshalled to insure the continued vibrant survival of Christianity; or, a revolution has taken place and the redressive machinery has failed. In this analysis, the crisis is located in the metaphor and observable in the ritual arena—the battle ground of the "social drama."

In our estimation, both paths of analysis are valuable and correctly isolate the forces which are impinging on Christian membership and faith. However, they need to be seen as complementary insights. Ritual and root metaphors are so intimately connected that a weakness or instability in one will engender a reaction in the other. A cloaking of the paschal mystery by sacramental rituals will neutralize its power to resolve binary-oppositions. An anti-structural challenge to the paschal mystery as structure will lead to a decreased participation in the sacraments which express and sustain membership and faith.

A perplexing question persists even after the Church's crisis is correctly grasped and its causes identified. Why is it happening today? All the evidence seems to point to our general crisis of culture. There is no doubt that at any time in human history tensions and transformations are present. Yet, there seems to be unique periods where major shifts in human self-understanding appear. These times are not so frequent that they become commonplace, yet they happen often enough so that we can note their presence. We live in an age characterized by major cultural upheaval and change which tamper with the fundamental unconscious presuppositions of what it means to be human, of what it means to live in a world with others, and of what is the future human destiny. In this age, every culture is confronted with the issue of its survival. No dispensation has been issued to Christian culture. Its crisis of faith and membership is spawned in the contemporary crisis of culture.

The contemporary challenge to Christian culture need not be interpreted as a totally negative phenomenon. It can be a purifying and strengthening experience if the Church can appropriately respond to and find satisfactory answers for a searching humanity. A successful ecclesial "apologetic" can materialize, if the Church will avoid symptoms of the crisis and honestly admit what it really involves, if it will emphasize those activities, resources, and redressive machinery which are essential to its existence and bypass, at least for a time, more peripheral elements and issues, and if it will demonstrate how the paschal mystery actually offers ultimate meaning for people who experience *today's* binary-oppositions.

The Church does appear to be appropriating the real challenge of our times. The Second Vatican Council was a momentous step in this direction. Throughout its documents, one senses a commitment to dialogue with a real World, real people, and real questions. This initial step has encouraged further penetration. Many post-Conciliar decrees and documents have returned to faith and membership as key ecclesial elements. This is the thrust of the ritual revisions eminating from the Council and the sacramental preparation programs which have been formulated to support them. The most potent examples of this orientation are the scholarly articles and emerging diocesan programs which face the question of adult initiation in the Church.

Strong redressive machinery is being marshalled by the Church to "do battle" with the real challenges it faces. The Church is equipping itself to "make a defense for the hope that is in her." This is recognizable in three areas. First, the Church has undertaken a renewal of her structures, rituals, and teachings so that the paschal mystery stands out clearly as the center and guiding principle of its faith. Second, the Church has returned to the task of evangelization as an essential characteristic of its mission and purpose. There is a growing realization that to insist on the "gift" character of faith is not a dispensation from preaching the word, but a greater responsibility to spread the Jesus story. Third, the Church has indentified itself with the plight of the poor and all who are oppressed and has vigorously pursued the causes of social justice and human dignity. The Church's redressive machinery has returned to the central responsibilities of being God's people i.e., to be a sign to the nations of God's loving concern, to offer true worship, and to care for the poor.

The Church also shows signs of demonstrating how the paschal mystery gives meaning to the significant tensions confronting contemporary humankind. It is speaking to the issues of abortion, population, use of human resources, peace, personal freedom, human rights, etc. For some the Church's voice may be only a whisper. But if it is, the whisper is growing louder. More importantly, the Church appears to be placing actions behind its words. It is establishing support systems, offering human resources, and dispensing financial backing so that persons will have the real option of choosing values and making decisions commensurate with the values of the paschal mystery as they apply in dilemma situations.

In suggesting that redressive machinery is presently at work in the Church to meet head-on the cultural crisis of faith and membership is not to judge its successfulness or failure. To make a prognosis at this stage of the social drama is difficult, if not impossible. Will the Church survive the crisis? Will Christ's paschal mystery be vindicated as the root metaphor which gives ultimate meaning to life? Will Christian faith and membership flourish in our new age? Time will answer these questions. Knowing the real crisis and mobilizing proper redressive machinery, however, are important steps toward insuring that the Christian community has a future in human history. From a Christian point of view, God will not fail the Church in the present age. But, will the Church be responsible and cooperate with God? If it does, how will this be concretely expressed in Christian culture.

In our dialogue with the behavioral sciences, much has been learned about ritual. These insights have fostered the development of a sacramental theology that can answer many questions which were previously unanswered. In the end, however, the theological inquiry is not drawn to a close but is called to continue the journey of reflecting on the mystery of faith in ever new arenas and situations.